für Jeff

taz Santa tir Cyrils
ce rinnon

The Beginnings of German Literature

For the German-speaking peoples under the Carolingians (c.
A.D. 750–950), the dominant literary tongue was Latin, the
lingua franca of the Christian West. Before the eighth century
only isolated words, legal terms, and proper names had found
their way from the vernacular into manuscripts. Cyril Edwards's
collection of essays examines the breakthrough into literacy of
the dialects known collectively as Old High German in the
south and Old Saxon in the north. In an introductory essay,
Edwards surveys the recording and survival of the earliest
continuous German texts. This leads into seven essays, each
inspired by a fresh look at the manuscripts. Two are concerned
with the Wessobrunn Prayer, the earliest religious poem in
German. A third looks at the destructive application of acids to
medieval manuscripts in an attempt to read barely legible
letters; it concentrates upon the *Hildebrandslied*, the only
surviving Old High German heroic lay, and the ninth-century
eschatological poem, the *Muspilli*. Two studies are devoted to
the Merseburg Charms, pagan survivals in a Christian
manuscript, invoking gods familiar from the Old Norse
pantheon. A study of the earliest traces of the love-lyric follows,
poems that slipped through the net of censorship imposed by the
Christian Church. The final essay is concerned with the Ossian
of the period, an ingenious forgery which was a cause célèbre
in the nineteenth century, the Old High German Lullaby.

Cyril Edwards is a Lecturer in German at St. Peter's College,
Oxford and an Honorary Research Fellow of University College
London. He has published numerous articles on medieval
German literature and co-edited a book on the medieval German
lyric. He is currently preparing a new translation of Wolfram
von Eschenbach's *Parzival* and *Titurel*.

Studies in German Literature, Linguistics, and Culture

Edited by James Hardin
(*South Carolina*)

The Beginnings of German Literature

Comparative and Interdisciplinary Approaches to Old High German

Cyril Edwards

CAMDEN HOUSE

First published 2002
by Camden House

Camden House is an imprint of Boydell & Brewer Inc.
PO Box 41026, Rochester, NY 14604–4126 USA
and of Boydell & Brewer Limited
PO Box 9, Woodbridge, Suffolk IP12 3DF, UK

ISBN: 1–57113–235–x

Library of Congress Cataloging-in-Publication Data

Edwards, Cyril W.
    The beginnings of German literature: interdisciplinary and comparative
approaches to Old High German / Cyril W. Edwards.
        p. cm. — (Studies in German literature, linguistics, and culture)
Includes bibliographical references and index.
ISBN 1-57113-235-X (alk. paper)
        1. German literature — Old High German, 750–1050 — History and
criticism. I. Title. II. Studies in German literature, linguistics, and culture
(Unnumbered).

PT183 .E35 2002
830.9'001—dc21

                                                              2001043137

A catalogue record for this title is available from the British Library.

This publication is printed on acid-free paper.
Printed in the United States of America

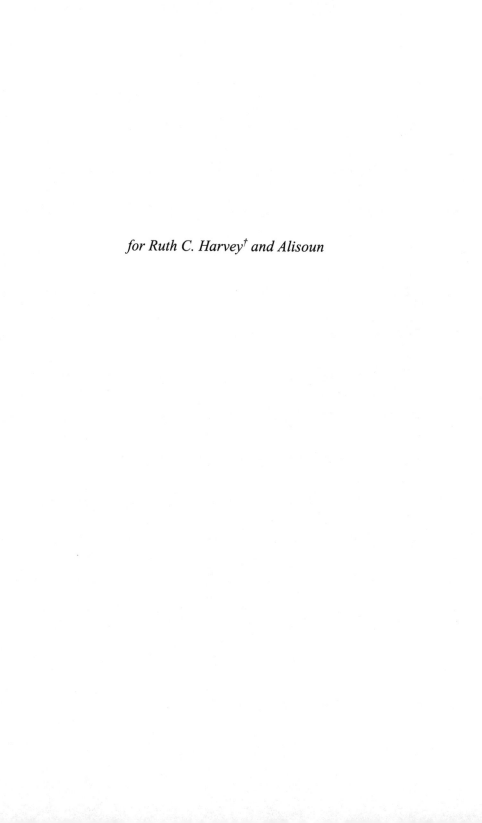

for Ruth C. Harvey[†] and Alisoun

Contents

Illustrations

I am indebted to the following libraries and archives for the provision of photographs:

    Bayerische Staatsbibliothek, Munich;

    Landesbibliothek und Murhardsche Bibliothek der Stadt Kassel;

    Domstiftsbibliothek Merseburg;

    Stiftsbibliothek St. Gallen;

    Bibliothèque Royale, Brussels; and

    Österreichische Nationalbibliothek, Vienna

Acknowledgements

A N INTERDISCIPLINARY STUDY of this kind has inevitably necessitated co-operation with colleagues in a wide range of fields, co-operation which has invariably been a pleasure because of the willingness of colleagues to sacrifice their time and permit me to benefit from their expertise. First and foremost, my two collaborators deserve mention here: Jennie Kiff-Hooper, now of the University of Leeds, who contributed codicological and art-historical experience to my second article on the Wessobrunn Prayer; Andrea Hodgson, formerly of King's College London, who researched the liturgical background to the prayer written on the same leaf as the Merseburg Charms.

For my introduction to Old High German I am indebted to my Oxford tutors, Ruth Harvey and Peter Ganz. At Goldsmiths' College in London I first came to teach the subject, and was blessed with enthusiastic colleagues and students. I was privileged to teach with and try my ideas out on Peter Christian, John Flood and David McLintock. It is David McLintock to whom I owe the greatest debt, to his infallible memory and profound knowledge, and to his readiness to consider even the most outré suggestions with patience, generosity, wit, and, on occasion, credence. His revision of J. Knight Bostock's *Handbook on Old High German Literature* (1955; revised edition 1976) has been an invaluable guide to me, as to a generation of students and scholars. Richard Wilson has been kind enough to read through some of the chapters in advance; he and Charles Relle have attempted to compensate for my inadequate Greek and Latin. Carolyne Larrington and Henrietta Martin-Twycross have read through and helped with the sections involving knowledge of Old Norse; Joy Jenkyns has kindly translated some of the Anglo-Saxon passages. I am also indebted to the readers from Camden House who scrutinised the original manuscript.

Other colleagues who have selflessly contributed their expertise are mentioned in the text or in footnotes. Many of them, like my two collaborators, I have met through the Earlier Medieval Seminar at the University of London's Institute of Historical Research, in which forum several of these ideas were first tried and tested. The Seminar is not only the best forum for medievalists in Britain, but the sociable atmosphere after the hawkish discussion has been a source of constant delight, despite the endless search for a suitable watering hole.

These chapters have taken shape through being given as papers in London, Oxford, Bristol, Munich and Göttingen. I am grateful for the many helpful responses from the audiences, and also to my students who have discussed these ideas in class, both in Oxford and in London. During my time at Goldsmiths' I received funding for visits to libraries in Germany and Austria; in particular, a visit to libraries in the former German Democratic Republic was sponsored by the College and the British Council. In 1998 the Faculty of Medieval and Modern Languages of the University of Oxford funded further visits to Munich and Vienna.

Librarians in England, Scotland, Germany, Austria, Switzerland, Italy and Belgium have provided friendly assistance, facilitating access both to manuscripts and to obscure secondary literature, and supplying photographs which have proved invaluable: the Bayerische Staatsbibliothek and the Österreichische Nationalbibliothek deserve particular mention here.

The two essays on the *Wessobrunn Prayer* are revised versions of articles published in 1984 and 1989; the first is printed here with kind permission of the editors of *Medium Aevum*, the second with that of John L. Flood, editor of *"mit regulu bithuungan." Neue Arbeiten zur althochdeutschen Poesie und Sprache* (Göppingen, 1989). The essay on the beginnings of the German lyric is an expanded version of a paper included in *Theodisca: Beiträge zur althochdeutschen und altniederdeutschen Sprache und Literatur in der Kultur des frühen Mittelalters* (Berlin, 2000); I am grateful to Wolfgang Haubrichs for permission to publish it.

Finally I would like to thank Nigel Palmer and Peter Christian for their wise counsel.

C. W. E.
JULY 2001

Preface

THE BREAKTHROUGH TO LITERACY of any culture is an object of fascination. Hieroglyphics, runes, ogam — all these early writing systems commanded special prestige because of their rarity, because the skill behind the execution of the system resided in the hands of a minority. The runemaster carves his name with self-evident pride at the end of his inscription: "I, FakaR, inscribed this"; "I, ErilaR, wrote these runes." It was a pride in craftsmanship, in special powers that could, in some societies and on some occasions, cross the border of the everyday world, into magic. In these essays runes form something of a leitmotif, clearly present in the oldest German religious poem, the Wessobrunn Prayer, as in the earliest survival of German heroic literature, the *Hildebrandslied*, and lurking, it will be argued, beneath the surface of the Merseburg Charms, whose origins lie in the pre-Christian world. Yet these runes are an anomaly, in that the writing system employed for the earliest German texts was the Roman alphabet.

In contrast to the Old Icelandic runemaster, the Old High German poet emphasises his indebtedness to the oral tradition: "Dat gafregin ih mit firahim" [That I found out by asking among men]; "Ik gihorta dat seggen" [I heard tell].Yet the German-speaking lands of the early Middle Ages had long been literate, or, to be more precise, had long been ruled by a literate hierarchy, before their native tongues found their way into writing. Such literacy as existed before the latter part of the eighth century among the Franks, the Bavarians and the Alemanni was, however, in the language of the Christian Church, in Latin. It is in the eighth century that we find the earliest surviving continuous texts written in German; prior to that German was limited to proper names or occasional glosses in Latin texts. The relationship between Latin and German in the period finds an effective symbol in the transmission of the Lorsch Bee Charm, a charm intended to control a swarm of bees, written upside-down in the lower margin of a Latin manuscript (Vat. pal. lat. 220, fol. 58) containing a collection of sermons. When I requested a photograph of the leaf from the Vatican Library, the first I was sent showed the Latin text with perfect clarity, whilst the German charm was out of focus.[1]

The pride of the rune-master is singular, individual. The writer of Old High German, on the other hand, is reticent to the point of anonymity, with few exceptions. Nevertheless, an upsurge of pride in the vernacular is detectable. It finds voice, highly articulate voice, in the mid ninth century, in the work of the first German author whose identity is known to us, the Alsatian monk Otfrid von Weißenburg. One of Otfrid's prefaces to his gospel harmony, the *Liber evangeliorum*, "CUR SCRIPTOR HUNC LIBRUM THEOTISCE DICTAVERIT," forms the best contemporary explanation of the incipience of writing in Old High German. For Otfrid, the lack of vernacular literacy is an anomaly and, somewhat grandiosely, he seeks to place Frankish on the same literary level as Greek and Latin: "Wánana sculun Fránkon éinon thaz biwánkon, / ni sie in frénkisgon bigínnen, sie gotes lób singen?" [Why should the Franks alone desist from singing God's praise in the Frankish tongue?]

The late eighth and early ninth century saw various attempts at a break-through into German, at the conversion of an oral tongue to a literary language. The evidence suggests that these attempts were for the most part autonomous and regional. Predominant, however, and acting to some extent as a centrally based linking structure, was the religious impulse. Throughout the German-speaking regions, the desire to spread religious doctrine and practice could only materialise, could only reach the majority of the people through the vernacular. The Lord's Prayer, baptismal vows, creeds — the central texts of the Christian mission — were translated into the various German dialects. The same impulse underlay biblical translation. Early translations focused on the gospels: the "Isidore Group" of translations, dating from the late eighth century, includes fragments of a translation of Matthew's Gospel. The *Diatessaron*, the gospel harmony ascribed to the second-century Greek or Syrian author Tatian, supplied the Latin base for no less than three major texts, the Old High German prose *Tatian*, Otfrid's *Liber evangeliorum* and the Old Saxon *Heliand*. The Wessobrunn Prayer and the *Muspilli* are freer treatments of biblical themes, which originate from the same religious impulse. The contextualisation of these early texts is often difficult to the point of impossibility; we cannot know how wide an audience they reached. But both the early attempts at translation and the ventures into the vernacular suggest a desire to reach as wide an audience as possible.

Pride in the vernacular expressed itself independently of the religious impulse in various ways. It may underlie the recording of the *Hildebrandslied*, whose opening line emphasises the link between oral culture and the Germanic past. Perhaps it is to be seen in the title assigned to the *Ludwigslied*, the first German political poem, written in the late ninth century. Titles are rare in early medieval literature, but here the scribe insists upon the unusual nature of his undertaking, prefacing the poem with a heading in rustic capitals: "RITHMUS TEUTONICUS." On a more theoretical, linguistic plane, an awareness of the problems of orthography is apparent. The Latin writing system was to a certain extent inadequate as a medium to express the new consonants which had arisen as a consequence of the First and Second Sound Shifts. This inadequacy was clearly apparent to the anonymous eighth-century translator of the Isidore frag-ments, whose orthography reveals an extraordinary subtlety in the attempt to represent the sounds of Old High German. For Otfrid von Weißenburg this interest also takes systematic shape and is discussed in his preface "AD LIUT-BERTUM," which anticipates the flowering of Old High German orthography towards the end of the period, in the writings of Notker III of St Gall.

The localisation and dating of many, indeed of the majority of Old High German texts, is rendered problematic by the fact that they survive as copies, not in the form in which they were first recorded in writing. Scribes and adaptors stemmed from different areas and different times. Most were monks, and monks might move from one monastery to another; the texts they copied were even more mobile. It would be illogical, in the absence of a standard language, to expect a thinking scribe to copy the dialect-based idiom and orthography of his source; scribes were not slavish photocopiers. In consequence dialect mix is a prevalent and often perplexing phenomenon in the Carolingian era. It does not contradict the impulse towards accuracy in the representation of sounds in writing, but rather reflects the complexity of a polydialectal society creating and transmitting a multi-layered literature.

The studies which form this book concentrate upon those early texts which mark a break with the dominant Latin culture. An introductory survey of the manuscript transmission of the earliest German texts serves here as a preamble to seven essays which address themselves to the shorter poetic texts of the period. Each of these approaches is informed by a fresh look at the manuscripts in which the texts are transmitted.

Two of these essays address themselves to the Wessobrunn Prayer. The first is comparative in nature, while the second attempts a contextualisation based upon the manuscript which preserves the poem, Clm. 22053. Bywaters of scholarship are charted in two further essays: the fourth chapter examines the employment of reagents to facilitate the reading of medieval manuscripts, which has led to the emergence of an additional line in the *Hildebrandslied*. The final chapter investigates what is, in all probability, a forgery — the *Ossian* of the field, the Old High German lullaby.

The two essays on the Merseburg Charms, like those on the Wessobrunn Prayer, are informed by the belief that these early texts require a pluralist approach. On the one hand, the codical context must be explored; on the other, the generic isolation of the texts invites recourse to a comparative method. The occurrence of the names of pagan gods is taken as the basis for a fresh look at the analogues of the charms.

The penultimate essay investigates the traces of secular lyric poetry in the period — forbidden texts, which survived in the face of censorship prompted by the hostility of the Church. These earliest German lyrics have received scant critical attention, for two reasons. Firstly, they are chronologically isolated; secondly, they are perceived as scatological. Scholarship has preferred to focus almost exclusively upon courtly love, which is generally seen as an "invention" of the twelfth-century renaissance. This schematisation ignores the paradox that in the thirteenth century and later many love-lyrics composed at courts were far from "courtly"; recent work on Neidhart von Reuental, for example, has freed the corpus from the shackles of earlier scholarly censorship.[2] For C. S. Lewis, the corollary of the "invention" of courtly love was that "'Love,' in our sense of the word, is as absent from the literature of the Dark Ages as from that of classical antiquity."[3] The schism perceived by Lewis created, or rather consolidated, an anthological and critical tradition. It is rare for either German anthologies or comparative studies to consider these early German lyrics. Bernard O'Donoghue finds no place for them in his wide-ranging anthology of "the courtly love tradition," on the grounds that "An historical survey of the writings we are concerned with can conveniently begin at the turn of the eleventh century. where Lewis places the origin of courtly love."[4] Roger Boase and Rüdiger Schnell similarly conform to this "convenient," if circular, scholarly practice.[5] Even the wider net cast by C. Stephen Jaeger ignores the OHG lyrics, presumably because they do not fit into the pattern of "Ennobling Love," although Jaeger does accord the Cambridge Songs brief consideration in his survey of pre-courtly love.[6] Love is various in nature, time and place. The neglected early medieval evidence demonstrates that love existed prior to courtly love in Germany, even in the cold climate of the Dark Ages.

C. W. E., July 2001

Notes

[1] See Cyril Edwards, "German vernacular literature: a survey," in *Carolingian Culture: Emulation and Innovation*, ed. Rosamond McKitterick (Cambridge: Cambridge UP, 1994), 141–70, Illustration 3.

[2] See, for example, Ingrid Bennewitz, "Die obszöne weibliche Stimme. Erotik und Obszönität in den Frauenstrophen der deutschen Literatur des Mittelalters," in *Frauenlieder — Cantigas de amigo. Internationale Kolloquien des Centro de Estudos Humanísticos (Universidade do Minho), der Faculdade de Letras (Universidade do Porto) und des Fachbereichs Germanistik (Freie Universität Berlin) Berlin 6.11.1998; Apúlia 28.–30.3.1999*, ed. Thomas Cramer et al. (Stuttgart: S. Hirzel, 2000), 69–84; Cyril Edwards, "Die Erotisierung des Handwerks," in *Liebe in der deutschen Literatur des Mittelalters. St. Andrews-Colloquium 1985*, ed. J. Ashcroft, D. Huschenbett, W. H. Jackson (Tübingen: Niemeyer, 1987), 126–48.

[3] C. S. Lewis, *The Allegory of Love: A Study in Medieval Tradition* (London: Oxford UP, 1936), 9.

[4] Bernard O'Donoghue, *The Courtly Love Tradition*, Literature in Context, 5 (Manchester: Manchester UP, 1982), 3.

[5] Roger Boase, *The Origin and Meaning of Courtly Love* (Manchester: Manchester UP, 1977); Rüdiger Schnell, *Causa Amoris. Liebeskonzeption und Liebesdarstellung in der mittelalterlichen Literatur*, Bibliotheca Germanica, 27 (Bern: Francke, 1985).

[6] C. Stephen Jaeger, *Ennobling Love. In Search of a Lost Sensibility* (Philadelphia: U. of Pennsylvania P, 1999).

Abbreviations and Works Frequently Cited

AAWG   Abhandlungden der Akademie der
Wissenschaften, Göttingen

ADB   *Allgemeine Deutsche Biographie*

ATB   Altdeutsche Textbibliothek

Bischoff, "Paläographische Fragen"
      Bernhard Bischoff, "Paläographische Fragen
deutscher Denkmäler der Karolingerzeit," *Frühmittelalterliche Studien*, 5 (1971): 101–34.

Braune, *Lesebuch*   *Althochdeutsches Lesebuch*, ed. by Wilhelm Braune,
17th ed., rev. by Ernst A. Ebbinghaus (Tübingen:
Niemeyer, 1994).

Cgm   Munich, Bayerische Staatsbibliothek, Codex
germanicus monacensis

Clm   Munich, Bayerische Staatsbibliothek, Codex
latinus monacensis

DTM   Deutsche Texte des Mittelalters

DVJS   *Deutsche Vierteljahrsschrift für Literatur und
Geistesgeschichte*

EETS   Early English Text Society

FuF   *Forschungen und Fortschritte*

GAG   Göppinger Arbeiten zur Germanistik

GGA   *Göttingische Gelehrte Anzeigen*

GRM   *Germanisch-romanische Monatsschrift*

Handbook   J. Knight Bostock, *A Handbook to Old High German
Literature*, 2nd ed., rev. by K. C. King and David R.
McLintock (Oxford: OUP, 1976).

MGH   Monumenta germaniae historica

MGH Cap.   MGH Capitularia

MGH Conc.   MGH Concilia (Legum Sectio III)

MGH SRG   MGH Scriptores rerum germanicarum in usum
scholarum saec. VI–IX

MHG   Middle High German

MIÖG	*Mitteilungen des Instituts für Österreichische Geschichtsforschung*
MLR	*Modern Language Review*
MSD	Müllenhoff, Karl and Wilhelm Scherer, *Denkmäler deutscher Poesie und Prosa aus dem VIII.–XII. Jahrhundert*, 3rd ed., rev. by Elias von Steinmeyer (Berlin: Weidmann, 1892; repr. Berlin/Zürich, 1964).
OHG	Old High German
OGS	*Oxford German Studies*
OS	Old Saxon
PBB	*Beiträge zur Geschichte der deutschen Sprache und Literatur*
PL	Patrologia Latina
PMLA	*Publications of the Modern Language Association*
Verfasserlexikon	Achim Masser, *Die deutsche Literatur des Mittelalters. Verfasserlexikon*, 2nd ed., rev. by Kurt Ruh et al. (Munich and New York: de Gruyter, 1977–2001)
ZfdA	*Zeitschrift für deutsches Altertum*
ZfdPh	*Zeitschrift für deutsche Philologie*

Introduction: The Recording and Survival of the Earliest German Texts

AS THEY FOUND THEIR WAY INTO WRITING, the German vernaculars of the Carolingian period, those dialects known collectively as Old High German in the south, and Old Saxon in the north, spawned what may be termed a "minority literature." Well over 95% of the texts from this time were written in Latin, the literary language of the Church, of the law, of the learned hierarchy. Literacy was taught through the medium of Latin, and even in the later Middle Ages writers who had a command of German but none of Latin were few in number.[1] An ambivalent attitude to the vernacular can be discerned in this earliest period of literacy in German. On the one hand, the desire of the Church to reach a wider public led to a large number of translations into the vernaculars, or the composition of texts which were translation-based; on the other hand there was a stigma attached to the vernacular, which finds its most eloquent expression in the prefaces to the verse adaptation of the *Diatessaron* by Otfrid, written in the South Rhenish monastery of Weissenburg (Wissembourg) between 863 and 871. Otfrid speaks in derogatory fashion both of the language which is his medium, and the secular oral culture in conscious opposition to which he has composed his *Liber evangeliorum*. His awareness of the unusualness of what he is undertaking is clear from the title he gives to the first chapter: "Cur scriptor hunc librum theotisce dictaverit" [Why the writer composed this book in German]. In one of the prefaces to the work, addressed to Liutbert, Archbishop of Mainz, he contrasts the fledgling Frankish tongue with Latin: "Hujus enim linguae barbaries ut est inculta et indisciplinabilis" [For as the barbarian nature of this language is uncultivated and cannot be learned by teaching]. He describes his poetic undertaking as having been motivated by a specific occasion when monastic and secular culture came into collision: "Dum rerum quondam sonus inutilium pulsaret aures quorundam probatissimorum virorum eorumque sanctitatem laicorum cantus inquietaret obscenus" [When some time ago the sound of useless things struck the ears of the most tried and tested men and the obscene song of laymen disturbed their sanctity]. His intent is that the pious "cantus" of his gospel harmony shall drown out the sounds of such secular voices.[2] Otfrid wishes to harness the vernacular to his own, Christian ends. At the same time he recognises that it is associated with a kind of culture which he finds offensive: for Otfrid, secular culture is obscene and barbaric, an offence to piety. Religious culture and lay culture are here in direct opposition.

This ambivalence in attitude to the vernacular is reflected in the character of the earliest texts which have survived. A twofold typology may be attempted here: on the one hand, the majority of the texts clearly originated with the blessing of the Christian Church, and many of these, such as the baptismal oaths (Braune XVI)[3] and the confessional formulae (Braune XXII), can be directly associated with the Church Councils and the missionary activity which characterised the reign of Charlemagne and his successors. A second category, however, comprises texts to which the Church objected and which it condemned in its edicts — what might be termed anti-establishment literature. Two kinds of texts are readily identifiable as belonging to this category: the magico-medical charms, and the early traces of the love-lyric. The former were regarded as suspect because of their associations with heathendom, the latter because of their erotic content. More problematic is the sole surviving trace of the heroic lay in Old High German, the *Hildebrandslied*, written down early in the ninth century. According to Charlemagne's biographer Einhard, Charlemagne gave orders for the preservation in writing of "barbara et antiquissima carmina."[4] It is, however, impossible to prove, so fortuitous is the form in which the *Hildebrandslied* survives, whether its recording was inspired by this interest on the part of the hierarchy.

To what extent is this binary typology reflected in the transmission of the texts in the manuscripts? No written survival can be in an absolute sense fortuitous. Nevertheless, the typology outlined above does to a certain extent colour the manner in which the written record was made. The charms written down in the Carolingian period survive as "fillers" on originally blank leaves, flyleafs, or in the margins of theological manuscripts. The Merseburg Charms, discussed in two essays below, are typical in this respect. The fact that the *Wiener Hundesegen* (Braune, XXXI, 2), a charm for the protection of dogs that guard cattle, and *Contra Vermes* (XXXI, 4a), an Old Saxon charm against disease-causing worms, are preserved together with Latin charms serving similar purposes points to a utilitarian function behind their being recorded, rather than their having survived because of any intrinsic interest in them as specimens of vernacular literature. The Lorsch Bee Charm, a late ninth- or early tenth-century entry, written upside-down in a sermon manuscript, typifies the way in which survival can verge upon the fortuitous:

> Kirst imbi ist huc*z*e. nu fliuc du uihu minaz. hera
> fridu frono. In munt godes gisunt heim zi comonne.
> sisisizi bina inbot dir san*ct*e maria hurolob ni habe du. zeholce
> ni fluc du. noh du mir nin drinnes. noh du mir nint uuin
> nest sizi uilu stillo vuirki godes uuillon.

> [Christ, the bee-folk is out! Now fly, my cattle, back / In holy peace, in God's authority, so that you may arrive home hale. / Alight, alight, bee: the Virgin Mary commanded you. May you have no leave: To the wood / flee not, nor escape me, nor deprive me of anything. / Sit quite still, work God's will.]

Here, unusually, a link exists between the proscriptions of the Church and the survival of a charm. The Decretal of Burchard of Worms and the Arundel Penitential condemn as "maleficium" the use of "incantantiones" to steal bees or honey.[5] Honey was as essential to the diet of the monastery as sugar is to the modern kitchen, and it is perhaps surprising that so little early literature relating to bees has survived. The Lorsch Bee Charm makes no specific reference to theft; it is presumably intended to control a swarm. However, in the Anglo-Saxon bee-charm (Cambridge, Corpus Christi College, MS. 41, p.182) there is a suggestion that the charm is intended to ward off a thief, a hostile magician:

Wið ymbe nim eorþan, oferweorp mid þinre swiþran handa under
þinum swiþran fet, and cwet:
  Fo ic under fot, funde ic hit.
  Hwæt, eorðe mæg wið ealra wihta gehwilce
  and wið andan and wið æminde
  and wið þa micelan mannes tungan.
And wiððon forweorp ofer greot, þonne hi swirman, and cweð:
  Sitte ge, sigewif, sigað to eorþan!
  Næfre ge wilde to wuda fleogan.
  Beo ge swa gemindige mines godes,
  swa bið manna gehwilc metes and eþeles.

[*Concerning a swarm of bees. Take earth in your right hand, cast it
under your right foot and say:*

'I have it under foot; I have found it.
Behold! Earth avails against all kinds of creatures,
it avails against malice and evil jealousy,
and against the mighty tongue of man.

When they swarm, scatter earth over them and say:
'Alight, victorious women, alight upon the earth!
Never turn wild and fly to the woods!
Be just as mindful of *my* benefit
as is every man of his food and his fatherland.][6]

The Anglo-Saxon charm lacks the buzzing alliteration of its OHG equivalent. Like the Lorsch charm, however, it is a marginal entry. The manuscript is an eleventh-century copy of the Anglo-Saxon translation of Bede's *Historia Ecclesiae*, which also contains the poem *Solomon and Saturn*. Its margins preserve a large number of shorter texts, all written in a neat eleventh-century hand. Among these are three other metrical charms. Two of these are, like the Vienna Dog Charm, intended to prevent theft of cattle (Dobbie, 9 and 10). A third (Dobbie, 11) is intended to guarantee safe-conduct on a journey.

It invokes God, Abraham and Isaac, and other Old Testament figures, as well as Mary, Peter and Paul. The Anglo-Saxon bee-charm is written in the left margin of the page, following a Latin prayer, "Pietatem tuam quesumus domine nostrorum absolue uincula delictorum." Neither the German scribe who recorded the Lorsch charm nor the Anglo-Saxon scribe saw any ideological discrepancy between recording a charm and recording a theological text. The co-existence of magic and religion persisted throughout the Middle Ages, disregarding the vitupera- tive condemnation of charms by the Church. Gawan, an exemplary Christian knight in Wolfram von Eschenbach's *Parzival*, written in the first decade of the thirteenth century, sees no conflict between the use of magic and his Christian faith:

> Gâwan die wunden verbant
> mit der vrouwen houbtgewant,
> er sprach zer wunden wunden segen,
> er bat got man und wîbes pflegen.

[Gawan bound up the wound with the lady's headdress. He pronounced a wound-blessing upon the wound. He asked God to take good care of both man and woman. *Parzival* 507,21–24.]

Another, cognate approach to the problem of the rationale behind the writing down of the earliest texts is to look at the transmission in terms of whether a text is a unicum, or exists in multiple copies. Two important reservations are necessary here. First, the losses incurred in the course of the last millennium are, of course, incalculable. Nevertheless, it may be significant that in recent decades, particularly with improved access to the libraries of Eastern Europe, a host of finds dating from the High Middle Ages has emerged, while very little dating from the earliest period has been found. Moreover, the transmis- sion of the surviving OHG texts is uneven in date. The ninth, middle century is the richest of the first three centuries of German literature, both in vernacular book production and original composition. There appears to have been something of a lull in the writing of original texts both in the vernacular and in Latin in the tenth century, a lull which contrasts sharply with the flourishing of ornamental book production and the rise of Ottonian architecture.[7] On the whole, it seems likely that what has survived is not the peak of a literary iceberg, but the consequence of literary activity encouraged by the Church under Charlemagne and his immediate successors.

The issue is further complicated by the fact that many OHG texts survive in the form of later copies, the originals of which may in some cases be centuries older than the surviving texts. The *Fuldaer Beichte* (*MSD* XXIII) and the *Ältere bairische Beichte* (Braune XXII.1a), for example, are thought to date from the reign of Louis the Pious (814–40), but survive only in copies made in the tenth and eleventh centuries.[8]

Proceeding with due caution, we may note, however, that before the middle of the tenth century, unica are the norm. This applies to those poetic texts which have come to be regarded as central to our understanding of the literary period, such as the *Hildebrandslied*, the *Wessobrunner Gebet*, the *Muspilli* and the *Ludwigslied*, all of which survive only in one manuscript. Even towards the end of the first two centuries the unicum remains customary. This isolation intensifies the problems of dating and contextualisation which affect most early medieval texts; linguistically, too, the isolated nature of the survivals has frequently led to circular arguments, such as Willy Krogmann's approach to the language of the Wessobrunn Prayer, which takes the Prayer as evidence for an early stage of undiluted Bavarian.[9]

It is perhaps instructive to look at the exceptions, those texts which survive in multiple transmission. Here there would appear to be a clear relationship between transmission and the functionality of a text. The synods and capitularies of 813 had advocated the translation of model sermons into the Romance and German vernaculars, but few examples survive to show that this edict was put into practice. A translation of Isidore's treatise *De Fide Catholica contra Judaeos* is preserved in fragments in two manuscripts: Paris Bibl. nat., cod. 2326, dating from the late eighth or early ninth century, and the Monsee-Vienna Fragments (Vienna, ÖNB, Cod. 3093) of the early ninth century; the latter include fragments of translations of the anonymous treatise, *De vocatione gentium*, and of the 76th sermon of St. Augustine, together with a further fragmentary sermon of a dozen lines. In Old Saxon a ninth-century fragment of a homily of Bede survives (Düsseldorf, Landes- u. Stadtbibliothek, cod. B 80 4⁰, fol. 153ʳ). The only other instance of double transmission of a sermon is the *Exhortatio ad plebem christianam* (Braune X). Both manuscripts of the *Exhortatio* translation (Kassel, Cod. theol. quart. 24 and Munich, Clm. 6244) are Bavarian in origin and were written in the first quarter of the ninth century. The text is presented bilingually, in parallel columns, like the OHG Tatian translation, suggesting that the priest had the option of preaching in Latin or in German. It is not until the eleventh century that we find further translations of sermons into the vernacular.[10] This gap between the ninth and the eleventh century coincides with the pattern we have already observed.

The most substantial early text to be translated into Old High German was the *Diatessaron*, the gospel synopsis attributed to the Syrian or Greek author Tatian, which dates back to the second century A.D. Here a strikingly similar pattern of transmission obtains for the early ninth-century prose translation of the Latin Tatian and for the two poetic reworkings in the vernaculars, Otfrid's *Liber Evangeliorum* and the Old Saxon *Heliand*. The earliest German rendering of the Tatian, the prose Tatian, survives complete in only one manuscript, Codex Sangallensis 56 (G), written as a parallel text to a Latin version. The original of the Oxford manuscript, Ms. Junius 13 (B), probably had the same format, but Peter Ganz has shown that this copy, made in the late sixteenth or seventeenth century, is to some degree independent of the St. Gall version.[11] Excerpts from the Tatian dating from the late ninth or early tenth century are preserved in the manuscript of the Old High German *Gespräche* (Paris, Bibl. nat., Ms. lat. 7641), and evidence exists of at least two further manuscripts which are now lost.[12] Otfrid's adaptation into rhyming verse survives in three ninth-century manuscripts and in fragments of a fourth, dating from the tenth century.[13] That such a huge work, some 7,000 lines, was copied so often and within such a short space of time points to the active interest and collaboration of several monasteries. The same conclusion may be drawn from the transmission of the *Heliand*, the Old Saxon adaptation of the Diatessaron in alliterative verse. Four of the five surviving manuscripts are thought to date from the middle or second half of the ninth century; anomalously, the most complete, the Cotton manuscript, dates from the second half of the tenth century.[14] The question of the extent to which these versions of the *Diatessaron* were intended to reach beyond a monastic audience is a vexed one, typifying the problems in contextualising the earliest German texts. Otfrid's dedications suggest a desire to reach an aristocratic public, while the *Praefatio in librum antiquum lingua Saxonica conscriptum*, published by M. Flacius Illyricus in 1562 and generally held to be a preface to the *Heliand*, the ninth-century OS version of the Tatian, states that its aim is to communicate divine precepts "non solum literatis, verum etiam illiteratis" [not only to the literate, but also to the illiterate.) This professed aim coincides nicely with the much-debated "Germanicisation" of the gospel text that confers upon the *Heliand* its unique character, the employment of vocabulary and local colour which must have been intended to bridge the gap between the Biblical events and their northern, newly-converted audience. Thus Christ, for example, is seen as a *landes uuard* [a guardian of the land], and Herod is cast as a *boggebo* [a giver of rings].[15]

Multiple transmission of texts of such central importance to the purposes of the Church comes as no surprise. Much more surprising is the number of magical charms which, in a relatively small total corpus, survive in more than one manuscript. The Church councils and penitentials are vehement in their condemnation of *maleficium*, black magic; their brief extends, however, to a wide range of pagan practices, which includes medicinal magic. Indeed, the *Admonitio generalis* of 789 prohibits all kinds of magic.[16] The surviving German charms — in contrast to, for example, some of the Old Irish and Old Icelandic ones, — belong primarily to the province of white magic, although even in this small corpus there would appear to be one exception, the First Merseburg Charm, which, at least if taken literally, applies magic to warfare.

Pro Nessia, a charm to expel worms or snakes from the diseased body, survives in a Bavarian version written at the bottom of a leaf in the middle of the tenth century:

Gang uz, Nesso, mit niun nessinchilinon,
uz fonna marge in deo adra, vonna den adrun in daz fleisk,
fonna demu fleiske in daz fel, fonna demo velle in diz tulli.
Ter Pater noster.

[Go forth, Worm, / with nine wormlets. / forth from the marrow into the
vein, / from the vein into the flesh, / from the flesh into the skin, / from the
flesh into this spear.
Pater noster three times.]

The combination of magic and the Lord's Prayer typifies the way in which the
OHG charms have survived. Against disease, all means were valid. The OS
cognate of this charm, *Contra vermes*, differs only in the rubric and the final
formula, an appeal to the Lord: "Drohtin, uuerthe so" [Lord, let this be so].[17]
Worms were the early medieval equivalent of bacteria, held responsible for a
variety of diseases.[18]

Contra caducum morbum (Braune XXXI, 8), the charm against epilepsy
which will be discussed in the context of the Merseburg Charms below, also
survives in two manuscripts (Paris, Bibliothèque Nationale, Cod. nouv. acq.
Lat. 229, which also contains *Ad equum errẹhet* (Braune XXXI, 7), and
Munich, Clm. 14763). The narrative introduction of the Trier charm *Incantan-
cio contra equorum egritudinem quam nos dicimus spurihalz* (Braune XXXI,
9.B.2), preserved with other charms in marginalia in a tenth-century manuscript, is a variant of the Second Merseburg Charm. Christ and St. Stephen
replace the gods P[h]ol and Uuodan, and again prayer is incorporated into the
charm, magic taking on a Christian cloak:

Quam Krist endi sancte Stephan zi ther burg zi Saloniu[n]: thar uuarth
sancte Stephanes hros entphangan. Soso Krist gibuozta themo sancte
Stephanes hrosse thaz entphangana, so gibuozi ihc it mid Kristes fullesti
thessemo hrosse. Pater noster. Uuala Krist, thu geuuertho gibuozian thuruch
thina gnatha thessemo hrosse thaz antphangana atha thaz spurialza, sose thu
themo sancte Stephanes hrosse gibuoztos zi thero burg Saloniun. Amen.

[Christ and St. Stephen came to the city of Saloniun: there St. Stephen's
horse was lamed. Just as Christ then cured St. Stephen's horse of that laming,
so I cure this horse with Christ's authority. Pater noster. Hail Christ, you who
deigned to cure by thy grace this horse of the laming or this "spurihalz," as
you cured St. Stephen's horse at the city of Saloniun. Amen.]

In the case of the charms, the most probable explanation for multiple
transmission is that the written texts reflect a widespread oral tradition. As they
were written down, they took on an increasingly Christian character.

The texts which form the subject of the essays comprising this book are all
unica in terms of transmission (if we disregard the Trier analogue of the

Second Merseburg Charm). The Wessobrunn Prayer, probably the oldest surviving German poem, was copied with considerable care and attention to scribal ornament, although the fact that the text was in a dialect or stage of the language with which the scribe was not totally familiar led to some errors. It is the only one of the texts treated here which forms an integral part of the manuscript in which it is written, yet its close analogues suggest that it may be an interloper, rather than a text of purely German origin. The transmission of the *Hildebrandslied* is as problematic as every other aspect of this earliest survival of German heroic poetry, but the fact that it was written down on end-leaves suggests that the scribes who recorded it knew that it was an anomaly. The *Muspilli* (Clm. 14098, fols. 61ʳ, 120ᵛ, 121ʳ⁻ᵛ), the earliest German eschatological poem, is remarkable for the incompetence of the hand which wrote it in the flyleafs and lower margins of a manuscript devoted to a beautifully written Latin sermon. The subordinate position of the *Hildebrandslied* and the *Muspilli*, combined with the fact that end-leaves are more prone to fade than the main body of a manuscript, had dire consequences: it led directly to that treatment with reagents in the nineteenth century which is discussed below. In the case of the *Muspilli*, the use of these chemicals has obscured large parts of the text, in all probability permanently.

The Merseburg Charms were written down in the early tenth century, on the originally empty flyleaf of a missal. The three earliest survivals of German secular lyric similarly survive on flyleafs or in margins. The OHG Lullaby (*Schlummerlied* or *Wiegenlied*) was rescued from the binding of a late medieval manuscript by its "discoverer," Georg Zappert. The mode of transmission confirms that the texts studied here are, with the exception of the Wessobrunn Prayer, fortunate survivals, fish that slipped through the net of a hierarchy uncertain of or antagonistic towards their nature.

Notes

[1] Compare Karin Schneider, *Paläographie und Handschriftenkunde für Germanisten. Eine Einführung*, Sammlung kurzer Grammatiken germanischer Dialekte, B. Ergänzungsreihe Nr. 8 (Tübingen: Niemeyer, 1999), 1.

[2] *Otfrids Evangelienbuch*, ed. Oskar Erdmann, 6th ed. rev. by Ludwig Wolff, ATB, 49 (Tübingen: Niemeyer, 1973): *Ad Liutbertum*, lines 63–64; 5–7; 11–12. Compare Walter Haug, *Literaturtheorie im deutschen Mittelalter. Von den Anfängen bis zum Ende des 13. Jahrhunderts: eine Einführung* (Darmstadt: Wissenschaftliche Buchgesellschaft, 1985), 25–44.

[3] References are to the *Althochdeutsches Lesebuch*, ed. Wilhelm Braune, 17th ed. rev. by Ernst A. Ebbinhaus (Tübingen: Niemeyer, 1994); henceforth referred to as *Lesebuch*.

[4] Einhard, *Vita Karoli Magni*, ed. O. Holder-Egger, MGH SS rer. Germ. (Hanover: Hahn, 1911), trans. Lewis Thorpe (Harmondsworth: Penguin, 1969), c. 29.

[5] Cyrille Vogel, "Pratiques superstitieuses au début du XIe siècle d'après le *Corrector sive medicus* de Burchard, évêque de Worms (965–1025)," in *Études de civilisation médiévale (IXe–XIIe siècles): Mélanges offerts à Edmont-René Labande* (Poitiers: Centre d'Études Supérieures de Civilisation Médiévale, 1974), 751–61 (esp. 759–60).

[6] *The Anglo-Saxon Minor Poems*, ed. Elliott van Kirk Dobbie, The Anglo-Saxon Poetic Records, 6 (New York: Columbia UP, 1942), 125; the translation is that of Kevin Crossley-Holland, *The Anglo-Saxon World. An Anthology* (1982; repr. Oxford: Oxford UP, 1999), 151. I am indebted to Christopher de Hamel and Gill Cannell of Corpus Christi College, Cambridge, for a photocopy of the charm.

[7] Cf. Horst Dieter Schlosser, *dtv-Atlas zur deutschen Literatur. Tafeln und Texte*, 2nd ed. (Munich: Deutscher Taschenbuch Verlag, 1985), 35, and the diagrams, 32 and 34.

[8] Cf. J. Knight Bostock, *A Handbook on Old High German Literature*, 2nd ed. rev. by K. C. King and D. R. McLintock (Oxford: Clarendon Press, 1976; henceforth: *Handbook*), 156.

[9] Willy Krogmann, "Die Mundart der Wessobrunner Schöpfung," *Zeitschrift für Mundartforschung* 13 (1937): 129–49.

[10] Cf. Karin Morvay and Dagmar Grube, *Bibliographie der deutschen Predigt des Mittelalters*, MTU, 47 (Munich: C. H. Beck, 1974), 1–8.

[11] Peter Ganz, "MS Junius 13 und die althochdeutsche Tatianübersetzung," *PBB* 91 (1969): 28–76.

[12] Cf. Ganz, 30–32.

[13] Cf. *Handbook*, 190–91; Werner Schröder, "Otfrid von Weißenburg," in *Die deutsche Literatur des Mittelalters. Verfasserlexikon*, 2nd edn by Kurt Ruh et al. (Berlin: De Gruyter, 1977–2001) (henceforth: *Verfasserlexikon)*, vol. 7, cols. 179–80; *Otfrids* Evangelienbuch, ed. Erdmann / Wolff, VI.

[14] Burkhard Taeger, "Heliand," *Verfasserlexikon*, vol. 3, cols. 960–61.

[15] For an introduction to the problems of contextualisation, see Cyril Edwards, "German vernacular literature," in *Carolingian Culture: Emulation and Innovation*, ed. Rosamond McKitterick (Cambridge: CUP, 1994), esp. 152–57.

[16] *MGH Cap.* I, 58.

[17] *Pro nessia* is in Munich, Clm. 18524b, from Tegernsee; cf. Bernhard Bischoff, "Paläographische Fragen deutscher Denkmäler der Karolingerzeit," *Frühmittelalterliche Studien* 5 (1971): 101–34 (126–27; 130–31); *Contra vermes* is on fol. 188^v of Vienna, ÖNB, Cod. 751, probably early tenth-century.

[18] Cf. A. Kuhn, "Indische und germanische segenssprüche," *Zeitschrift für vergleichende Sprachforschung* 13 (1864): 49–74 and 113–57.

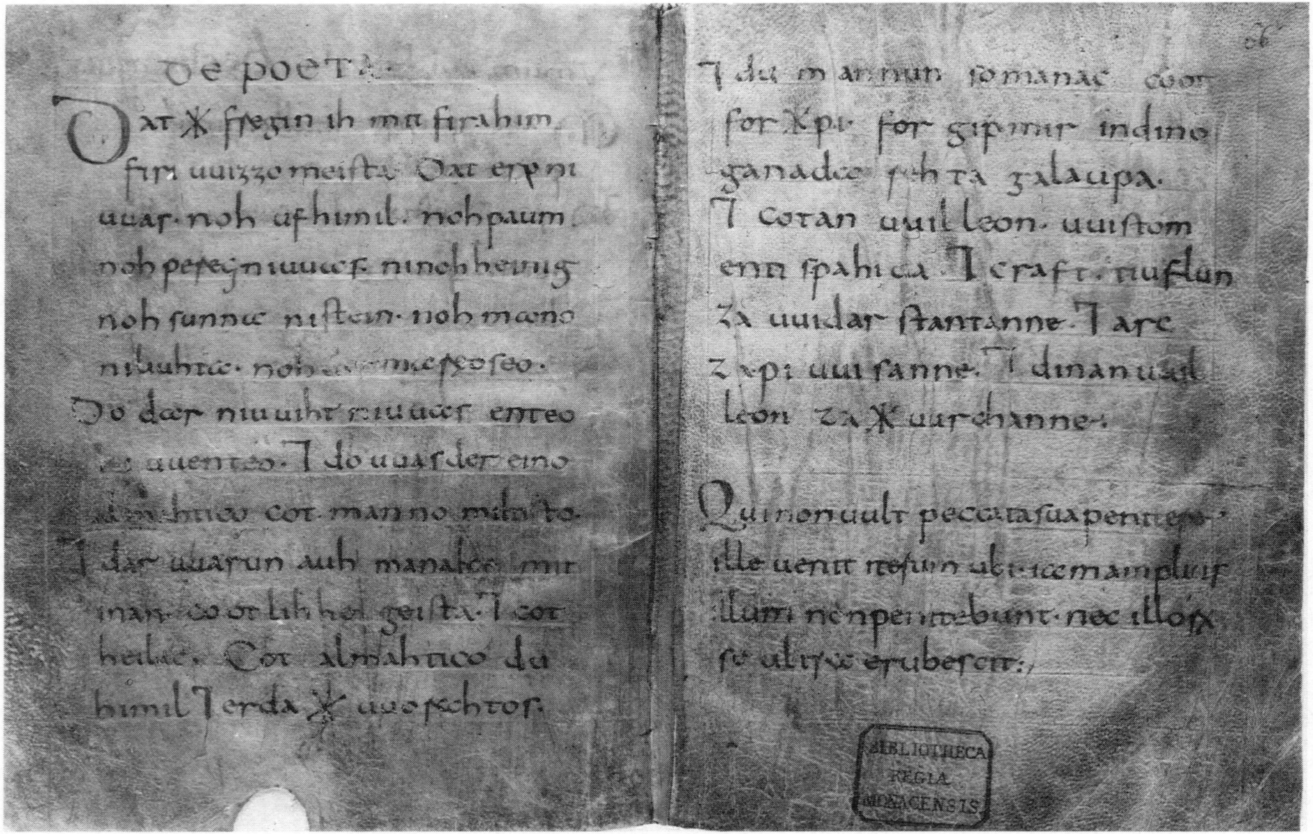
De poeta
BIBLIOTHECA
REGIA
MONACENSIS

1: *Tōhû wābōhû*:
The *Wessobrunner Gebet* and its Analogues

a) Clm 22053, fols. 65ᵛ–66ʳ (illustration 1):

De Poeta.
Dat ＊fregin ih mit firahim / firi uuizzo meista.
Dat ero ni / uuas. noh ufhimil.
noh paum / noh pereg niuuas.
ninohheinig / noh sunna nistein.
noh mano / niliuhta. noh der marẹo seo. /   5
Do dar niuuiht ni uuas enteo / ni uuenteo.
⌐do uuas der eino / almahtico cot.
manno miltisto./ ⌐dar uuarun auh manake mit / inan.
cootlihhe geista. ⌐cot / heilac.
Cot almahtico du / himil ⌐erda ＊uuorahtos. /   10
⌐du mannun so manac coot / for ＊pi.
for gipmir indino / ganada rehta galaupa. /
⌐cotan uuilleon. uuistóm / enti spahida.
⌐craft. tiuflun / za uuidar stantanne.
⌐arc / zapi uuisanne. ⌐dinan uuil / leon za ＊uurchanne.¹

b) Braune/Ebbinghaus, *Althochdeutsches Lesebuch*, § XXIX:

De Poeta.
Dat *ga*fregin ih mit firahim   firi uuizzo meista,
Dat ero ni uuas   noh ufhimil,
noh paum <. . .>   noh pereg ni uuas,
ni <. . .> nohheinig   noh sunna ni s*c*ein,
noh mano ni liuhta,   noh der marẹo seo.   5
Do dar niuuiht ni uuas   enteo ni uuenteo,
enti do uuas der eino   almahtico cot,
manno miltisto,   *enti* dar uuarun auh manake mit inan
cootlihhe geista.   *enti* cot heilac <. . .>

Cot almahtico, du himil *enti* erda *ga*uuorahtos, *enti* du mannun   10
so manac coot for*ga*pi, forgip mir in dino ganada rehta galaupa
enti cotan uuilleon, uuistóm *enti* spahida *enti* craft, tiuflun za
uuidarstantanne *enti* arc za piuuisanne *enti* dinan uuilleon za *ga*uurchanne.

[Of the Creator
This my questioning among men determined, greatest of wonders,
That there was neither earth nor heaven above,
Nor tree, nor mountain was there,
Nor anything, nor did the sun shine,
Nor the moon beam, nor the glorious sea.
When there was nothing of ends nor turnings,
And then there was the one Almighty God,
Kindest of men. And there were also many with him,
Divine spirits. And God Holy,
God Almighty, you who created heaven and earth,
And bestowed so many good things upon men,
Bestow upon me in your grace true faith,
And good will, wisdom and intelligence,
And power to withstand devils,
And to shun evil, and to work your will.]

The *Wessobrunner Gebet* has been described as the least problematic of the alliterative poems surviving in Old High German.[2] This scarcely does justice to the speculation to which these twenty-two lines of manuscript have given rise over the past two and a half centuries. It is sometimes the case that, faced with a consensus, we would like, as Jeffrey Ashcroft says in his analysis of the early songs of Walther von der Vogelweide, to introduce "Chaos in die Ordnung";[3] but, with regard to the *Wessobrunner Gebet*, it seems requisite to go one stage further, and to introduce, or rather reintroduce, chaos into the chaos, in the hope of casting some light upon the almost primaeval darkness which still lies upon the face of what is probably, if only in terms of its transmission, our oldest German poem.[4]

The attention of scholars has been drawn again and again to the early lines of the poem (1–6 in the *Lesebuch*), which appear to lay "un-Scriptural stress on the pre-material void or chaos."[5] Explanation for this has been sought in quarters as far afield as the Old Norse *Vǫluspá* and the Vedic Sanskrit *Rig-Veda*,[6] and it has commonly been held that these lines reflect pagan beliefs, or at least have their origin in an attempt to oust pagan beliefs concerning the beginning of the world, as reflected in Bishop Daniel's letter to Boniface.[7] In fact, the natural phenomena which are described as being absent prior to the Creation in the *Wessobrunner Gebet* are readily identifiable with those described as being created by the Word of God in the first chapter of Genesis, the sole exceptions being *pereg*, which can be traced to Psalm 90.2, Psalm 104.6 or Proverbs 8.25,[8] and *stein*, which is in any case generally amended to *scein*. It is at least conceivable that the poet obtained his stress upon the void by simply inverting the ideas he found in Genesis and other Old Testament accounts of the Creation. Line 6, "Do dar niuuiht ni uuas enteo ni uuenteo," would then act as a summary of the negative picture that has been presented, leading into the climax of the early part, the introduction of the divine presence.

But line 6 presents us with considerable difficulties, in terms of both form and meaning. Like the majority of the lines of the poem as it appears in the manuscript, it does not alliterate in accordance with the poetic conventions observed in Anglo-Saxon, Old Saxon or Old Norse verse. Leslie Seiffert suggested that the OHG ear would regard the *ni* and the *uuiht* as two distinct entities, enabling the *uu* sounds in the line to alliterate, albeit in the wrong places, yielding the scheme *aaxa*.[9] Perrettt adopted a more radical solution and, objecting to the 'proclitic double negative,' suggested *iuwiht*, following Grein.[10] This would give the more acceptable scheme *abab*, with the vowels *iu* and *e[nteo]* alliterating; but Perrett supported this emendation by referring to "the odd appearance of the unattached *n* in *niuuiht*," though the facsimile which he reproduced shows clearly that *n* is one letter which is never used to form a ligature by the scribe.

Perrett is one of a minority of scholars[11] who have drawn attention to "the rhyme-couple in line 6b." He fails to find any parallel to this "additional ornament"; elsewhere in early Old High German texts, however, rhyme does occur in predominantly alliterative texts. The two Merseburg charms employ rhyme in the conjuring formula; and it appears to be present in the alliteratively defective line 61 of *Muspilli*. Conversely, in Otfrid's depiction of the Annunciation the phenomenon of alliteration supporting end-rhyme obtains (1.5.5–6,10–12). More significantly, the rhyming infinitives at the end of the *Wessobrunner Gebet* itself bolster the poetic effect at a point where the alliteration is so weak that even the Grimms, in their otherwise admirably conservative edition, felt obliged to supply *tugida* before *enti craft*.

Rhyme-pairs similar to *enteo ni uuenteo* are a frequent ornament in Anglo-Saxon alliterative poetry. Kluge cited a plethora of examples, one of which, *side and wide* (*Genesis A*, 118) reminded Baesecke of *enteo ni uuenteo*.[12] The end-rhyme *ende*: *wende* occurs from time to time in early and classical Middle High German; one such occurrence is in the twelfth-century poem *Das Himmelreich*:

> Selbe ne hast du [*sc*. got] anegenge noh uerwesenten ente
> dannen ne magen dih die stete noh die wente
> deheine halben umbegeben noh umbescriben
> uerrer noh naher. uz oder in getriben. (33–36).[13]

[You Yourself have neither beginning nor decaying end. / Hence neither places nor walls can / surround or circumscribe You in any way, / nearer nor farther, nor drive You out or in.]

A closer parallel to *enteo ni uuenteo* occurs in the late thirteenth-century Creation hymns of the North German didactic poet Der Meißner:

> Got vater vnde din goteliche kraft.
> du wende an ende endehaft.
> von meisterscaft.
> almehtich wunderere . . .
> Dv were ouch e.
> dine wunder ne.
> noch din lob keyn syn mvchte halb durch grvnden
> Du nichtes icht.
> vnde ichtes nicht.[14]

[God the Father and Your divine power, / You turning without final end, / of mastery / almighty miracle-worker / . . . You have always existed. / Neither Your wonders / nor Your praise could any mind half penetrate. You something of nothing, / and nothing of anything.]

The rhyme-pair resurfaces in the *Bremisches Wörterbuch*, which lists *von Ende to Wende* and *von Ende bet to Wende* as meaning "von einem Ende zum andern," and gives as an example: "Ik weet mine Lekse von Ende bet to Wende."[15] Von der Hellen thought that he had heard the phrase in the locality of Geestemünde.[16] His implication is that the poet of the *Wessobrunner Gebet* is drawing upon a popular Low Saxon idiom, but if this were true one might expect to find rather more frequent occurrences of the rhyme-pair.

Von der Hellen also draws our attention to another of Der Meißner's hymns, in which the significance the poet attaches to *wende* becomes somewhat clearer:

> Merket wie got gewundert hat
> Besunder die vier wende
> viur. erde. wazzer vnde luft
> hant manigerleye wunder.
> Her begyn ane begyn.
> wer ist syn rat.
> her ende vnde doch an ende
> her aller tieft eyn tiefe gruft. (*HMS*, 102a)

[Mark what miracles God has wrought, / the four walls, one after the other: / fire, earth, water and air / possess many wonders. / He who is a beginning without a beginning — / who is His counsellor? / He is an end and yet without ending, / of all depths a deep chasm.]

We should hesitate to regard Der Meißner as an authority on the meaning of the phrase in the *Wessobrunner Gebet*, but the coincidence of context, and moreover the negatives "Du nichtes icht. vnde ichtes nicht" in the first hymn do suggest that Der Meißner is drawing in some significant measure on the same phraseology as we find in the OHG poem. Four centuries separate the texts, and there is no obvious line of communication, but the resemblance is striking.

Perrett also addressed himself to the meaning of line 6. Of the two rhyming words, *enteo* is the less problematic. The sense of a spatial line or border is confirmed by Notker's usage in the prologue to his Boethius translation, where it corresponds to *fines* in the Latin model: "Uuér zuîvelôt romanos íu uuésen állero rîcho hêrren. únde iro geuuált kân ze énde dero uuérlte?"[17] A similar sense obtains in the Monsee Fragments, where "venit a finibus terrae" is rendered by "quam fǫna entum lantes."[18] Perrett believed that *enteo* might have been suggested by the phrase "cuncta . . . extenta locorum spatia" in Bishop Daniel's letter. *uuenteo* was thought by Jacob and Wilhelm Grimm and subsequent scholars to be a synonym for *enteo*, meaning "Grenze, *extremitas*," but, again working from Bishop Daniel's letter, and the challenge to the pagans to say whether they believed that the world had always existed *sine initio*, Perrett argues that, while *enteo* refers to space, *uuenteo* refers to time. His interpretation confers new importance upon *do* and *dar*, which are seen in the following lines, *"enti do uuas der eino almahtico cot. manno miltisto. / enti dar uuarun auh manake mit inan. cootlihhe geista,"* to refer to time and space respectively, forming a chiastic antithesis to *enteo* and *uuenteo*.

The argument is ingenious, but weakened by Perrett's own admission that "whether *wenteo* was ever *understood* [my italics] as referring to time or timelessness may well be doubted." In the Cotton MS of the *Heliand*, *giuuand* does occur in variation with *endi*, apparently referring to time: *"Neo endi ni kumid, / thes uuîdon rîkeas giuuand, the* he giuualdan scal" (267–68).[19] In Modern German the time connotation is well established, *die Wende* being awarded the accolade of "das Wort des Jahres" for 1982 by no less an authority than Broder Carstensen.[20] But the only close OHG parallel suggests that the Grimms were correct in interpreting *uuenteo* as "boundaries," as the genitive plural of OHG *uuant*, rather than *uuenti*; in the interlinear version of the Trier capitulary of 818, we read "inneneuuendiun theru selveru grāsceffi . . . ūzzeneuuendiun theru grāsceffi,"[21] a sense confirmed by the lines from *Das Himmelreich* quoted above.

If we can find parallels in Old Testament accounts of the Creation for all the nouns in lines 2–5, ought we not to look there also for an explanation of line 6? Klaeber paraphrases: "also es war keine Scheidung da," and points to Genesis 1.6, "et dividat aquas ab aquis."[22] Following *der marǫ seo*, this absence of watery divisions would then constitute another poetic inversion of the Genesis account, and might have found further inspiration from other biblical references to the division of the land and the waters, such as Job 26.10, Job 38.8ff, Psalm 104.9, Jeremiah 5.22, all of which refer to God placing a *terminum* beyond which the waters may not pass. But "Do dar niuuiht ni uuas enteo ni uuenteo" seems to have a wider, more cumulative sense than this, summing up the depiction of the primaeval void.[23]

Wackernagel maintained that "die mosaische Genesis sagt nichts von einer ungeschaffenen Materie,"[24] and this categorical assertion seems to have deterred the majority of scholars from looking further. The most pertinent statement in Genesis would seem to be I.2, "Terra autem erat inanis et vacua." While this line in the Vulgate offers us synonymia, and two negatory adjectives, it scarcely provides an obvious springboard for "Do dar niuuiht niuuas enteo ni uuenteo." But the Septuagint proves more helpful. The glosses in Clm. 22053 reveal a knowledge of Greek on the part of the compiler of the MS, or of his teachers;[25] in the Septuagint the earth is described as ἀόρατος καὶ ἀκατασκεύαστος. Both words are rare: ἀόρατος means "unseen, invisible, obscure," but two of the classical scholars I consulted suggested, independently, that it may be a false etymology from *horos,* "boundary"; ἀκατασκεύαστος means "not properly prepared or constructed," occurring in Theophrastos, of a drug, and apart from that only in Enoch 21.1: "And I proceeded to where things were chaotic. And I saw there something horrible: I saw neither a heaven above nor a firmly founded earth, but a place chaotic and horrible."[26] The Greek has then two negatory adjectives, both with the *alpha* privative, the negative prefix; the obscurity of the two words is a reflection of the problems posed by the Hebrew, which has at this point the phrase *tōhû wābōhû.* The copulative particle, *wā,* joins two words which are obscure in the extreme.

It appears that the Hebrew religion, in a process analogous to the Christianization of elements of the Germanic vocabulary such as *Muspilli,* drew upon older, "pagan" religions for the formulation of its ideas about the Creation. *Tōhû* is defined as meaning "formlessness, confusion, unreality, emptiness," though lexicographers admit that the "primary meaning" is "difficult to seize." It has been traced back to the Babylonian *Ti'amat,* the primaeval dragon of chaos, goddess of Creation, mother of the gods. *Bōhû,* marginally the rarer of the two words, denotes "emptiness," and only ever occurs in conjunction with *tōhû.* An Arabic parallel means "be empty"; the word may be related to *Baau,* the nocturnal mother goddess in Phoenician mythology. By the time of the writing of Genesis both these words, it is thought, would have become dead metaphors and lost all association with their originally quite distinct mythological circles.[27] Thus the *Jerusalem Bible* translates the phrase in Genesis 1.2 as "trackless waste and emptiness," "a formless void."[28] The same phrase in Jeremiah 4. 23 is rendered as "a formless waste"; here the prophet is describing the chaos that will come at the end of the world, and the imagery used is similar to that found in the *Wessobrunner Gebet,* and in the *Muspilli:*

> I looked to the earth, to see a formless waste;
> to the heavens, and their light had gone.
> I looked to the mountains, to see them quaking
> and all the heights astir.
> I looked, to see no man at all,
> the very birds of heaven had fled,
> I looked, to see the wooded country a wilderness . . .

There is no reference to the sea, but both trees and mountains, *poum* and *pereg*, are here. The presence of this pair in the *Wessobrunner Gebet* is not merely the result of *Stabreimzwang*, the need to provide an alliterating stave, still less a reminiscence of the Alpine landscape,[29] but a reflection of the fact that the beginning and end of the world are in biblical tradition described in terms of the same natural phenomena.

The only other occurrence of the phrase *tōhû wābōhû* also refers to the destruction of the world by Yahweh, when the void will recur, erasing the lines that have been created:

> [Their land] will be the haunt of pelican and hedgehog,
> the owl and the raven will live there;
> over it Yahweh will stretch the measuring line of chaos
> and the plumb-line of emptiness. (Isaiah 24.11)

The connotation of "tracklessness," an absence of finite lines or boundaries, is common to *tōhû wābōhû* and line 6b of the *Wessobrunner Gebet*. It might be that the OHG poet, intrigued perhaps by the Vulgate or the Greek text of Genesis 1.2, referred to the Hebrew original, and then constructed the rhyme-pair as a conscious or unconscious echo of the formally similar Hebrew phrase.

Such speculation demands that a route be posited whereby the two texts might have come into association. We do meet with some acquaintance with Hebrew elsewhere in Clm. 22053: on fol. 94ʳ the Hebrew name for God, *el*, occurs; more significantly, the legend of the *Discovery of the Holy Cross*, which is the first continuous text in the manuscript, includes the prayer of Judas, based upon a common Hebrew prayer found in its earliest form in 1 Chronicles 29.10ff. The Hebrew words have been divided wrongly, suggesting dictation rather than faulty copying; other fragments of Hebrew follow the prayer (fol. 70ᵛ). Glenys Waldman suggests that "the scribe(s) of the model(s) for the Wess. Prayer Ms. knew enough Hebrew to be able to recite some prayers."[30] The poet of the *Wessobrunner Gebet* might have consulted a Jew learned in the Scriptures concerning Genesis 1.2, or he might have found a reference to the Hebrew text in a commentary.

The first learned Jew known to have settled in Germany was Moses ben Kalonymos, who came to Mainz in the second half of the ninth century.[31] However, in the year 829 Hrabanus Maurus sent to Hilduin of St. Denis a commentary on the books of Kings, and he states in his preface that has inserted sections for which he has consulted a learned Hebrew.[32] This Jew has been the subject of some controversy. While historians such as Katz and Baron readily accept his existence, theologians are more sceptical. They point out that the commentaries of Hrabanus Maurus are on the whole derivative, constitut-ing a compendium of earlier patristic commentaries — "parasitic copying," as Laistner describes them.[33] Laistner traces another reference to a Hebrew in Hrabanus's commentary on Genesis back to a letter of Jerome to Damasus.[34]

The phrase *modernis temporibus*, which Hrabanus twice employs to describe his Jew, the second occasion being his dedication to Louis the Pious of the commentary on Chronicles,[35] may not after all mean that he was a contemporary of Hrabanus, as Angelomus of Luxeuil (*c.* 845–55) has similar "tantalisingly vague" references to an "unknown Jewish scholar."[36]

A further reference to Hebrew occurs in Hrabanus's commentary on Matthew, *à propos* the Aramaic word *racha* in Matthew 5.22. This passage is also discussed on fol. 70ᵛ of the *Wessobrunner Gebet* manuscript. Rieger traces Hrabanus's interpretation back to Claudius of Turin, and ultimately to Augustine.[37] The two apparently derivative quotations do not, however, refer specifically to a Jew of modern times. Whether or not this Hebrew existed, and whether or not he was the author of the anonymous *Quaestiones Hebraicae in libros Regum et Paralipomenon*, reference to the Hebrew seems to have been an established principle of Hrabanus Maurus in the construction of his commentaries, and the idea of a Jewish contemporary — perhaps a convert to Christianity — being consulted is not inherently unlikely.

The early decades of the ninth century constitute one of those rare periods when anti-Semitism was at a relatively low ebb in Europe. Charlemagne had sent Isaac, a Jew, with the ambassadorial party to Harun al Rashid, Caliph of Baghdad, perhaps as interpreter, in 797. Louis the Pious appointed a *magister Judaeorum*, who may or may not have been a Jew himself, as overseer of the Jews, and Agobard, Bishop of Lyons, claims that "Carolingian magnates preferred the prayers and blessings of rabbis to those of Christian clergymen and that rustic Christians had shifted their market-day from Saturday to Sunday so that they could attend the synagogue-service instead of Mass."[38] Conversions were by no means uncommon, and not all the conversion traffic was one-way.

The most fascinating case, analysed by Cabaniss,[39] is that of Bodo, a nobleman of Alemannic stock, educated for the Church in Aachen and attached to the entourage of Hilduin of St Denis, to whom Hrabanus Maurus, abbot of Fulda, dedicated his commentary on Kings. Bodo was a personable young man, very much a court favourite. Walahfrid Strabo, pupil of Hrabanus, employed as royal tutor, composed some rather sickly verses in honour of Bodo's blonde Teutonic beauty, which end: "Candide, care vale, carissime semper ubique / Pusio candidule, candide pusiole." [Fair one, dear one, goodbye dearest always and everywhere, / Little fair boy, fair little boy]. By 838 Bodo had risen to become court chaplain and royal deacon to Louis the Pious, and, apparently sickened by the laxity of Louis's court, and the fact that "regardless of the solemn vow of chastity, many women had often yielded to his persuasive charms and fond embraces in the very sanctuaries of Aix-la-Chapelle," resolved to go on a pilgrimage to Rome. Louis accorded him a retinue befitting his station, but whether he ever actually reached Rome is uncertain. At some point Bodo made the acquaintance of some Jews, and on 22 May 839 he was circumcised. He renounced the tonsure, grew a beard, changed his name to Eleazar, exchanged clerical garb for a military habit, married the young daughter of one of his Jewish friends and persuaded his nephew also to adopt the Jewish religion. Not content with this, he sold the very retinue Louis had accorded him to Mohammedan slave-traders. Perhaps feeling that Aachen was now too hot to hold him, Bodo emigrated to Moorish Spain, where greater tolerance was accorded to Jews.

The reaction at Louis' court was one of incredulity. The Emperor himself could not believe his ears, and for days his household was grief-stricken over the mournful news. Various motives were attributed to Bodo: treason, avarice, concupiscence, allegiance to the devil. Meanwhile, in Spain, Bodo-Eleazar became a zealot and tried to persuade all his acquaintances to embrace Judaism, or failing that Islam. The last we hear of him is in 847, when the Christians of Moorish Spain sent a formal petition to Charles the Bald and the bishops of the Empire, tearfully imploring them to recall the apostate, who was making life unbearable for the Mozarabaic Christians.

In his commentary on Genesis, Hrabanus Maurus is concerned to explain the whereabouts of God at the time of the Creation, since we are told that He created not only the earth, but also heaven. Hrabanus, without particular reference to his Hebrew source at this point, locates God in a higher heaven, *superius illud coelum*, and this heaven is filled with the most blessed hosts of angels, *beatissimis angelorum agminibus*, who were created before men. As Leitzmann points out, this idea derives from older commentaries, such as those of Augustine and Bede, and it seems likely that it owes its presence in the *Wessobrunner Gebet* to such a commentary.[40] Hrabanus proceeds to interpret "Terra autem erat inanis et vacua" as meaning that the earth was covered with water, constituting the abyss. The earth itself was formed of "atoms of darkness," and only when these came into light did it possess form. The formless matter was then circumscribed by God with boundaries, *finibus*. Hrabanus also refers to the creation of the four elements, *die vier wende* in the words of Der Meißner. The phrase *inanis et vacua* seems to have exercised a peculiar fascination on Hrabanus, for it occurs again in his Matthew commentary, to explain *racha*: "Aliter *racha* proprie verbum Hebraeorum est, et interpretatur κοινὸς, id est, inanis aut vacuus" [Otherwise *racha* is properly a word of the Hebrews, and means O, that is, vain or empty — *PL*, CVII, col. 806.]

Chronology seems at first to militate against the hypothesis that the *Wessobrunner Gebet* might be a by-product of Hrabanus Maurus' concern with Genesis. The *Commentaria in Genesim* is dedicated to Freculph, Bishop of Lisieux, and the exchange of letters which constitutes its preface bears the date 819. In the correspondence Hrabanus is given the title of abbot, but he was only elected in 822.[41] The biographies suggest that Hrabanus' first commentary was that on Matthew, dating from the year 822.[42] The first mention of Freculph as a bishop is in 825, when he was sent to Rome to supply the French bishopric's view on idolatry.

The *Wessobrunner Gebet* manuscript contains three dates which offer a clue as to the time of its composition or copying: the document recording the liberation of the slave Herimotas (fol. 66ᵛ), which is in a different hand from the greater part of the manuscript, and may have had the function of a public statement, was composed during the reign of *rege nostro carolo*. As Waldman shows, Charlemagne did not cease to be known as *rex* when he became Emperor, and so the document, or its original, might date from any time between 768 and 814.[43] The other two dates occur on the last page of the manuscript (fol. 99ᵛ), in what may again be a different, and is now in parts a barely legible hand. In the course of some chronological observations the years 814 and 815 are mentioned, the latter year being singled out as particularly significant: "et in eod*em* anno defunctus gloriossimus carolus rex et constitutus fuit filius ei*us* hludouuigus rex In regn*um* suum" [and in that year the most glorious King Charles died and his son Louis was made king in his kingdom]. Both these pages occur at ends of sections of the manuscript and contain matter extraneous to the content of their sections; they might have been entered on these final pages at any time during the compilation or copying. Bischoff believes that the manuscript may have been compiled during "eine längere Reihe von Jahren."[44] We are still very much in the dark as to the precise function of the manuscript, but it may well, like the manual of Walahfrid Strabo, abbot of the Reichenau, have been the life-long property of a monk, his own personal copy and encyclopaedia.[45] At all events, we can only admit with Waldman (p. 11) that 814–15 is at best an approximate date. But much, of course, depends on how big a gap in time exists between the *Wessobrunner Gebet* as it has survived and what we imagine to be the poem's date of composition.

The argument that the *Wessobrunner Gebet* is a corrupt copy of a much older text rests in part on the assumption of metrical or semantic lacunae. Three of these have been enshrined in the *Althochdeutsches Lesebuch* since Braune's first edition of 1875.[46] As recently as 1958, Ernst Ochs likened the *Wessobrunner Gebet* to "einer Ruine, die man am besten so beläßt, wie sie überliefert ist," and then proceeded to spoil the effect of his apt simile by proferring two new conjectures as to the lacunae.[47] The meticulous English scholarship of the last half-century has moved away from this approach and sought to plug the holes by taking us back to the original manuscript. Much, not least the glosses on fols. 61ᵛ–63ʳ, suggests that the copying, if not the compilation, of the manuscript took place in Bavaria, and it seems unlikely that a scribe should miss out whole words of a text in a language that was at least close to his own. Opinions vary as to the carefulness of the scribe responsible for the greater part of this still inadequately explained miscellany, but Waldman's study suggests that, while the scribe makes copying errors of considerable magnitude in the first part of the manuscript, omitting whole columns in the legend of the discovery of the Holy Cross which occupies fols. 1ᵛ–21ʳ, such errors are rare in the later sections. The texts before and after the *Wessobrunner Gebet*, while haphazard in arrangement and incoherent enough to suggest to Waldman "a sort of stream-of-consciousness thinking,"[48] are not characterized by the omission of whole words.

The first point at which the *Lesebuch* posits a lacuna is after *paum* in line 3. The line makes perfect sense as it stands in the manuscript, but underlying the assumption of a gap is the theory that the original of the poem alliterated perfectly in accordance with the conventions of Old English verse; line 4, on this basis, is also seen as deficient, and with regard to lines 6–9 considerable doubt has been expressed as to whether the poet has here been attempting to produce alliterative verse of the same purity as we allegedly find in lines 1, 2 and 5. Lines 10–13 in the *Lesebuch* are dismissed as prose, and possibly a later addition, although Ganz has stressed that these lines do employ alliteration and that the punctuation suggests that the scribe was aware of this. Ganz's approach shows at the very least that the "prose" part of the prayer is no more irregular in metre than the rest of the text, and that to posit lacunae on a purely metrical basis is to make assumptions with regard to the competence and intentions of the original poet which we can neither prove nor disprove. Nevertheless, the division of the text into two is almost universally accepted, and more adventurous scholars have not hesitated to reconstruct three, or even four distinct original poems.[49]

With regard to the apparently defective line 4, McLintock argues that *ni* as a copulative conjunction is alien to Old High German except in the two instances in the *Wessobrunner Gebet*, *enteo ni uuenteo*, and *ninohheinig*, and thus points away from High German provenance.[50] *noheînic* as a pronominal adjective is however attested in the *Monsee Fragments* (XXX,5). Grienberger and Schirokauer see it as a pronoun referring back to *paum* and *pereg*; Schirokauer translates: "Nicht Baum noch Berg war da, nicht einer."[51] Perhaps the closest parallel is *Muspilli*, lines 51–52: "*so* inprinnan*t* die perga, poum ni kistentit / *enihc* in erdu." It would seem, then, that the positing of a gap in line 44 may rest solely on metrical grounds.

The third lacuna in the Braune edition marks the gap between what the editors of the *Lesebuch* consider to be the complete poem and its prose appendage. Here Perrett has adduced one of the Anglo-Saxon analogues of our poem, the seventh-century *Cædmon's Hymn*, which consists of nine lines of alliterative verse in praise of the Creator:

> Nu scylun herȝan   hefænricæs uard,
> metudæs mæcti   end his modȝidanc,
> 3 uerc uuldurfadur   sue he uundra ȝihuæs,
> eci dryctin,   or astelidæ;
> he ærist scop   ælda barnum
> 6 heben til hrofe,   haleȝ scepen,
> tha middunȝeard   moncynnæs uard;
> eci dryctin   æfter tiadæ
> 9 firum foldu,   frea allmectiȝ.
> Primo cantauit Caedmon istud carmen.[52]

[Now <we> must praise the guardian of the kingdom of heaven, / the Creator's might and purpose, / the work of the glorious father, as he, of each and every wonder, / eternal Lord, established the beginning; / he first created for the children of men / heaven as a roof, holy Creator, / the middle-earth, guardian of mankind; / the eternal Lord afterwards / made the earth for men. Lord Almighty.]

The poem's length coincides perfectly with the first part of the text of the Wessobrunn Prayer, as edited by Braune, and ends with a similar half-line. Even the most cursory glance at Anglo-Saxon alliterative verse yields a large number of parallels to *cot heilac* as a syntactically isolated half-line, for example: *halig Drihten* (*Genesis B*, 240, 247, 251); *aelmihtig God* (*Dream of the Rood*, 106); *frea almihtig* (*Genesis A*, 117). Perrett argues that "the grammatically unrelated *enti cot heilac* of line 9 does most effectively emphasise the *theme* of the poem, which is taken up as in a Response by the first words of the prose, *Cot almahtico*."[53] Perrett's suggestion that 9b is an anacoluthon, but nevertheless a complete half-line in the Anglo-Saxon mould, would gain conviction if we were to adopt Ganz's suggestion that the ⌐-symbol is not necessarily to be taken as representing *enti*, but may be read as a metrical pause. The deletion of *enti* in line 7 yields a *Do . . . do* link such as is common in Middle High German, and makes the poem appreciably tighter. As is, however, pointed out by Schwab, when the symbol occurs elsewhere in the manuscript it stands for Latin *et*.[54] Moreover, prayers such as the *St Emmeramer Gebet* and the *Lorscher Beichte* employ *enti* with cumulative force in a manner that has been compared with that of the *Wessobrunner Gebet*.[55]

But is (*enti*) *cot heilac* necessarily an *Abzeile*? No matter how we attempt to edit lines 7–11, metrical difficulties present themselves. Even Ganz's adherence to the punctuation of the manuscript produces the clumsy line: "*enti cot heilag*. Cot almahtico du himil *enti* erda gauuorahtos."[56] Seiffert suggests an interlocking, if non-metrical, pattern of alliteration: "al*m*ahtico cot *m*anno *m*iltisto enti . . . *m*anake mit inan *c*ootlihhe geista enti *c*ot heilac *C*ot almahtico."[57] It seems that at this point in the text, if not elsewhere, the ideas which the poet wishes to express take precedence over metrical principles. The presence of the angels at the Creation is part of the doctrine he has absorbed from patristic interpretation of Genesis, and the stress upon God as *manno miltisto* is integral to the meaning of the poem, providing the link between *deus omnipotens* and God the helper of contemporary man: "Gott heisst hier nun *milti* wegen der in der Schöpfung kundgegebenen unendlichen Güte."[58] While the punctuation provides no obvious solution to our problem here, it is helpful to remember that the punctuation is primarily a metrical device; moreover, the scribe's employment of capitals is inconsistent, as can be seen from line 2: "Dat ero ni uuas. . . ." The first editor of the *Wessobrunner Gebet*, Bernhard Pez, in his *Thesaurus Anecdotorum Novissimus* (1721), took these factors into account, and printed: "Cot heilac, Cot almahtico du himil / erda   gauuorahtos

<. . .>." Wackernagel in 1827 similarly interpreted the point after *cot heilac* as a less than final pause.[59] The Grimms in 1812, however, took the point and the capital to mark the end of a sentence, and almost all subsequent editors have either followed them with depressing unimaginativeness, or made three dots out of one.

The other Anglo-Saxon poem that has been adduced for comparison is *The Wonders of Creation* from the Exeter Book, dating from *c.* A.D. 1000.[60] At first sight this poem appears to have little in common with the *Wessobrunner Gebet*; it is longer (102 lines), much more diffuse, and, like *Cædmon's Hymn*, places no stress on the primaeval void. It nevertheless provides a useful analogue: its beginning suggests that it belongs to an older tradition of Creation poetry, and it lays great stress on the acquisition of knowledge about the Creation by word of mouth. The poem opens as a dialogue between an inexperienced man and a wiser speaker who is to impart knowledge to the former on the basis of his asking, *fricgan* (3); this was how mankind acquired wisdom long ago, by always asking, *á fricgende* (14), and the studious man should even now *ascian* (17) about the secrets of the Creation. The parallel with the opening of the *Wessobrunner Gebet* is unmistakable. The summary of a Creation lay in *Beowulf* similarly lays stress on the wisdom of the minstrel: "Saegde se þe cūþe / frumsceaft fira   feorran reccan <. . .>" [90a–91: One who was able to relate from long ago the creation of men recited <. . .>.] It seems likely that there is more to this than an oral formula, such as introduces the *Hildebrandslied*, or even the "Sô gifragn ik," which introduces the thirty-second and fifty-fourth fitts of the *Heliand*.[61] The stress upon knowledge about the Creation being the privilege of a learned minority may well reflect a missionary function underlying the genesis of the Creation lay. Bede's account of the conversion of King Sigbert of Essex (650–60) by King Oswy of Northumbria anticipates Bishop Daniel's letter to Boniface in emphasizing the importance of the Creation doctrine: "for Sigbert . . . was then king of that nation, and a friend to King Oswy, who, when Sigbert came to the province of the Northumbrians to visit him, as he often did, used to endeavour to convince him that those could not be gods that had been made by the hands of men. . . . That God is rather to be understood as . . . almighty, eternal, the Creator of heaven and of earth and of mankind, . . . whose eternal abode must be believed to be in Heaven."[62] A. S. Cook saw *Cædmon's Hymn*, composed in the monastery of Hild at Whitby, whither Oswy had committed his daughter for tutelage, as reflecting Oswy's stress on the Creation as a conversion ploy. Cædmon, of course, had no need to underline the basis of his wisdom, for he had, like the *Heliand* poet after him, his calling from God.[63]

The ending of *The Wonders of the Creation* is also significant for an attempt to locate the *Wessobrunner Gebet* within a literary tradition. Having described the wonders of the Creation and the eternal bliss of the inhabitants of heaven, the poet turns to the life of man upon earth. The power of God as revealed in the Creation is made the basis of a prayer:

forþon scyle mon gehycgan þæt he meotude hyre
æghwylc ælda bearna forlæte idle lustas
læne lifes wynne fundige him to lissa blisse
forlæte heteniþa gehwone sigan
mid synna fyrnum fere him to þam sellan rice: ⁊

[So let one resolve to obey God; let each of the children of men forsake vain desires, the fleeting pleasures of life, and aspire to the bliss of heavenly joys. Let him let every evil fall away from him along with sinful vices, and let him go to the better kingdom.]

                              The Wonders of Creation, 98–102.[64]

Despite its late date, the Anglo-Saxon poem's combination of an account of the Creation with a prayer constitutes a strong argument for the unity of composition of the *Wessobrunner Gebet*.

    The Wonders of Creation accords pride of place to the sun, which it describes as *forðmære tungol* (line 69), "the ever-famous," or "ever-glorious star." The same adjective *marƣo* in the *Wessobrunner Gebet* has been the source of some controversy. Docen interpreted it as meaning "glänzend, schimmernd," and was followed in this by Grienberger and Baesecke; Müllenhoff argued that the sense was "herrlich"; Schirokauer contended that the unusual employment of the definite article meant that *der marƣo seo* referred to "das Weltmeer, das germanische Mythenmeer."[65] The sense in *The Wonders of Creation* is open to ambiguity, but the adjective also occurs in *The Dream of the Rood* (line 12): "eall þeos mære gesceaft" [all this glorious creation]; in *Genesis B* (line 299) to describe the Lord: "mæran Drihten"; and also in the *Heliand* (line 269): "mâri theodan." In the *Vǫluspá* it is the newly created earth, *miðgarð*, that is described as *mæran* (str. 4). The parallels confirm that the word is employed to describe the glory of the Creator, and the reflected glory of the phenomena created by Him.

    The close resemblances between the *Wessobrunner Gebet* and its Germanic cognates return us inevitably to the question of the poem's provenance. Four kinds of evidence have been sifted and resifted over nearly two centuries in attempts to establish the true soil from which the *Wessobrunner Gebet* sprang: the palaeographic and orthographic; phonological and morphological; the lexis and style of the poem; and the suggestions of a literary tradition. The palaeographic evidence has been the subject of a long dispute between Baesecke and Bischoff. Baesecke held that the two most striking palaeographic features, the Tironian abbreviation for *et* and the star-rune, derive from Anglo-Saxon scribal practice, and that therefore the poem was translated from Anglo-Saxon into Franconian in Fulda, finding its way from there to St Emmeram.[66] The presence of the symbols in, for example, a Regensburg manuscript produced during the time of Bishop Baturich (817–47) is attributed by Baesecke to the personal contact between Baturich and Hrabanus Maurus. Bischoff, while accepting that both abbreviations are Anglo-Saxon in origin, sees no reason to locate the compilation of Clm. 22053 outside Bavaria, and has variously suggested Benediktbeuern, Staffelsee and Hesselohe.[67] In the course of this dispute a clear distinction has not always been drawn between the compilation of the manuscript and the copying of all or part of it, though there is a tacit assumption that at least some of the manuscript has been copied.

Ute Schwab argues that Bischoff's suggestion of Staffelsee is doubtful on the grounds that it had only a very limited library, the only commentaries there being Jerome on Matthew, and a commentary on the Psalms. Her study of the star-rune leads her to reject the thesis of Anglo-Saxon provenance; the presence of the rune in Bavarian manuscripts is seen rather as the result of a complex development over a long period of time on the Continent, involving Irish, Frisian and possible Italian influences.[68] Schwab draws upon the work of René Derolez, who points out that the attribution of the introduction of runes into continental manuscripts to Hrabanus Maurus is an over-simplification.[69] From Alcuin's time onwards runes were introduced as abbreviations and, in particular, for aesthetic effect; Anglo-Saxon teachers and scribes were for the most part responsible for this.

But that the star-rune is new to the scribe of Clm. 22053 is strongly suggested, as Schwab herself points out,[70] by the only other occurrence of the rune in the manuscript, in the glosses which precede the *Wessobrunner Gebet* on fol. 63[r]. The scribe uses a star-rune, but this time with a horizontal stroke through it rather than the correct vertical stroke that we find in the *Wessobrunner Gebet*, to precede the word *kazungali*, long held because of an extraordinary combination of faulty memory and hearsay to refer to the oldest named German poet, but now recognized as the gloss for *poetica*.[71] Before the symbol there is an erasure which suggests an earlier botched effort; it is as if the scribe is practising his skill with the unfamiliar symbol before he employs it in the *Wessobrunner Gebet*, the ornamentation of which suggests that it is intended to occupy pride of place in this part of the manuscript. Such deliberation is scarcely compatible with the omission of words.

For the scribe at least the rune appears to correspond to the *ka* sound. Since Hoffmann's privately published edition of the *Wessobrunner Gebet* in 1825, the rune has been interpreted as *ga-* on the basis of *ganada* and *galaupa*.[72] Krogmann, following C. A. Mayer, sees the scribe of the *Wessobrunner Gebet* as differentiating with almost Notkerian finesse between Bavarian *g* "in palataler Umgebung" and *c* (*k*) "in velarer Umgebung."[73] *kazungali* and *cholonne* (fol. 62[v]) would suggest otherwise; it seems likely that the scribe found *g* in the prayer he was copying, but he may have treated it inconsistently. In *pereg* he alters *c* into uncial *g*; *constantinuses puruc* and *salzpuruc* (62[v], 63[r]) suggest that *c* was the form that came naturally to him. The emendation here may imply that the scribe subsequently failed to change the *c* back to the poem's original *g*; *đ* and *d* in the *Hildebrandslied* offer a similar discrepancy. We cannot be certain that the *c* of *cot, coot, cotan, cootlihhe* was in the scribe's original, and this of course could have drastic implications for our view of the poem's alliteration, not to mention its linguistic provenance.

The other orthographical evidence that suggests that the poem as we find it in Clm. 22053 is a copy of an older original consists in three probable scribal errors. *ero* in line 2 has possible cognates in later texts, but the evidence is far from convincing.[74] On Fischer's *Schrifttafel*, the photography reveals a slanting stroke to the right below the *o* which, although not there in earlier facsimiles, is quite clear to the naked eye in the manuscript today.[75] At this point, and in the *as* of *uuas* in the following line, the ink is somewhat darker than the rest of the text. It may be that the slanting stroke indicates the scribe's consciousness that he has made an error in omitting the dental. Secondly, the *st* ligature in *nistein* (4) is thought to be a mistake for *sc*; as Grienberger points out, the configuration of the ligature in *stein* differs slightly from the ligature in *meista, miltisto, geista, uuistóm* and *uuidarstantanne*. Finally, lines 42 and 43 of the *Hildebrandslied* suggest that the *e caudata* in *marẹo* (5) might belong more properly in *seo*. The *e caudata* is common in the Latin texts in the manuscript, for instance in the Latin Creation poem on fols.37ᵛ–40ʳ, where it generally stands for *æ*, but in *çeli* appears to be wrongly placed below the consonant rather than the vowel.[76] All this suggests a scribe who makes occasional spelling errors, particularly when writing a language presumably rarely entered into manuscripts by him, rather than the kind of copier who is prone to omit words. Taken in conjunction with the generally careful employment of the *punctus*, which may have been omitted after *firahim* and *nohheinig* because the margin suggested the end of a half-line or line, the orthographical evidence suggests a fairly accurate reproduction of what the scribe had before him, but it does not take us very far in establishing the poem's provenance.

The twenty-one lines of manuscript have permitted the adoption of four extreme positions with regard to the linguistic provenance of the poem, or its supposed archetype. It has been variously held that this was Franconian (Reinwald, in a letter to Docen, Carl von Kraus,[77] Baesecke), Old Saxon (Docen, Wackernagel, Müllenhoff, Scherer, Rieger[78]), Anglo-Saxon (Braune, Baesecke again, Perrett) and Bavarian (Kögel,[79] C. A. Mayer, Krogmann). The last two opposing stances were taken up as recently as 1937, when Krogmann argued that both poet and scribe were Bavarian, and 1938, when Perrett reconstructed the Anglo-Saxon original of the poem. Since then scholarship has with a few exceptions chosen to rest its pen on the subject of the language of the *Wessobrunner Gebet*, perhaps in mute acknowledgement of the inadequacy of the evidence and the consequent insuperability of the problem.

It seems probable that the truth lies somewhere between the extremes, that the text as it has survived is a dialect mix of some kind, a geographical and chronological hybrid. But here too the possibilities and the suggestions that have been made are myriad. The possible approaches to the first word of the text, *Dat*, may serve as an illustration. The spirant *ʒ* resulting from shifted *t* is not to be found in our short poem in final position; in medial position it occurs only in *firiuuizzo*, corresponding to OS *firiwit*, OE *fyrwet*. We cannot of course be sure that when our scribe wrote a *t* he always intended a *t* to be pronounced; this *t* may be a reflection of conservative orthography. It may, however, indicate that either poet or scribe was writing at a time or in an area where the shift had not taken place. Yet if the word were Old Saxon or Anglo-Saxon in origin we would expect *that*, or perhaps a *ðat* such as we find in the early lines of the *Hildebrandslied*. It may, of course, be that a scribe was attempting to transpose an older or geographically alien text into Bavarian, and failed to do so with regard to this word in the first two lines; or such a common word, even in Upper German, may have preserved the unshifted *t* in the spoken language as a relic form. It would even be possible to apply McLintock's theory concerning the more complex dialect mix that confronts us in the *Hildebrandslied*;[80] thus *dat* and such elements of vocabulary as we cannot satisfactorily explain from what survives in OHG would be evidence of a deliberately archaizing intention. This is similar to the approach of Kögel, and of Steinmeyer, who speaks of a "Rhapsodensprache, von der wir aus dem engeren Deutschland blutwenig wissen."[81] Krogmann also argues from ignorance, this time our ignorance of pre-ninth-century Bavarian. By the time his monodialectal argument comes to consider *dat* it has become somewhat circular, so that he is delighted to claim the unshifted form as the "wertvollste Gabe" of the poem to our reconstruction of Old Bavarian.[82]

We have already seen, in our consideration of the word *marȩo*, that lexical elements in the *Wessobrunner Gebet* can be explained by reference to cognates in Anglo-Saxon, not to mention Old Saxon and Old Norse. These links extend to *gafregin*, *firahim*, *firiuuiȝȝo*, *ufhimil*, *manno miltisto*; perhaps also the copulative use of *ni*, and the preposition *mit* in the sense of "among."[83] Perhaps the most convincing of these parallels is the use of *geista* to mean angels.[84] *Genesis A* (line 1875) describes the angels as *halige gastas*. The idea of the presence of the angels at the Creation derives from commentaries, but the formulation of the idea suggests an Anglo-Saxon influence at work, and the same applies to the phrase *manno miltisto* (OE *manna mildost*), which is so central to the unity of the thought of the poem. Krogmann's consideration of these parallels restricts itself to the feasibility of the existence of these lexical elements in OHG; he deliberately ignores "den Inhalt des Liedes"[85] and the similarities in content that other scholars have found in the different Germanic languages.

The lexical parallels and the Anglo-Saxon literary analogues point in the same direction, to an area where the influence of Anglo-Saxon missionaries was prominent. De Boor, considering the resemblances between the *Wessobrunner Gebet* and the ON *Vǫluspá*, comes to the conclusion that in Iceland too "christliche Gedanken dem Norden in angelsächsischer Prägung zugekommen sind."[86] The linguistic evidence can only be of limited value in helping us determine the provenance of the poem, but that too is not inconsistent with the hypothesis that a Bavarian scribe was copying a poem by an author from further north. This poet's — probably decorative — use of the star-rune, a device unfamiliar to the copyist, suggests Anglo-Saxon scribal practice. Taken together, the four kinds of evidence point to a "collaboration"[87] between Anglo-Saxon and German cultures, but the difficulty remains of trying to establish the concrete form which this collaboration took. Baesecke and Perrett have argued for a direct translation from an Anglo-Saxon poem, but if that were the case one might have expected a more rigid adherence to Anglo-Saxon poetic conventions. More attractive is the suggestion that an Anglo-Saxon monk and a High German-speaking monk collaborated in producing a German poem; or perhaps an Anglo-Saxon missionary, whose German was good, but not perfect, was the author. He would be familiar with the literary traditions of his homeland, and would be attempting in his target language a poetic prayer on a subject he knew to have been treated in Anglo-Saxon alliterative verse. A lively interest in Genesis existed in the Anglo-Saxon stronghold of Fulda; there were commentaries present in the library on which the poet might have drawn; and Hrabanus Maurus's Jew may explain the mysterious phrase *enteo ni uuenteo*. The end-product cannot be dismissed as a "vereinfachte christliche Kosmogonie."[88] Its apparent simplicity derives from the perfect fusion of Christian doctrine and poetic skill; one might more appropriately apply to it Hermann Gunkel's words concerning its ultimate source, the first chapter of Genesis: "Diese Schilderung des Uranfangs ist gerade in ihrer Einfachheit großartig und eindrucksvoll."[89]

Notes

[1] / denotes the end of a line in the manuscript. The original's use of points to mark alliteration has been preserved.

[2] J. Sidney Groseclose and Brian O. Murdoch, *Die althochdeutschen poetischen Denkmäler*, Sammlung Metzler, 140 (Stuttgart: J. B. Metzler, 1976), 45.

[3] Jeffrey Ashcroft, "Die Anfänge von Walthers politischer Lyrik," in *Minnesang in Österreich*, Wiener Arbeiten zur germanischen Altertumskunde und Philologie, 24, ed. Helmut Birkhan (Vienna: K. M. Halosar, 1983), 1–14 (1). Terry Fenton argues that the concept of chaos has itself been superimposed anachronistically upon Genesis 1.2. See Fenton, "CHAOS IN THE BIBLE? Tohu vavohu," in *Jewish Education and Learning, published in honour of Dr. David Patterson on the occasion of his seventieth birthday*, ed. Glenda Abramson and Tudor Parfitt (Chur & London: Harwood Academic Publishers, 1993), 203–20. I am indebted to Jill Hughes of the Taylorian Library for drawing my attention to this article.

[4] On the relative dates of the *Wessobrunner Gebet* and the *Hildebrandslied*, see Hans Fischer, *Schrifttafeln zum althochdeutschen Lesebuch* (Tübingen: Niemeyer, 1966), 15*.

[5] Ruth C. Harvey, in an unpublished lecture given in Oxford in 1972.

[6] The parallel with the *Vǫluspá* was first adduced by F. D. Grater, "Das älteste deutsche Gedicht," *Bragur* V:i (1796): 118–55 (132), that with the *Rig-Veda* by Robert A. Fowkes, "Eastern echoes in the *Wessobrunner Gebet?*" *Germanic Review* 37 (1962): 83–90.

[7] Cf. Gustav Ehrismann, *Geschichte der deutschen Literatur bis zum Ausgang des Mittelalters, I: Die althochdeutsche Literatur*, 2nd ed. (Munich: C. H. Beck, 1932), 133–34.

[8] Theodor von Grienberger, "Althochdeutsche Texterklärungen," *PBB* 45 (1921): 212–38 (237); cf. W. Perrett, "On the *Wessobrunner Gebet* — I," *London Medieval Studies* 1,ii (1937): 134–38 (134); Gemma Manganella, "Il 'caos' del *Wessobrunner Gebet*," *Istituto Orientale di Napoli, Annali, Sezione Germanica* 8 (1965): 285–91 (esp. 289–91).

[9] Leslie Seiffert, "The metrical form and composition of the *Wessobrunner Gebet*," *Medium Aevum* 31 (1962): 1–13 (6–7). That the Grimms shared this view is clear from the red strokes in their edition, *Die ältesten deutschen Gedichte aus dem achten Jahrhundert: Das Lied von Hildebrand und Hadubrand und das Weißenbrunner Gebet* (Kassel: Thurneissen, 1812), 80.

[10] W. Perrett, "On the *Wessobrunner Gebet* — II," *London Medieval Studies* 1,ii (1938): 139–49 (139); C. W. M. Grein, "Das Wessobrunner Gebet," *Germania* 10 (1865): 310.

[11] Perrett, II, 144; the Brothers Grimm, 83–84. OHG combinations of alliteration and end-rhyme are commented upon in *Handbook*, 302–03. Peter F. Ganz adduces a Latin parallel in "Die Zeilenaufteilung im 'Wessobrunner Gebet'," *PBB* (Tübingen) 95 *Sonderheft* (1973): 39–51 (47).

[12] F. Kluge, "Geschichte des Reimes im Altgermanischen," *PBB* 9 (1883): 422–50 (esp. 424ff.); Georg Baesecke, *Der Vocabularius Sti. Galli in der angelsächsischen Mission* (Halle: Niemeyer, 1933), 123; cf. also Baesecke, *Das lateinisch-althochdeutsche Reimgebet 'Carmen ad deum' und das Rätsel vom 'Vogel federlos'* (Berlin: Wissenschaftliche Editionsgesellschaft, 1948), 26–27.

[13] Ed. Albert Leitzmann, *Kleinere geistliche Gedichte des XII. Jahrhunderts* (Bonn: A. Marcus und E. Weber, 1910). I am grateful to David Yeandle of King's College, London, for the opportunity to consult the Hamburg *Frühmittelhochdeutsches Wörterbuch* on microfilm.

[14] Text according to the Jena manuscript. Cf. Friedrich Heinrich von der Hagen, *Minnesinger. Deutsche Liederdichter des zwölften, dreizehnten und vierzehnten Jahrhunderts*, 4 vols (Leipzig: J. A. Barth, 1838–61), vol. 3, 93b. The parallel was first adduced by Karl Müllenhoff, *De Carmine Wessofontano et de versu ac stropharum usu apud Germanos antiquissimo* (Berlin: Typis academicis, 1861), 19.

[15] *Versuch eines bremisch-niedersächsischen Wörterbuchs*, ed. Bremisch Deutsche Gesellschaft, 5 vols (Bremen: Georg Ludewig Forster, 1767), vol. 1, 307 and vol. 5, 227; cf. MSD, 2, 6.

[16] Eduard von der Hellen, "Zur Kritik des Wessobrunner Gebetes," *Germania* 31 (1886): 272–80 (276).

[17] *Notker der Deutsche. Boethius, "De consolatione Philosophiae," Buch I/II* (*Die Werke Notkers des Deutschen. Neue Ausgabe. ATB*, 94), ed. Petrus W. Tax (Tübingen: Niemeyer, 1986).

[18] George Allison Hench, *The Monsee fragments* (Strasbourg: K. J. Trübner, 1890), VII, 9; cf. also XXXI, 20: *usque ad extremum terre = untaz. aerda. enti.*

[19] *Heliand und Genesis*, ed. Otto Behaghel, 9th ed. rev. Burkhard Taeger, *ATB*, 4 (Tübingen: Niemeyer, 1984).

[20] Broder Carstensen, "Wörter des Jahres 1982," *Deutsche Sprache* 1983 (2): 174–87 (174).

[21] Braune, *Lesebuch*, XIX, 5–7. The parallel was adduced by Rudolf Kögel and Wilhelm Bruckner, *Geschichte der althoch- und altniederdeutschen Litteratur*, (*Grundriss der germanischen Philologie*) ed. Hermann Paul et al., II,VI,2, 2nd rev. ed. (Strasbourg: K. J. Trübner, 1901–09), 92.

[22] Fr. Klaeber, "Zum Wessobrunner Gebet," *Archiv für das Studium der neueren Sprachen* 174 (1938): 204.

[23] The Oxford copy of the von Eckardt facsimile suggested that the importance of this summarizing line was indicated even by the colours of the manuscript. Up to and including this line it appeared that the scribe had etched over the black ink of every letter with yellow. Indeed the *Wessobrunner Gebet* itself appeared to be the only text in the whole manuscript favoured with both red and yellow illumination. A glance at the original manuscript in the Staatsbibliothek, however, revealed no such features, and other copies of the 1922 facsimile diverge further in respect of colour. Let this prove a salutary warning to users of facsimiles.

[24] Wilhelm Wackernagel, *Das Wessobrunner Gebet und die Wessobrunner Glossen* (Berlin: Schmidt, 1827), 18.

[25] Cf. fols. 54ʳ, 62ʳ; Perrett I, 134–35.

[26] I am grateful to Sebastian Brock of the Oxford Institute of Oriental Studies, Richard Wilson of Birkenhead and Charles Relle of Blackheath High School for their assistance; translations of Enoch are rare, perhaps because of what the Reverend Oesterley, in his introduction to R. H. Charles's translation of *The Book of Enoch* (London: SPCK, 1912) terms "repellent passages."

[27] The definitions are from Francis Brown, Samuel R. Driver, Charles A. Briggs, *A Hebrew and English Lexicon of the Old Testament* (Oxford: Clarendon Press, 1977), 1062. The major scholarship on the origins of the Creation myth is by Hermann Gunkel in *Schöpfung und Chaos in Urzeit und Endzeit: eine religionsgeschichtliche Untersuchung über Gen 1 und Ap Joh 12* (Göttingen: Vandenhoeck und Ruprecht, 1895); he gives in translation the Babylonian sources, one of which was adduced as an analogue of the *Wessobrunner Gebet* by the Grimms on the basis of its anaphoric negatives. Cf. also Gunkel, *Genesis*, 7th ed. (Göttingen: Vandenhoeck und Ruprecht, 1966), 103–04. Gunkel's theories are accepted by more modern scholars such as Gerhard von Rad in *Genesis: A Commentary*, trans. John H. Marks, 3rd rev. ed. (London: SCM Press, 1963), 48; Norman H. Snaith, *Notes on the Hebrew Text of Genesis I–VIII* (London: The Epworth Press, 1947), 8; *The Jerome Biblical Commentary*, ed. Raymond Edward Brown, Joseph A. Fitzmyer and Roland Edmund

Murphy (London: Geoffrey Chapman, 1968), 10. I am indebted to Chris Cook, formerly of the Religion Department, Goldsmiths' College, and Dr Helmut Hasche for their assistance with the Hebrew.

[28] Quotations in English are from *The Jerusalem Bible*, ed. Alexander Jones (London: Darton, Longman & Todd, 1966).

[29] C. A. Mayer, "Die Heimat des Wessobrunner Gebets." *Alemannia* 31 (1903): 161–70 (168).

[30] Glenys A. Waldman, "The Wessobrunn Prayer Manuscript, Clm. 22053: a transliteration, translation and study of parallels" (diss., Pennsylvania State University, 1975), 70.

[31] Solomon Katz, *The Jews in the Visigothic and Frankish Kingdoms of Spain and Gaul* (Cambridge, Mass.: The Mediaeval Academy of America, 1937), 70.

[32] *PL*, CIX, col. 10. Migne dates the preface to 834.

[33] M. L. W. Laistner, "Some early medieval commentaries on the Old Testament," *Harvard Theological Review* 46 (1953): 27–46 (37). Equally sceptical is Stadtrabbiner Dr Rieger, "Wer war der Hebräer, dessen Werke Hrabanus Maurus benutzt hat?" *Monatsschrift für Geschichte und Wissenschaft des Judentums* 68 (1924): 66–68. This scepticism is not shared by Katz (69); Salo Baron, *A Social and Religious History of the Jews*, 2nd ed. (New York: Columbia UP, 1952–69), IV, 256; nor by Beryl Smalley, *The Study of the Bible in the Middle Ages*, 2nd ed. (Oxford: Basil Blackwell, 1952), 43. Bernhard Blumenkranz, *Les Auteurs chrétiens latins du Moyen Âge sur les juifs et le judaïsme* (Paris: Mouton, 1963), adduces a number of additional passages in which Hrabanus refers to Hebrew, and where the exegesis does not appear to be derivative (190, n. 1).

[34] Laistner, 27.

[35] *PL*, CIX, col. 281A; cf. Rieger, 66; Laistner, 30; Franz Wutz, *Onomastica Sacra, Untersuchungen zum Liber interpretationis nominum Hebraicorum des hl. Hieronymus*, Texte und Untersuchungen zur Geschichte der altchristlichen Literatur, Bd. 41, 3. Reihe, 11 (Leipzig: J. C. Hinrichs, 1914–15), 788.

[36] Laistner, 38. Blumenkranz views these references as "un pillage constant de l'œuvre de Raban Maur" (179).

[37] Rieger, 67.

[38] Alan Cabaniss, "Bodo-Eleazar: a famous Jewish convert," *Jewish Quarterly Review* 43 (1952/53): 313–28 (321), quoting from Agobard, *De Insolentia Judaeorum* (*PL*, CIV, col. 74B). Subsequent quotations are from Cabaniss's account of the Bodo story. Cf. also Blumenkranz, 184ff.

[39] Cabaniss, *art. cit.*

[40] Albert Leitzmann, "Zu den kleineren ahd. Denkmälern," *PBB* 39 (1914): 548–58 (551ff.).

[41] Mechthild Sandmann, "Hrabanus Maurus als Mönch, Abt und Erzbischof," in *Hrabanus Maurus und seine Schule. Festschrift der Rabanus-Maurus-Schule*, ed. Winfried Böhne (Fulda: Rabanus-Maurus-Schule, 1980), 23.

[42] *ADB* 27, 72; Sandmann, 20.

[43] Waldman, 11.

[44] Bernhard Bischoff, *Die südostdeutschen Schreibschulen und Bibliotheken in der Karolingerzeit, I: Die bayrischen Diözesen*, 2nd ed. (Wiesbaden: O. Harrassowitz, 1960), 20.

[45] See Bernhard Bischoff, "Eine Sammelhandschrift Walahfrid Strabos (Cod. Sangall. 878)," in Bernhard Bischoff, *Mittelalterliche Studien: Ausgewählte Aufsätze zur Schriftkunde und Literaturkunde*, vol. 2 (Stuttgart: Anton Hiersemann, 1967), 34–51.

[46] Ganz, 44.

[47] Ernst Ochs, "Das Wessobrunner Gebet," *Archiv für das Studium der neueren Sprachen* 194 (1958), 43.

[48.] Waldman, 415.

[49] Cf. Ganz (43), discussing these nineteenth-century attempts to "edit" the text.

[50] D. R. McLintock, "The negatives of the Wessobrunn Prayer," *MLR* 52 (1957): 397–98.

[51] Theodor von Grienberger, "Ahd. Texterklärungen," *PBB* 45 (1921): 212–38 (237); Arno Schirokauer, "*Der mareo seo*," *PMLA* 65 (1950): 313–18 (317).

[52] *Three Northumbrian Poems: Caedmon's Hymn; Bede's Death Song; and the Leiden riddle*, ed. A. H. Smith, rev. ed. (Exeter: U of Exeter, 1978).

[53] Perrett, II, 147.

[54] Ute Schwab, *Die Sternrune im 'Wessobrunner Gebet': Beobachtungen zur Lokalisierung des clm. 22053, zur Hs. BM Arundel 393 und zu Rune Poem V. 86–89*, Amsterdamer Publikationen zur Sprache und Literatur, 1 (Amsterdam: Rodopi, 1973), 3.

[55] Cf. Seiffert, 9–10.

[56] Ganz, 50.

[57] Seiffert, 7.

[58] Wackernagel (as note 24), 59.

[59] Bernhard Pez, *Thesaurus Anecdotorum Novissimus* (Vienna: sumptibus Philippi, Martini & Joannis Veith fratrum, 1721); Wackernagel, 11.

[60.] *The Exeter Book, Part II*, ed. W. S. Mackie, EETS, OS, 194 (London: Oxford UP, 1934), 48–55.

[61] Bernhard Joseph Docen, *Miscellaneen zur Geschichte der teutschen Literatur* (Munich: Scherer, 1807), 21; *Handbook*, 175–76.

[62] Bede, *Ecclesiastical History*, 3, 22, quoted by A. S. Cook, "King Oswy and Cædmon's Hymn," *Speculum* 2 (1927): 67–72 (67). For a wide-ranging survey of the relationship between the early Church and Germanic vernacular literature, see Patrick Wormald, "Bede, 'Beowulf' and the conversion of the Anglo-Saxon aristocracy," in *Bede and Anglo-Saxon England*, ed. Robert T. Farrell, British Archaeological Reports, 46 (Oxford: British Archaeological Reports, 1978), 32–95.

[63] Cf. *Handbook*, 182.

[64] *The Exeter Book, Part II*, 54–55.

[65] Docen, 23; Grienberger, 237; Baesecke, *Der Vocabularius Sti. Galli*, 120; *MSD*, II, 5; Schirokauer, 315.

[66] *Der Vocabularius Sti. Galli*, 122ff.; *St. Emmeramer Studien* (1922), 444 (= *Kleinere Schriften zur althochdeutschen Sprache und Literatur* (Bern and Munich: Francke, 1966), 47).

[67] Bernhard Bischoff, "Paläographie," in *Deutsche Philologie im Aufriß*, ed. Wolfgang Stammler and Günter Schade, 2nd ed. (Berlin: Erich Schmidt, 1957), I, col. 408; idem, *Die südostdeutschen Schreibschulen*, I, 18ff.; cf. also Waldman, 8ff.

[68] Schwab, 15; 36–37; 53–54.

[69] René Derolez, "Die 'hrabanischen' Runen," *ZfdPh* 78 (1959): 1–19. The problem of the runes had already been broached by Wilhelm Weidmüller in "Das *Wessobrunner Gebet* und seine 'Runen'," *Volk und Schrift* 10 (1939): 2–11.

[70] Schwab, 3.

[71] Cf. O. Denecke, "Vom Dichter Kazungali," *Zeitschrift für Bücherfreunde* 6:1 (1914): 19–30.

[72] Wackernagel, 30.

[73] Mayer, 162; Willy Krogmann, "Die Mundart des Wessobrunner Gebets," *Zeitschrift für Mundartforschung* 13 (1937): 129–49 (134).

[74] Cf. Krogmann, 139–40.

[75] Fischer, 15; Erich Petzet and Otto Glauning, *Deutsche Schrifttafeln des IX. bis XVI. Jahrhunderts aus Handschriften der K. Hof- und Staatsbibliothek in München*, 1 (Munich: C. Kuhn, 1910), No. 1; Magda Enneccerus, *Die ältesten deutschen Sprach-Denkmäler, in Lichtdrucken hrsg.* (Frankfurt a. M.: Enneccerus, 1897), tables 9–10; Annette von Eckardt, *Die Handschrift des Wessobrunner Gebets. Geleitwort von Carl von Kraus* (Munich: Kurt Wolff, 1922).

[76] Cf. Otto Mazal, *Lehrbuch der Handschriftenkunde. Elemente des Buch- und Bibliothekswesens*, 10 (Wiesbaden: L. Reichert, 1986), 111: "Der Diphthong *æ* war schon in vorkarolingischer Zeit durch *e* caudata dargestellt worden, seine Vollform wurde in karolingischer Zeit dennoch Regel. Das *e* caudata verdrängte des weiteren im 10. und 11. Jahrhundert den Doppellaut und wurde im 12. Jahrhundert durch einfaches *e* ersetzt."

[77] *Zeitschrift für die österreichischen Gymnasien* 47 (1896): 340–41.

[78] M. Rieger, review of *Der Heliand und die angelsächsische Genesis*, by Eduard Sievers, *ZfdPh* 7 (1876): 114–16 (116).

[79] Kögel (as note 21), 90.

[80] D. R. McLintock, "The language of the *Hildebrandslied*," *Oxford German Studies* 1 (1966): 1–9.

[81] Steinmeyer, *Die kleineren althochdeutschen Sprachdenkmäler*, 19.

[82] Krogmann, 149.

[83] On *firahim* see W. Wackernagel, "Der Heliand und das Wessobrunner Gebet," *ZfdPh* 1 (1869): 291–309 (300); on *firiuuiʒʒo*, Joseph Schmidt, "Die germanischen präpositionen und das auslautsgesetz," *Zeitschrift für vergleichende Sprachforschung*

26 (1883): 20–45 (25); on *manno miltisto*, L. Whitbread, "Line 8a in the *Wessobrunner Gebet*," *MLR* 34 (1939): 426–27; on *ni*, McLintock, "Negatives"; on *mit*, Krogmann, 136.

[84] Cf. Baesecke, *Der Vocabularius Sti. Galli*, 120.

[85] Krogmann, 136.

[86] *Germanische Altertumskunde*, ed. Hermann Schneider, 2nd ed. (Munich: C. H. Beck, 1951), 341.

[87] Perrett, II, 147.

[88] Groseclose and Murdoch, 47.

[89] Gunkel, *Genesis*, 104. I am much indebted to the late Leslie Seiffert for the care with which he edited the first version of this essay for *Medium Ævum*, and to Richard Wilson for his assistance with its revision.

Cum trxensisent septem dies clamabat
iudex delacu dicens· Obsecrouos
educiteme &ego ostendcemuobis
crucemxpi. Auui ascenou
.... uas elacu·
....

Cum corcendirr& autem iudex
delacu &nerciebcer cirnuir ubi
iacer& crux· leuccuit uocé suã·

2: Clm. 22053, fol. 10ᵛ. Judas in the dry lake.

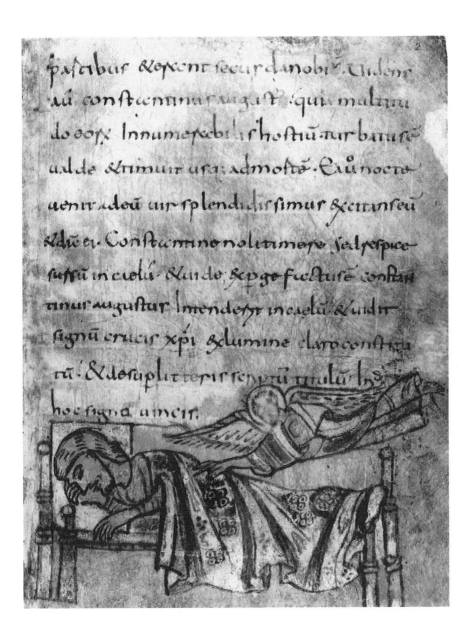

3: Clm. 22053, fol. 2ʳ. Constantine's vision.

Inquo loco ubi cruci fixura tantū ostet

inquo loco crucifixus ē tatitū ostendā

de mihi qui uocatur caluarie locus

ego faciem munda\ locum fortitan

Inueniam desiderium meū Iudas dix

neque locum noui quia nec expetentiuⁿ

Hatur. Beata helenc edix. p crucifixum

fan. re int ficiain ni fidixes fuen tuē.

Ethaec cū dixiss& iussit eū mitti in

lacū siccū. usq; in septem dies. sine cybo

manentem:-

DIS SUS OST.

UBI IUDAS IULAEUMY)

4: Clm. 22053, fol. 10ʳ. The dry lake.

Sedomnium bonorum semper
inuidus inimicur diabolur cumfu
rore uociferebat inaere dicens.
Quis iterum hic quinon permittit
me suscipere animas eorum.
ihu nazarene omnia superasti adec
ecce lignum tuum manifestast ad
uertis me. O iuda quidhocfecisti.

5: Clm. 22053, fol. 14ᵛ. The miracle of the Cross.

commendauit au eum beatahelena
epo qui inillotempore exet. qui &bap
tizauit eum Inxpo.

um inorcefetur adhuc beata hel
nce inhierofolyma. factum est
beatumenxin domi none acci
pere Inxpo;

6: Clm. 22053, fol. 16ʳ. Baptism scene.

2: *Ego bonefacius scripsi?* More Oblique Approaches to the Wessobrunn Prayer

(written in collaboration with Jennie Kiff-Hooper)

EVEN THOUGH we can clearly see the scribe's — or perhaps the colourist's — fingerprints on folios 18–21 of Clm. 22053, the Wessobrunn Prayer manuscript, there is much about it which remains a mystery. The codical context of the smaller OHG texts has all too often been ignored, the Germanist tending to treat the object of his interest with reference only to the slender corpus of comparable vernacular material, with circular arguments often resulting. Where the Wessobrunn Prayer is concerned, he has small excuse, for since 1922 a facsimile of the whole manuscript has been readily available; acclaimed as a technological masterpiece for its time, it is reliable in everything except the reproduction of the colours. In the same year there appeared the pioneering codicological approach of Georg Baesecke. The decade-long dispute between Baesecke and Bernhard Bischoff tended to obscure the possibilities which a combination of their approaches might offer. But in the 1970s two works appeared which in their different ways reopened issues, re-alerted attention to the puzzles of the codex. Ute Schwab's monograph, *Die Sternrune im Wessobrunner Gebet*, "ein buntes Kuckucksei," as she herself describes it in her introductory "Dankeswort," cast the net wider than any previous scholar in tracing influences on both the orthography and theology of the codex. Schwab's work was complemented by the massive thesis of Glenys Waldman.[1]

Any study of this kind must needs be accompanied by methodological caveats. The *opinio communis* is that Clm. 22053 is at least in part a copy of one or more earlier manuscripts. The palaeographic evidence suggests that the bulk of the copying was done at the same time, or perhaps by the same hand over a lengthy period of time. But we cannot know if a similar synchronicity obtained with regard to the original compilation, whatever its dimensions, and this renders suspect attempts to equate the provenance and date of other texts in the manuscript with that of the Wessobrunn Prayer itself. Against that, however, there are a number of unifying factors in this diverse material, and in particular, as we shall see, a concentration of these in that part of the codex which contains the Wessobrunn Prayer.

The majority of the texts are patristic in origin. This reduces the likelihood that they could give us a clue as to the date or provenance of the Wessobrunn Prayer itself. It may be possible to locate other copies of these texts, for instance in large monasteries where the contents of libraries can be pieced together, such as Fulda or St. Gall, whereas our knowledge of smaller monastic libraries is sporadic and limited, with occasional valuable exceptions such as Staffelsee, whose catalogue survives. But such an identification can provide no reliability with regard to establishing a point of origin. Much remains to be done in this respect, particularly with regard to those texts for which Schwab and Waldman have been unable to suggest parallels. Schwab attempts to trace the origin of a sample of what she considers the most important texts in that part of the codex which precedes the Wessobrunn Prayer. Waldman's approach, which tackles the whole codex, is careful to distinguish between "parallels" and "sources." This study will take a further sample of texts in the manuscript, particularly those in the proximity of the Prayer, and see what clues they provide us as to date, provenance and motives underlying the compilation.

With the exception of the first text, the ornamentation is exceedingly limited. There are very few large display initials at the opening of the individual texts, and those which do occur are limited to internal geometric or spot motifs. All of these initials are square capitals, which although commonly used in Anglo-Saxon manuscripts for this purpose, are not exclusively English. Uncial letter-forms are also used to open some of the texts, but they are on a much smaller scale and their decoration is confined to occasional colour-blockings. The addition of blocks of colour to some of these, as well as lesser initials which introduce individual chapters, suggests that an attempt was made to ornament them either by the scribe or the artist responsible for the illustrations. The square and uncial capitals were not the only forms of display capitals used by the scribe of the Wessobrunn manuscript. The rubrics contain a mixture of script types. The predominating script is uncial, yet there are examples of rustic letter forms. The rubrics are painted in some instances, and a few of the individual letters have been blocked with colour. Only at the beginning of the first text does there seem to be a deliberate attempt to employ a series of different-sized capitals to create a display layout, although there are pointers in this direction in the employment of capitals in the Wessobrunn Prayer itself. Throughout the manuscript, and despite the variety of the texts which it contains, the placing of the initials is, on the whole, very orderly. The adherence of the scribe to the confines of the ruled area allotted to the text, as well as the neatness of the script, suggests that this is the work of an experienced scribe. The script itself is Caroline minuscule, and a competent execution of a relatively new style of writing. If the manuscript is the work of a single scribe, he would seem to have encountered some problems with regard to the layout of the text in the latter part of the manuscript. On fols. 67^v–76^v the text has been contracted and the letter-forms become more angular, almost mimicking the spidery qualities found in many insular minuscules. A possible explanation for this is that the well-spaced Caroline minuscule had taken up more of the allotted text space than the scribe had foreseen, thus forcing the remaining text to be contracted to fit into the space that had originally been designated for it. At first glance this contraction of the script could be misinterpreted as a change of scribe; however, the individual letter-forms do not vary sufficiently to indicate that this is the case.

While the manuscript appears to be for the most part the work of one scribe, it is doubtful if the manuscript was considered to be a single entity at its conception. The reasoning behind this suggestion can be seen in the way in which the first text, the "Discovery of the Holy Cross" (fols. 1ᵛ–21ʳ), is joined to the remaining texts by an extract written in a different hand dating from the tenth century. This addition fills an area that was originally left blank at the end of the quire and continues onto the next quire. The "Discovery of the Holy Cross" has also suffered from unsympathetic cutting at the edges of the sheets, resulting in many of the illustrations being cut away at the edges. An example of this appears on fol. 10ᵛ (illustration 2), where the figure's nose and part of his hands have been lost. Also some of the drawings seem to disappear into the later binding. These features indicate that the manuscript was not only at one point a larger one that it is now, but also that the picture cycle was already *in situ* when it was trimmed and bound with the other texts at some point in the tenth century. This is not necessarily an argument against the miscellany being the work of one scribe, although it must be taken to indicate that "The Discovery of the Holy Cross" was not originally envisaged as part of the extant manuscript. The other texts do not seem to have suffered any severe trimming.

In the introduction to her thesis, Glenys Waldman suggested that "the trained art historian might find the illustrations (ff.2ʳ–20ʳ) for the legend of the 'Discovery of the True Cross' a good criterion for dating the Wessobrunn Prayer Ms. (or at least that first section of it)" (p. 15). The Wessobrunn manuscript contains what is probably the earliest version of the 'Discovery of the Holy Cross' to be illustrated in the West. A sequence of eighteen illustrations highlights parts of the narrative, dwelling particularly upon the extensive interrogations of the Jews by St. Helena, and the "persuading" of Judas to reveal the whereabouts of the cross by throwing him into a dry lake and depriving him of food. The precise origin of the drawings found in the Wessobrunn manuscript remains unclear. Two early iconographical parallels have been adduced by Karl Wiegel.[2] An initial in the Gellone sacramentary (Paris, BN, MS lat. 12048), dating from the second half of the eighth century, shows Judas with his hoe, digging for the True Cross, and three vertical crosses with a symmetrical arrangement of nails. One of seven frameless drawings in Vercelli, Bibl. Capitolare, MS CLXV, dating probably from the last quarter of the eighth century, shows the handing over of the Cross to St. Helena. Its bottom part again portrays Judas with a hoe, unearthing the (horizontal) crosses. The drawings illustrate a text of the *Canones Conciliorum*, and the connection with Constantine and the First Ecumenical Council explains the presence of such a drawing in this context. Neither of these illustrations accompanies a text of *De Inventione Sanctae Crucis*, although it is conceivable that they may derive from a cycle such as that found in Clm. 22053, and in the case of the

Vercelli manuscript this is strongly suggested by the compression of two chronologically distinct events into the same drawing.

Stylistically the illustrations in Clm. 22053 seem to draw heavily upon the influence of Late Classical and Byzantine art. It is not beyond the realms of possibility that Syriac lectionaries may have played a part in this pictorial tradition. The illustrations certainly depict some features which are usually associated with a period much earlier than that in which they were executed. The bed on which Constantine rests (fol. 2^r; illustration 3) is not of a type which is generally found in Carolingian MSS of the early ninth century, and the representation of an oblong pillow as opposed to the more usual bolster is almost unknown. However, it is an illustration that lacks the "clutter" found in many other "bedroom scenes"; there are no curtains twisted elegantly around pillars as there are in most pseudo-classical and de luxe Carolingian illuminations. The action of the scene is kept to the bare essentials of the narrative, a worried Constantine with his hand to his head in fitful repose, and the angel bringing the message of victory. Yet the drawing does include some surprises: the artist has not included a cross in this drawing; the phrase "In this sign thou shalt conquer" forms part of the last line of the text and is not an integral part of the illustration. The drawing of the angel superimposes itself upon some letters of the text, indicating that this picture, along with the other seventeen, was added after the text had been completed.

Another unusual illustration in this cycle shows Judas in the dry lake. This part of the narrative is broken down into two separate sections. On fol. 10^r (illustration 4) the lake is depicted as a rectangular box, viewed at an oblique frontal, with two soldiers on either side of it. In the second drawing, on fol. 10^v, the artist employs a "before and after" sequence, showing Judas being pulled from the lake, and then in prayer, probably a reference to his conversion. Although the drawings of the Wessobrunn artist are on the whole crude, if not rustic, this particular illustration is dramatic and more animated than most. There are other drawings in the cycle which display a striking composition, such as the miracle of the cross, where the artist suggests the circular movement of the crosses being passed over the body of the dead man (fol. 14^v; illustration 5). However, in a scene that readily lends itself to a "before and after" composition to highlight the miracle, the artist chooses not to use it. The illustration of the baptism (fol. 16^r; illustration 6) clearly shows the Mediterranean influence at work, and iconographical parallels can be found in Byzantine manuscripts (for example, Vatican Cod. Urb. gr. 2, fol. 67^v and Paris BN Cod. gr. 1528, fol. 182^r). The large tub used for the baptism in the Wessobrunn manuscript can be traced in Carolingian manuscripts of this period and even appears in manuscripts which were being illustrated in England in the tenth century, such as the Æthelstan Psalter (Oxford, Bodleian Library, Rawlinson B 484, fol. 85).

The artist of "The Discovery of the True Cross" could be regarded as conservative in his use of colour and ornamentation. Whether the artist who drew the picture-cycle was also responsible for the highlighting of the illustration in red, yellow and blue, or for the occasional gold leaf, is open to debate. Some of the figures which have been partly cut away by the severe trimming are blocked with colour, suggesting that the paint was applied prior to the tenth-century rebinding. However, in other parts of the Wessobrunn manuscript fingerprints can be seen which may imply that some of the paint was applied during the tenth century. It is therefore only possible to say that the picture-cycle of "The Discovery of the Holy Cross" is probably contemporary with the text. On the whole the figures are rather monumental, solid and static, and are unlike those traditionally associated with the Carolingian period, as epitomised in the Ebbo Gospels and the Utrecht Psalter. Yet there are a few parallels. The solid figures found in the Stuttgart Psalter (Stuttgart, Württembergische Landesbibliothek, Biblia folio 23) bear some comparison with the Wessobrunn manuscript. On the whole, iconographical invention is not synonymous with the Carolingian era. Some manuscripts appear to follow Late Classical exemplars faithfully, while others only added small innovations. Provincial scriptoria were slightly more experimental than the larger schools, although the quality of their work was greatly inferior. It is impossible to determine whether the Wessobrunn artist was being faithful to his exemplar or not. The positioning of the illustration in relation to the appropriate piece of text is not always accurate, although adequate space is always left for the drawing. It is possible that the Wessobrunn picture-cycle formed part of a well-established pictorial tradition, and that this manuscript is the sole survivor. Yet it is equally possible that the artist was using one existing exemplar, or maybe more, depicting the story of Helena and the discovery of the True Cross as he understood it.

In conclusion, the Wessobrunn manuscript would seem to be a product of a provincial Carolingian scriptorium. The actual geographical location of the scriptorium itself is impossible to establish with any certainty. The destruction of the monastery at Wessobrunn in the tenth century and its subsequent rebuilding probably resulted in this manuscript being given as a gift to replace some of those texts, or teaching aids, that had been lost. It is possible that the "Discovery of the Holy Cross" actually arrived at Wessobrunn bound separately from the miscellany with which it was later joined, although it may have been bound together elsewhere. It is also possible that all the texts in the Wessobrunn manuscript were given as a personal gift to the house, although there is no real evidence to suggest this. Given the quality of the manuscript, it is unlikely to be the product of any of the major scriptoria at work at this time, and the precise influences upon the artist cannot be determined with any certainty. The eternal problem with dating by reference to art history is that it all rests upon comparisons, and when the text has no obvious exemplar, textual antecessor or internal dating that is beyond question, we are left in the realms of possibles and maybes that defy most attempts to place manuscripts within a secure historical framework.

The second section of the codex, from fol. 22ʳ to fol. 66ᵛ, is subdivided thematically by Waldman into three sections: "A Theological Miscellany"; "Geography"; "The Wessobrunn Prayer and the Seven Liberal Arts." Ehrismann views the ordering of the manuscript with perceptive, not to say deceptive clarity. He holds that the Wessobrunn Prayer is an integral part of "ein lateinisches Kompendium über Gegenstände der sieben freien Künste," which begins with the heading *MENSURA EST* on fol. 57ᵛ.[3] The definition of *mensura* follows Isidore's Etymologies verbatim. The territorial divisions and measurements on fols. 58ʳ–59ʳ are also taken from Isidore, but are exemplified and given German glosses. A further subdivision is indicated by the heading *MENSURAM. VIARUM* in capitals, blocked in colour, on fol. 59ʳ. Here too, the scribe follows Isidore. At line 9 of fol. 59ᵛ the relationship between Clm. 22053 and Isidore starts to be more problematic. There are two garbled lines, *ostendit et non donat. pugnat pro eo orbis terrarum* [He shows (it) and does not give; he fights for it of the lands of the world,] which may or may not refer to Hercules, the founder of the measurement *stadium*, and then another heading in capitals: *HIERONIMUS AIT*. This would seem to be a blind; what follows draws in part on Isidore's "De Europa," but consistently shows great interest in the geography of Germany, and of Bavaria in particular. Isidore's description of the Danube is at first followed faithfully, but then the text offers a folk etymology of *peigirae*. The word is derived from *baugo* [ring], and *Uer* [man]. Schwab (p. 133, note 190) argues that *Baugo enim aput illos corona dicitur* proves the etymology is not Bavarian in origin. Whether or not this be the case, the insertion of this etymology into Isidore's discussion "De fluminibus" certainly indicates a special interest. Isidore is finally deserted altogether for a wider-ranging geography lesson with glosses, introduced by the headings on fol. 61ʳ: *HEC NOMINA DE VARIIS PROVINTIIS* and on fol. 62ᵛ *DE CIUITATIBUS.*

A definition of the seven liberal arts begins with a capitalised heading at line 2 of fol. 63ʳ: *SEPTEM ARTE[S] SUNT LIBERALES ID SUNT. PER QUAS LIBRI SCRIBUNTUR.* The list that follows comprises grammar, rhetoric, geometry, arithmetic, music, astronomy and astrology. The broad definition of *grammatica* as *Litteratura*, meaning the science of letters in general, is a fair reflection of the importance attached to grammar in Carolingian education.[4] That Isidore is not the sole source for the list of the liberal arts in Clm. 22053 is clear not merely from the definitions, but also from the divergences in order which begin at the third art, which in Isidore's list is dialectic or logic. Clm. 22053 omits this, but includes both *astronomia* and *astrologia*. No absolute orthodoxy prevailed in the late eighth century with regard to the order of the *artes*, or even the constituent parts of such a list. Clm. 22053's definition of astronomy as *medicina* may have been influenced by the important role that the stars played in medieval medicine, for instance in determining the appropriate time for bleeding. Isidore appends to the liberal arts a discussion of the importance of medicine, and considers whether it should be classed among them, but attaches no importance to astrology in this context.[5] Clm. 22053's list and definitions appears to be uniquely its own, suggestive, as is much else in the manuscript, of badly taken lecture notes rather than faulty copying.

The same explanation may account for the contradictory views concerning grammar that follow the definitions, or they may be extracts from a chrestomathy of a kind that was becoming popular in the Carolingian period.[6] The first quotation contains two striking images:

> Sicut purpura uestes decorat. sic aedificat grammatica linguam nostram canonicam. Sicut tela non habens licium ad nullum opus perfectum sine illo perficitur. Ita et omnis scriptura absque cramaticam. inordinata esse multorum est inchoandum sed paucorum finiendum:ʻ

> [As purple decorates clothes, so does Grammar build our prescribed language. As the warp not having a thread is made for no perfect work without it. Thus the whole scripture would be all out of order but for grammar. Many are capable of beginning but few of finishing.]

The punctuation mark with which the quotation concludes commonly denotes the end of an item in the manuscript, for instance after the Latin invocation which follows the Wessobrunn Prayer (fol. 66ʳ). Here it precedes an erasure, which appears to be of a comment in a later hand; of this Waldman can read only *nua enim*. Then there follows a second quotation in direct opposition to the first:

> Ars crammatica. inimica est deo. Ars spiritus sancti. humilitas. caritas castitas benignitas. Non est sapientia qui coequari possit caritati. et humilitate quod est radix omnium bonorum.

> [The art of Grammar is hostile to God. The knowledge of the Holy Spirit: humility, charity, chastity, kindness. There is no wisdom which is equal to charity and humility, which is the root of all good.]

The contradictory quotations are a reflection of a recurrent controversy concerning the value of the study of pagan authors for the understanding of divine wisdom. Already in the third and fourth centuries, Laistner notes "the extreme of tolerance and even approval of the liberal arts on the one hand and uncompromising condemnation on the other, as well as a possible intermediate between the two." With the Carolingian Renaissance, the controversy became acute: "The truth would seem to be that, although there were always some who desired Gregory the Great's ban on secular learning to be put into effect, the majority of teachers and prelates took the more reasonable line of seeing in the study of the arts a valuable means to an end."[7] The first quotation represents what would be in the late eighth century the commonly held view. While Augustine and Jerome contradict themselves on the value of grammar, fluctuating between the position of the ascetic Christian and the humanist scholar,

Bede, Alcuin and Boniface would undoubtedly have entertained the more positive outlook. It finds impassioned expression in Hrabanus Maurus's defence of grammar (*PL* 107, 395–96). The more ascetic viewpoint, which rejected secular literature out of hand, relied on the authority of Gregory, one of whose homilies is the source of *DE CHRONICA* on fol. 65^r.[8] It is as if the scribe or author is being tapped on the shoulder, rebuked for his enlightened viewpoint and reminded of the essentials of the Benedictine Rule, and the erasure between the quotations may well be a reflection of continuing interest in the controversy. If either of these quotations could be traced, then it might be possible to identify the school of thought, if not the monastery, which spawned this part of the manuscript. But the Carolingian Renaissance saw a proliferation of grammars and short treatises on grammar which might be the source of these quotations.[9]

With another majuscule heading, the scribe reverts to *DE MENSURIS*. The tables of weights and measures follow Isidore, but again treat him with considerable freedom, incorporating German glosses. This section may be intended to serve as an example of geometry, the third art on the list, but if so, the second art, rhetoric, has been omitted from exemplification. Without any heading or clear sub-division, the text drifts for some three lines on fol. 64^r into material more appropriate to the fourth art, arithmetic, adducing the central terms *calculus* and *numerus*, and supplying German glosses. The last line of this page returns to *Mensura*, this time offering a slightly different definition to that taken from Isidore on fol. 57^v. (A further section *DE PONDERIBUS* and *DE MENSURIS* occurs in a separate part of the codex, on fol. 86^r.) At this point such sense of order as there has been disappears. In minuscule the faulty Greek *Decathologo* is glossed by the poor Latin *dedecemverbalegis*, and then the capitalised heading from fol. 59^v, *HIERONIMUS AIT*, is repeated; again, Waldman can find no parallel in Jerome. The catalogue that follows is not in any sense a decalogue, having only eight items, ending with *Vinum adebriendum*. The compiler is addicted to making lists, many of which involve numbers. Seven and four are, understandably, the favourites, and some of these lists have been parallelled by Schwab in an Irish *Liber de numeris* (p. 99 and p. 111, note 6). The codex seems here to be almost parodying its predilection for catalogues, and it is hard to see any connection between, for example, *Aqua adlauandum* and the seven liberal arts. There follows the Gregorian sermon *DE CHRONICA*, comparing the times of day with the ages of man. This precedes directly the Wessobrunn Prayer on fols. 65^v–66^r. *DE CHRONICA* might be taken as relating to arithmetic, but there is no obvious connection with the Wessobrunn Prayer. In the next section of the manuscript, on fol. 71^{r-v}, the scribe reverts to the ages of man in a freer treatment of Pope Gregory's sermon, this time linking them to figures from the Old Testament. This is the only obvious link between these two sections of the codex, and argues against *DE CHRONICA* being an integral part of any "discussion" of the seven liberal arts. Such discussion as we have is fragmentary and not well ordered. If the arts were to have been exemplified in sequence, then this sequence has been disrupted and curtailed. The discussion is not carried forward to the next section of the codex, the "biblical miscellany" which commences with the *UISIO QUAM UIDIT EZECHIEL* on fol. 67ʳ. Nor was the last, hair side, 66ᵛ, utilised to prolong it. This may have been simply because of the condition of the page, "erheblich berieben," as Bischoff describes it,[10] but it seems more likely that the compiler's source for the exemplification of the seven liberal arts was incomplete, or that his interest in them expired, perhaps as early as *DE MENSURIS* on fol. 63ᵛ.

The rubric *DE POETA*, which Ehrismann sees as meaning "vom Dichter, d.h. daß der Text ein Gedicht ist" (p. 147) can be parallelled not only within the "meteorologischen und geographischen Aufzeichnungen des Kompendiums," but is typical of headings in the whole codex. On the whole, I find Perrett's cautiously worded suggestion, "Of the Creator," a far more attractive explanation of *DE POETA* than the assertion that the title means that the prayer is an example of poetry.[11] In the latter case, it seems justifiable to ask why the scribe did not write more correctly *poetica*, the word he had glossed with *kazungali* three pages earlier. Perrett consulted Professor Soutar of Aberdeen, who wrote: "Even supposing it [*sc. poeta*] does not occur in the sense you desire in any of the authors before the ninth century, I see nothing to prevent ninth century authors from having so employed it. . . . If questioned for using *poeta* in this strange sense, they could turn on the questioner, and say its sense was Greek, and that it was really a Greek word." Such classical scholars as I have consulted have tended to react in the same way to the suggestion that *poeta* might mean "Creator," following Plato's usage.

To view the Wessobrunn Prayer as an example of poetry, and therefore an integral part of the Seven Liberal Arts, is to make it an even greater anomaly than it actually is, and to ask a little too much of the Carolingian Renaissance. Not before Notker, two centuries later, do we possess any vernacular material relating to the liberal arts, and even then we can scarcely talk of poetic composition. It makes far more sense to see the Prayer, with Seiffert,[12] as devotional, if not liturgical, in function, as an early example of the use of the vernacular for religious composition. Schwab too advocates the possibility "dass die bairischen Verse nicht ohne Sinnbezug zu den übrigen katechetischen Texten des Handbuches stehen" (p. 21), such as the Creed *Fides catholica* (fols. 36ᵛ–37ᵛ), its variant, the *Symbolum quod interpretatur conlatio* (fols. 44ʳ–45ʳ), dividing the items of the Creed among the twelve apostles, and *De principio coeli et terre* (fols. 37ᵛ–40ᵛ), the exegetical account of the Creation which Waldman (p. 209) links with Isidore's *Quaestiones in Veterum Testamentum: In Genesin*. The Latin invocation immediately following the Prayer, for which no source has been traced, points in the same direction.

While the Seven Liberal Arts do not seem to function well as a unifying factor in this section of the manuscript, there are other factors which suggest synchronicity in copying, and perhaps in composition. The star-rune, a botched attempt at which precedes the gloss *kazungali*, supplies a link between the *artes* and the Wessobrunn Prayer. The interest in Bavaria in the geographical section is matched by a degree of consistency in the language of the German material in the codex. A key element here is the "Sproßvokal," which is to be found in the geographical glosses in the suffix *-puruc*, in the Wessobrunn Prayer in *perec* and *gauuorahtos*, and in the names in the charter which backs the Prayer, *hiltipereht* and *chunipereht*. The most detailed analysis of the language of the Prayer is that of Willy Krogmann,[13] who argues that it is "rein bairisch" (p. 149), and dates from some time before 800, reaching back "kaum allzuweit in das 7. Jh." (p. 131). He considers each individual element of the language which earlier scholars had suggested might point to extra-Bavarian influence, and contends that its existence in an older form of Bavarian than we otherwise possess is perfectly feasible, concluding by claiming that the Prayer, by attesting *mit firahim*, *mit inan*, *enteo ni uuenteo*, *dat* and *ero*, "bereichert in dankenswertester Weise" our knowledge of Old Bavarian (p. 149). Not content with this circular argument, Krogmann attempts to claim for his reconstructed Old Bavarian a fine distinction in the quality of *g/k*: "Wg. *g* wird in palataler Umgebung durch *g* wiedergegeben . . . in velarer Umgebung, wenn wir von der auch sonst oft besonders behandelten Vorsilbe *ga-* absehen, durch *c(k)*" (pp. 133–34). He chooses to ignore the form *kazungali*, together with all the rest of the German material in the manuscript. The glosses and the proper names suggest that while in medial position there may have been some hesitation between *g* and *c/k*: *peigirolant*, *paigirae*, *reganespuruc*, *regino*, *Baugo*, *hludouuigus*, but *Baucueri* (fol. 60ᵛ), *g* had invariably shifted to *k* in initial and final position: *kazungali*, *creozolin*; *puruc*, *lancpartolant*. Moreover, Krogmann oversimplifies the problem of the quality of *g* after the "Sproßvokal." He argues that both *pereg*, the emendation in line 3 of the Prayer, and *perec*, which was what the scribe first wrote, are Bavarian, but fails to provide any explanation for them both being written by the same scribe. *kazungali # ganada*, and *perec # pereg* and the suffix *-puruc* are clear indicators that the original language of the Wessobrunn prayer was not unalloyed late eighth-century Bavarian. The scribe's emendation of *perec* to *pereg*, whereas in the glosses he wrote consistently *-puruc*, suggests strongly that the language of the Prayer was in some sense alien to him, but that he was attempting to transcribe it as accurately as he could. The force of the shift against which he is struggling is epitomised on fol. 63ᵛ, where *grammatica* is written twice with an initial *c* — one of many pointers that some of the texts in the codex were written down in haste from lectures. Others include the rendering of *Bellerophon* as *bellorum frons* on fol. 96ᵛ.

The nature of these discrepancies in the representation of the sound shift is of course highly problematic. They may be no more than a reflection of the Bavarian dialect in a time of transition, but the careful emendation of *c* to *g* invites a more complex explanation. Several immediately suggest themselves: the language of the Wessobrunn Prayer may have been felt to be geographically alien, or chronologically alien, or the scribe may have been attempting to create or retain an archaism, a relic form.[14] At all events, the emendation suggests that Krogmann's argument is too one-sidedly synchronous.

Curiously, only Baesecke and Romuald Bauerreiss have devoted much attention to the charter of manumission which backs the Wessobrunn Prayer (fol. 66ᵛ):[15]

> in nomine d*omi*ni d*ei* sal*uatoris* ih*esu* christi.
> Ego Iacob dimisi liber*um* ser*uum* n*ominatu*m. herimotan
> cu*m* licentia riholfo magistro n*ost*ro et rege n*ost*ro
> carolo. ante p*re*sente ortleipo comite
> in loco nunccupante hesilinloh. v. k*alendas* nou*embras*
> ut sit lib*er* int*er* liberos habeat licentia*m*. ire redire
> uendere negotiare sic*ut* c*et*eris liberis licitu*m* e*st*
> ac sic ab ingenuis parentib*us* p*ro*creatus fuiss*et*.
> Si q*ui*s contra hanc cartula*m* lib*er*tatis quilib*et*
> Inire temptauerit primitus In su*m* d. . .[?] Incur
> rat *et* conponat sic*ut* lex e*st*. *et* carta haec
> nihilominus firma p*er*maneat. *ecce* s*unt* testes
> regino p*res*byt*er* hiltipereht. tasso hato.
> marcheo. ehso. heriprant. chunipereht.
> s.afrih.[16] ego bonefacius scripsi;.

[In the name of the Lord God, our Saviour Jesus Christ, I, Jacob, have freed my slave Herimot with the permission of Riholf our master and our King Charles, in the presence of Count Ortleip in the place called hesilinloh, on the fifth day before the Kalends of November — so that he may be a free man among free men, that he may have leave to go, return, sell, negotiate just as it is granted to other free men as if he had been born of free parents.

If anyone at all tries to undertake anything against this charter of liberty, in the first place let him incur [illegible] and let him make it good just as is the law. And let this charter nevertheless remain in force. Here are the witnesses: Regino presbyter, Hiltipereht, Tasso, Hato, Marcheo, Ehso, Heriprant, Chunipereht, s [illegible letters] afrih. I, Bonefacius, wrote this.]

Waldman's tracings confirm Bischoff's view that the charter is in the same hand as the greater part of the codex. It looks very different from the Wessobrunn Prayer, but the latter has been accorded special significance by the generous ornamentation and the broad layout it is given. A comparison between the charter and other parts of the Latin material in the codex reveals far more similarities. The scribe is writing on the hair side of the last page of a quire, a difficult surface, and employing a different style of hand. Rosamond McKitterick suggests that "the chap had some formal notarial training,"[17] which would account for the extensive use of abbreviations, and the double *c* in *nunccupante*, which I have not found elsewhere in the manuscript. Inebriation, fatigue, cold, darkness, lack of time, lack of space, the nature of the document to be written down or copied — all these factors and more can affect the style of a hand, and create an erroneous impression that a different scribe is involved. The conventional wisdom, for example, holds that two scribes were involved in the writing down of the *Hildebrandslied*. "Scribe A" is regarded as responsible for the first leaf, but then, at the top of the second leaf, there is an effort to write in a more compressed hand, attributed to "Scribe B." A more probable explanation is that the same scribe, perhaps believing that otherwise he will not fit the lay into the limited area available to him, changes his hand; after 8½ lines he relaxes, and reverts to the larger forms attributed to "Scribe A." A similar problem occurs in the Vercelli Book, Vercelli MS CXVII, in the middle of the poem *Elene*, the Latin source of which is cognate with "The Discovery of the Holy Cross" in Clm. 22053. On fol. 131[b] "the writing becomes noticeably smaller," and certainly the difference is greater than that between "Scribe A" and "Scribe B" of the *Hildebrandslied*, but the Anglo-Saxonist sensibly concludes that "there are no grounds for assuming that the manuscript is in more than one hand."[18] In the case of the *Hildebrandslied*, it seems sensible to ask why more than one scribe should be involved in the writing of a short text, the survival of which hangs by such a tenuous thread.

What motive underlies the presence of the charter in Clm. 22053? The consensus is that it is a copy of an older document. This is possible, although it may be that it is a church's or monastery's own record of the manumission. What seems certain is that the charter must have been of significance to someone involved in the compilation, or copying, or commissioning, of the codex as a whole. If it is a copy of an older original, then it is unlikely to be far removed in date from the original, as its validity was apparently felt to still hold. There is no mention of the heirs of the freed slave, suggesting that it was copied in his lifetime. It is clearly no mere writing or copying exercise, and equally clearly has nothing to do with the seven liberal arts. The scribe names himself as Bonefacius, and Bischoff suggested (*Schreibschulen*, p. 20) that this might be the writer of the whole manuscript. The compiler or commissioner of the codex may be one of the key people mentioned in the charter: the slave-owner Jacob, the *comes* Ortleip, perhaps even the freed slave Herimot.

Baesecke strove to date and locate the charter by searching for a cluster of names with sufficient correspondence to the names in the manumission, particularly those of the witnesses. He concentrated his attention on the Regensburg records, where he found *Riholf, Chuniperht, Herimot, Ato, Hatto* and *Jacob*, albeit in different documents. He found the trace of a cluster in a document recording the presentation of a church in St. Emmeram to Freising in A.D. 772 by *Ortleip*, witnessed by *Riholf, Chuniperht* and *Regino*. But there are two dangers in the indiscriminate application of such an approach. Firstly, Baesecke chooses to ignore the fact that the majority of the names in the manumission are extremely common in Bavarian documents — the exceptions being Ortleip, the witness Tasso, the last, not fully legible witness, Eafrih or S.ifrih, and Bonefacius himself. Even in Fulda this name is rare, tending to be reserved for bishops, and in the charter it may be the given name of a monk. Secondly, Baesecke ignores the problems of rank: his Ortleip is not a *comes*, nor is his Richolf a *magister*. Later in his career, Baesecke shifted in his view of the provenance of the codex from Regensburg to Fulda,[19] and if he had based his cluster approach in Fulda, he could have found many of the right names there too, even a *Jacob* who gave land *cum mancipiis* to Fulda at the turn of the eighth/ninth centuries.[20] And one of the most common names in the Fulda Gesamtverzeichnis in the first quarter of the ninth century is Herim(u)ot.[21] The freed slave might conceivably have been a Fulda monk. But links like these can be reconstructed randomly in Freising, Fulda, St. Gall, Weißenburg, wherever enough names have survived.

A second approach that suggested itself was to use the place-name *in loco nunccupante hesilinloh* as a starting-point. In view of the Bavarian personal names, the linguistic evidence, and the interest in Bavaria and the Danube shown in the glosses, Bavaria seemed the obvious area for a search. The Klein-hesseloher See in Munich's Englischer Garten takes its name from Groß-hesselohe, now a southern suburb of Munich, which in the nineteenth century was a favourite destination for a country excursion. This Hesselohe is of respectable age; it is referred to in a document dated 776–778, which records the gift of Duke Tassilo III of Bavaria of *omnia, quae habuit Hatto ad Hesinloch, et omnia, quae ad ipsam villam pertinent* to the monastery of Schäftlarn.[22] The *hato* listed among the *testes* in the manumission is unlikely to have been such a munificent landowner.

The other Hesselohe in present-day Bavaria is a hamlet about a mile north of Tassilo's ducal residence, Neuburg on the Danube. This supplies a possible link with *Neapolis*, which occurs among the glosses DE CIVITATIBUS on fols. 62ᵛ–63ʳ. As Waldman points out, "All but four of the cities are within the boundaries of present-day Germany and Austria, and all were important religious centers (usually the seat of a [arch]bishop)" (p. 292). The list begins with Lyons, then a Frankish group: Strasbourg, Speier, Worms, Cologne; then comes Constantinople, then *Neapolis*, glossed as *civitas nova*, and finally the Bavarian dioceses of Regensburg, Passau and Salzburg. The fact that Regensburg is glossed twice: *Norica reganespuruc. Allofia radasponsa* led Waldman to argue anew that the Regensburg scriptorium might be the home of the codex.[23] What seems clear is that towards the bottom, the list is concentrating on an area familiar to the scribe or his source. The Geographer of Ravenna lists seven cities called *Neapolis*, but Waldman may be wide of the mark when she plumps for Naples.[24] There is a connection with the preceding Constantinople in that Naples was the Byzantine capital of southern Italy, an "independent enclave on the West coast, more or less autonomous from Constantinople," but as its "ducal and episcopal hierarchy remained independent of the Carolingian conquests,"[25] it is difficult to see why it should precede a list of Bavarian dioceses. More likely is that for the scribe at least *Civitas Nova* meant the Bavarian bishopric of Neuburg. Unfortunately this leads us into one of those controversies which church historians are fond of conducting with polemical heat. There appear to have been two Neuburgs which may have had bishops, and it seems possible that confusion already existed in the late eighth century. Bauerreiss argues that the only possible site for the bishop's seat is Neuburg am Staffelsee, on the island of Wörth, and Bischoff once considered Staffelsee as a candidate for the scriptorium behind the codex, although the list of books found there when the church was shut down *c.* 810 contains no pointers to the content of the Wessobrunn codex.[26] There is no archaeological evidence for a bishop's seat on the island of Wörth — "alles aus Holz, alles verbrannt," the locals told me when I rowed across to the island — and Friedrich Zoepfl has argued as polemically as Bauerreiss that Neuburg on the Danube was the site of Boniface's foundation, a ducal residence like the other Bavarian bishops' seats. Zoepfl argues that the seat may have shifted to Staffelsee in the time of Bishop Sintbert of Augsburg (797–807), and that this would explain the papal letter of 11 April 800, which refers to an *ecclesia Stafnensis*.[27] It may of course be pure coincidence that we have a *Hesilinloh* on fol. 66ᵛ of clm. 22053, and a *Civitas Nova* on fol. 62ᵛ, but the proximity of the hamlet and Neuburg on the Danube is at very least striking.

A third approach was suggested by the unusual formulation in the charter, *cum licentia riholfo magistro nostro et rege nostro carolo*. Charlemagne is not stated to be present at the freeing of the slave, which takes place *ante presente ortleipo comite*, but the reference to his legal authority suggests, as Baesecke already realised, an *ante quem non* of 788, in which year Tassilo, Duke of Bavaria, finally submitted himself to Frankish rule. It is highly unlikely that the freeing of a Bavarian slave prior to 788 would take place without reference to the authority of Tassilo. Baesecke's upper date was 800. This was based on *rege nostro*, as in 800 Charlemagne became Emperor of the Romans. But Charlemagne is still referred to as *rex* in the chronological notes — probably in a different hand — on the last folio of the codex. These refer to the death of Charlemagne in 814 and the accession of Louis the Pious *In isto anno* 815; they were probably written in 815 or soon thereafter, and certainly before the death of Louis the Pious in 840. But if Charlemagne's title is not sufficient evidence for a *post quem non* of 800, there is another pointer in that direction. If we accept a rough synchronicity for the compilation of the geographical glosses and the writing of the manumission, and if we accept that *Civitas Nova* means Neuburg, then it is unlikely that the glosses (or the charter) were compiled much after 800, for by 804 Neuburg had ceased to be a bishop's seat, being amalgamated with Augsburg, and thus falling under the archbishopric of Mainz.[28]

It is difficult to assess the proximity of Charlemagne to the charter, but his interest in Bavaria appears limited to the years 787–803. July 787 saw a military campaign in parts of Bavaria, with Charlemagne himself going as far as the Lech to meet with the army, probably at Lechfeld, near Augsburg. He is thought not to have gone into Bavaria itself.[29] In October 788 Charlemagne was in Würzburg, and then in Regensburg for the first time, returning to Francia later that year. Some time after March 791, he headed for *partibus Baioriae* from either Ingelheim or Worms, and in August 791 assembled an army to fight against the Huns in Regensburg. The campaign typified his preferred mode of travel, with part of the army marching east along the banks of the Danube, and part of it travelling by boat. His interest in travel by water is most clearly illustrated by the disastrous canal-building project of 793. The completed fragment can still be seen at Karlsgrab, north-east of the river Altmühl above Eichstätt. He returned from Austria along the southern bank of the Danube and spent the winters of both 791 and 792 in Regensburg, where he remained based until the autumn of 793. December 793 finds him in Würzburg, February 794 in Frankfurt. There is then a gap until August 803, when he is again *in Baioarium*, for the last time as far as our records of his itinerary show. Gauert finds three underlying motives: "Die Aufenthalte in Baiern waren bedingt durch die Unternehmungen gegen Herzog Tassilo, die Kriegszüge gegen die Awaren und Maßnahmen zur Eingliederung des Landes in das fränkische Reich."[30] Any one of these journeys, or even the canal-building project, might have taken Charlemagne to Neuburg on the Danube.

The charter, which bears little relation to the standard formularies, couples the name of Charlemagne with that of *riholfo magistro nostro*. One possible explanation is that Riholf represents the arm of ecclesiastical authority and Charlemagne the secular arm. *magister* has a wide range of meanings in medieval Latin, from a "slave-foreman, chief of a group of serfs" to a "provost." Here, however, it would seem to refer to someone of higher rank than the slave-owner Iacob, and possibly the *comes* Ortleip. *magistra* can denote an abbess, and the adjective *magisterialis* has the sense "episcopal."[31] Bauerreiss may well have been correct in suggesting that Riholf was none other than the archbishop of Mainz, the highest primate in Germany, and overlord of the diocese of Augsburg, which after *c.* 802 appears to have encompassed both Bavarian Hesselohes and Neuburgs. Riholf, a favourite pupil of Alcuin, was an energetic *missus*, and the records attest his presence in Fritzlar, where he was consecrated in 787; Mainz; Rome, with Charlemagne in 800–801; Erfurt; Fulda (twice); Aachen; Bleidenstat; and Schlitz. He died on 9 August 813.[32] Riholf appears to have been in Bavaria only twice. The first occasion was before he became archbishop. In 781, as *diaconus*, he participated in an embassy to Duke Tassilo, probably to Regensburg.[33] For the second journey to Bavaria, ten years later in 791, we have only the rather dubious authority of Notker the Stammerer, who, in his life of Charlemagne, directs a number of anti-episcopal anecdotes at "the holder of the most important see in Germany." As Lewis Thorpe notes, this implies Mainz, but Thorpe regards Richolf as "admirable in every way."[34] In truth, there is as little evidence for this view as for the picture painted by Notker. Notker's bishop is "vainglorious and greatly preoccupied with all manner of stupid things" (Thorpe, p. 108), and is tricked by Charlemagne into buying a stuffed mouse for an exorbitant price off a Jewish merchant. Placed in charge of Charlemagne's queen — whose name Notker gets wrong — during the expeditions against the Huns (in Regensburg from 791–793), the bishop is rebuked for daring to parade Charlemagne's golden sceptre "in place of his festal staff" (p. 110). Further anecdotes reveal him as a sadist, a drunkard, a man with no ear for music, in all a bishop "in name rather than in deed" (p. 111). It is probably pure coincidence that on fol. 36ʳ of the Wessobrunn codex, in the context of a list of twelve sinful abuses traced by Waldman to St. Augustine's *De duodecim Abusionum Gradibus*, *Episcopus neglegens* is repeated and accorded an editorial sign in another hand. Waldman (p. 201) suggests that "the later scribe had a special interest in a negligent bishop."

Riholf might have been deemed worthy of the title *magister* in its episcopal sense between 787 and 813. None of the other names in the charter appears in the Mainz *Regesta* during his reign, but this would be readily comprehensible if the charter originated in his Bavarian archi-episcopate. Jacob, the slave-owner, accords himself no title, and Rosamond McKitterick suggests he might be "a small free landowner or a merchant." The name is not necessarily Jewish, but one of a number of Old Testament names quite common in the Bavarian nobility.[35] The rare name Ortleip occurs in the Freising record of 722 referred to by Baesecke, although Störmer thinks this Ortleip must be a monk (*Adelsgruppen*, pp. 124, 133). In a Regensburg record of 822 there is a reference to a *Machelm filius Otleipi*, whom Störmer (*Früher Adel*, I, 105) thinks may be a vassal of the bishop of Freising, and perhaps identical with the Machelm who was ambassador to the Bulgars under Louis the Pious in 824. If *Ortleip comes* were this Machelm's father, place and time would again fit.

It is in the last resort simplistic to try to trace a Carolingian text or manuscript to a single monastery or scriptorium. This can provide no more than a partial answer to the question of provenance. Monks, particularly scholarly monks, were travelling creatures. They took their learning with them when they were promoted, or occasionally demoted; they passed it on to others by word of mouth, or by allowing manuscripts to be copied, borrowed, given, without any thought of draconian copyright law. Clm. 22053 reflects accurately such a lively and indiscriminate acquisition of knowledge. Learning, in the enlightened late eighth and early ninth centuries, was a corporate affair, fostered by a central government with an active interest in education. Nevertheless, the texts in the immediate proximity of the Wessobrunn Prayer — the list of the *artes* and the controversy concerning the value of grammar, the geographical glosses with their special interest in Bavaria, the manumission —, all these in combination point towards a unity of place and time. This in turn strongly suggests, although it cannot in the nature of things prove, that we should not look very far outside the monastic schoolroom of late eighth-century Bavaria for the genesis of the Prayer itself.

Appendices

1. German material in Clm. 22053 (other than the Wessobrunn Prayer and the manumission)

fol. 45ᵛ	patizar (for Balthazar)
fol. 58ʳ	zella. uuihiruN. hrindirarae
fol. 59ʳ	scaramez
fol. 60ᵛ	peigirae. Baucueri, Baugo
fol. 61ʳ	scottonolant
fol. 61ᵛ	uualholant
	auh uualholant
	uuasconolant
	uuascun
	franchonolant
	lancpartolant
	auh Lancpartolant
	prettonolant
	prezzun
	benauentolant
	suapa
fol. 62ʳ	peigirolant
	paigira
	iudeonolant
	auh uuandoli
	rapana (Ravenna)
fol. 62ᵛ	strazpuruc
	cholonne
	costantinusespuruc
	reganespuruc
	pazauua
	salzpuruc
fol. 63ʳ	kazungali
fol. 64ʳ	zantro. creozolin. chisilinc.
	zala.
fol. 83ʳ	chaharia (Zechariah)
fol. 84ʳ	taualun
	huntes satal
	distil
	uuipil
fol. 99ᵛ	hludouuigus

2. A List of Lists in the Wessobrunn Prayer Manuscript

fol. 35ᵛ	INCIPIT SENTENTIA SANCTI GREGORII. Sanctus gregorius dixit haec sunt XII. in hoc saeculo qui abuse fiant
fol. 40ᵛ	DICTA SALOMONIS

fol. 41ʳ	HAEC SUNT X UERBA LEGIS QUE LOQUUIUS SE DOMINUS AD MOYSEN DICENS
fol. 41ᵛ	List of four reasons why Christ was born of a betrothed rather than a *simplice virgine* (after St. Jerome and Bede).
fol. 43ʳ	DE SEPTEM FORMIS SPIRITU DICIT
fol. 46ʳ	QUATTUOR ALE SUNT QUE UOLANT AD CAELUM
fol. 48ᵛ	EX IIIIᵒ CREATURIS CONSTAT HOMO . . . ET DE IIIIᵒ ELIMENTIS HOMINUM
fol. 49ʳ	DE V SENSIBUS HOMINUM . . . ET V SUNT SPIRITUALES . . . DE CAUSAS .III. . . . DE CAUSAS .III.
fol. 49ᵛ	DE ALIIS .III. DICIT . . . DE ALIIS .III. DICIT
fol. 50ʳ	DE TRIBUS CAUSIS DICIT . . . DE VII DAMPNATIO SUNT PECCATORUM
fol. 50ᵛ	VII MUNERATIO IUSTORUM
fol. 51ʳ	SEPTEM MODIS REDEMITTERE ANIMAS DE INFERNO
fol. 51ᵛ	SEPTEM SCALES SUNT QUIBUS ASCENDITUR AD REGNA CAELORUM
fol. 52ʳ	DE VIIIᵒ VITIA PRINCIPALIA QUAE MERGUNT HOMINEM IN INFERNUM
fol. 54ʳ	DE SEX COGITATIONIBUS SANCTORUM
fol. 54ᵛ	Isidore's *De Conflictu Vitiorum et Virtutum*
fol. 56ʳ	DE EBRIETATE (after Isidore)
fol. 56ᵛ	DE SOBRIETATE
fol. 57ᵛ	MENSURA EST
fol. 59ʳ	MENSURAM VIARUM
fol. 61ʳ	HEC NOMINA DE VARIIS PROUINTIIS
fol. 62ᵛ	DE CIVITATIBUS
fol. 62ʳ	SEPTEM ARTES SUNT LIBERALES
fol. 63ᵛ	DE MENSURIS
fol. 64ᵛ	Decathologo. dedecemuerbalegis. HIERONIMUS AIT
fol. 65ʳ	DE CHRONICA
fol. 83ʳ	DE BESTIIS ANIMANTIBUS
fol. 85ʳ	DE SUPERNIS CREATURIS
fol. 86ʳ	DE PONDERIBUS . . . DE MENSURIS . . . DE DIEBUS ANNI ET TEMPORIBUS
fol. 93ᵛ	SEPTEM MODI SUNT PREDICATIONES . . . DE DEI NOMINE. Deus tribus modis adorator
fol. 95ᵛ	VII MIRACULI (MUNDI) (after Bede).[36]

Notes

[1] Annette von Eckardt, *Die Handschrift des Wessobrunner Gebets*. The faulty reproduction of the colours was noted by Kenneth C. King in 1967, as is clear from the correspondence between Professor King and the Munich librarian, Dr. Dressler, which David McLintock has kindly passed on to me; Georg Baesecke, "St. Emmeramer Studien," *PBB* 46 (1922): 430–94; Baesecke, *Der Vocabularius Sancti Galli*; Baesecke, *Vor- und Frühgeschichte des deutschen Schrifttums,* 1 (Halle: Max Niemeyer, 1940) and 2 (Halle: Max Niemeyer, 1950); Bernhard Bischoff, "Paläographie," in *Deutsche Philologie im Aufriß*, 2nd ed., 1, col. 498; Bischoff, *Die südostdeutschen*

Schreibschulen, 2nd ed., 1, 20; Ute Schwab, *Die Sternrune im Wessobrunner Gebet;* Glenys A. Waldman, "The Wessobrunn Prayer Manuscript clm 22053." My translations of Latin texts from Clm. 22053 are based upon those of Waldman.

[2] Karl Adolf, "Die Darstellungen der Kreuzauffindung bis zu Piera della Francesca," (diss. Cologne, 1973), 19ff. Wiegel discusses the evolution of the story of the Invention, and has detailed descriptions of all the drawings in Clm. 22053. The Gellone initial is reproduced in E. A. Lowe, *Codices latini antiquiores,* Part 5 (Oxford: Clarendon Press, 1950), facing 29, and discussed by Bernard Teyssèdre, *Le Sacramentaire de Gellone et la figure humaine dans les manuscrits francs du VIIIᵉ siècle* (Toulouse: E. Privat, 1959), 96–98. The Vercelli drawings are reproduced and described by Noemi Gabrielli, "Le miniature delle Omelie di San Gregorio," in *Arte del Primo Millennio,* Atti del IIº Convegno per lo studio dell' arte dell' alto medio evo tenuto presso l'Università di Pavia nel Settembre 1950, ed. Eduardo Arslan (Turin: Viglongo, 1950), 301–11 and plates CXLVIII–CLXIII. The drawing in question is fig. 17.

[3] Ehrismann, *Geschichte der deutschen Literatur bis zum Ausgang des Mittelalters, Erster Teil. Die althochdeutsche Literatur,* 146.

[4] Cf. Jean Leclercq, *L'amour des lettres et le désir de Dieu, initiation aux auteurs monastiques du moyen âge* (Paris: Éditions du Cerf, 1957), 50: "Or le grammaire carolingienne est le reflet de toute la culture de ce temps, et c'est en elle, au premier chef, que cette période apparaît comme une renaissance."

[5] Isidore, *Etymologiarum Liber* IV, *PL* 82, 183–98.

[6] Cf. M. L. W. Laistner, *Thought and Letters in Western Europe, A.D. 500 to 900,* 2nd ed. (London: Methuen, 1957), 221–22.

[7] Laistner, 28; 166; compare Henri de Lubac, *Exégèse Médiévale. Les Quatre Sens de l'Écriture,* Théologie, 41, 42 and 59 (Paris: Aubier, 1959–64), vol. 1, 75–76, 82; Leclercq, 41ff.

[8] On similar attitudes in the Carolingian period, cf. Laistner, 80; 166; on Hrabanus Maurus, 306–08.

[9] Cf. Vivien Law, "The study of grammar," in McKitterick, *Carolingian Culture,* 88–110.

[10] Bischoff, *Schreibschulen,* I, 20.

[11] Perrett, "On the *Wessobrunner Gebet* — I," 134.

[12] Seiffert, "The metrical form and composition of the *Wessobrunner Gebet,*" 10–13.

[13] Krogmann, "Die Mundart des Wessobrunner Gebets," 129–49.

[14] These problems I discuss in more detail in chapter 1, above.

[15] Baesecke, "St. Emmeramer Studien," 442–43; Romuald Bauerreiss, "Das frühmittelalterliche Bistum Neuburg im Staffelsee," *Studien und Mitteilungen zur Geschichte des Benediktiner Ordens* 60 (1946): 375–438 (430–32).

[16] Baesecke reads, with Pez (*Monumenta Boica* VII, (1766), 373), *Hesilinlih,* Waldman *hesilinlo* in line 5. The penalty in line 10 is illegible. The last witness was read by Pez as *Seifrih,* by Baesecke as *S.ifrih,* by Waldman as *eafrih.* The first letter looks like an *s,* but the second letter is illegible; the third may be an *a.*

[17] In correspondence, September 1986. I am indebted to Paul Fouracre, Peter Ganz, Tim Reuter, Tom Cain and many other colleagues for their assistance with this charter.

[18] *Cynewulf's 'Elene'*, ed. Pamela Gradon, rev. ed. (Exeter: U of Exeter P, 1977), 2; see the facsimile edition by Celia Sisam, *The Vercelli Book*, Early English MSS in Facsimile, XIX (Copenhagen: Rosenkilde & Bagger, 1976).

[19] *Der Vocabularius Sti Galli*, 120.

[20] Wilhelm Störmer, *Adelsgruppen im früh- und hochmittelalterlichen Bayern*, Studien zur Bayerischen Verfassungs- und Sozialgeschichte, 4 (Munich: Kommission für Bayerische Landesgeschichte, 1972), 82.

[21] *Die Klostergemeinschaft von Fulda im früheren Mittelalter*, ed. Karl Schmid, Münstersche Mittelalter-Schriften, 8 (Munich: W. Fink, 1978), vol. 8/3, 82.

[22] *Die Traditionen des Klosters Schäftlarn 760–1305*, ed. Alois Weissthanner, Quellen und Erörterungen zur bayerischen Geschichte, N.F., Bd. 10. Erster Teil (Munich: Beck, 1953) vol. 1, § 2. On the place-name and its etymology, see Karl Puchner, *Historisches Ortsnamenbuch von Bayern. Oberbayern, Bd. I. Landkreis Ebersberg* (Munich: Kommission für Bayerische Landesgeschichte, 1951), 40; 105; Sigmund Riezler, "Die Ortsnamen der Münchener Gegend," *Oberbayrisches Archiv für vaterländische Geschichte*, 44 (1887), 71.

[23] Waldman, "The Scriptorium of the Wessobrunn Prayer Manuscript," *Scriptorium* 32 (1978): 249–50.

[24] Waldman, "The German and geographical Glosses of the Wessobrunn Prayer Manuscript," *Beiträge zur Namenforschung*, N.F., 13 (1978), 261–305 (299).

[25] Chris Wickham, *Early Medieval Italy. Central Power and Local Society, 400–1000*, New Studies in Medieval History (London: Macmillan, 1981), 154; 78.

[26] Bauerreiss (note 15); Schwab (note 1), 15; Bischoff, *Schreibschulen*, 1, 19. The list is in *MGH Legum* 2,1 (Hannover, 1883), 251.

[27] Friedrich Zoepfl, *Das Bistum Augsburg und seine Bischöfe im Mittelalter* (Augsburg: Schnell & Steiner, 1955), 33–34.

[28] See F. Dörrer, "Die Kirchenprovinz Salzburg im Mittelalter," in *Atlas zur Kirchengeschichte*, ed. Hubert Jedin et al. (Freiburg i. Br.: Herder, 1970), § 46. Dörrer is sensibly non-committal concerning the location of Neuburg: "schließlich an der Grenze gegen die Alemannen das vermutlich kleine, infolge Quellenarmut nicht genau bestimmbare Bistum Neuburg (Residenz Neuburg auf der Staffelseeinsel oder Neuburg an der Donau?)."

[29] Johann Friedrich Böhmer, *Die Regesten des Kaiserreichs unter den Karolingern 751–918*, 1st ed., rev. by Engelbert Mühlbacher (Cologne: Böhlau, 1889), 120ff.

[30] Adolf Gauert, "Zum Itinerar Karls des Großen," in *Karl der Große: Lebenswerk und Nachleben*, ed. Wolfgang Braunfels et al. (Düsseldorf: L. Schwann, 1966–68), 1, 307–22 (318).

[31] Jan Frederik Niermeyer, *Mediae Latinitatis Lexicon Minus* (Leiden: E. J. Brill, 1984), 624–25.

[32] Johann Friedrich Böhmer, *Regesta archiepiscoporum Maguntiniensum: Regesten zur Geschichte der Mainzer Erzbischöfe* (Innsbruck, 1877; repr. Aalen: Scientia Verlag, 1966), vol. I, 45–55.

[33] On the problem of identification see Theodor Schieffer, "Erzbischof Richulf (787–813)," *Jahrbuch für das Bistum Mainz* 5 (1950), 333.

[34] *Einhard and Notker the Stammerer. Two Lives of Charlemagne*, trans. with an introduction by Lewis Thorpe (Harmondsworth: Penguin, 1974), 110; 191.

[35] Störmer, *Adelsgruppen*, 81–82; 89; and *Früher Adel. Studien zur politischen Führungsschicht im fränkisch-deutschen Reich vom 8. bis 11. Jahrhundert* (Stuttgart: A. Hiersemann, 1973), vol. 1, 42. Störmer thinks the Jacobs may be connected by kinship, and that the name may be reserved for offspring destined for the Church.

[36] This list has no pretensions to be exhaustive. Abbreviations are here as expanded by Waldman. The interdisciplinary nature of this study has involved the unselfishly given assistance of scholars too numerous to mention, but I feel particularly indebted to James Simpson and Anette Syndikus for their help with the seven liberal arts.

7: Clm. 14098, fol. 61ʳ. The first surviving leaf of the Muspilli.

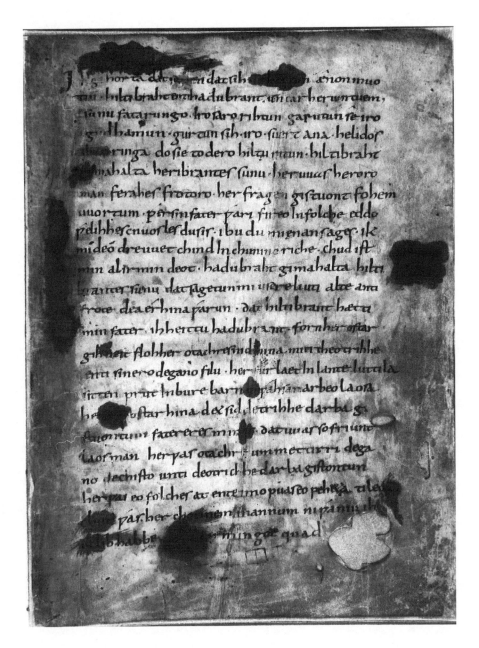

8: Landesbibliothek und Murhardsche Bibliothek der Stadt Kassel, Cod. theol. 2° 54, fols. 1ʳ and 76ᵛ. The Hildebrandslied.

9: *Landesbibliothek und Murhardsche Bibliothek der Stadt Kassel, Cod. theol. 2° 54, fols. 1ʳ and 76ᵛ*. The Hildebrandslied.

3: "Unlucky Zeal": The *Hildebrandslied* and the *Muspilli* under Acid

PERHAPS THE MOST VALUABLE LESSON that medieval studies can teach is a sense of historical perspective. The final part of the last millennium, to the detached eye of the medievalist, seemed to be characterised to an ever-increasing extent by instances of what might be termed the triumph of science over mind. This essay will concern itself with one small triumph of the kind, one which has, however, a long and respectable history behind it.

Preparing his edition of the minstrel romance *Thomas of Erceldoune* for his *Popular Ballads and Songs* (1806), the Scottish antiquarian Robert Jamieson (1780?–1844) found himself confronted with considerable problems in the Cambridge manuscript (Cambridge University Library MS Ff.5.48): "The Camb. MS. from which the editor made the above transcript, has suffered by rain-water nearly as much as the Cotton has by fire; a great part of each page having become entirely illegible by the total disappearance of the ink. By wetting it, however, with a composition which he procured from a bookseller and stationer in Cambridge, the writing was so far restored in most places, that, with much poring, and the assistance of a magnifying glass, he was able to make it out pretty clearly. The greatest difficulty he met with was from the unlucky zeal and industry of some person, who, long ago, and in a hand nearly resembling the original, had endeavoured to fill up the chasms, and, as appeared upon the revival of the old writing, had generally mistaken the sense, and done much more harm than good."[1]

The ease with which Jamieson was able to obtain a "composition" from the Cambridge stationer and apply it to the manuscript is unsurprising. In Cambridge, as in libraries all over Europe, medieval manuscripts had been the victims of this particular kind of "unlucky zeal" on the part of scholars, as they sought to restore faded medieval ink by reconstituting it, using various acid-based reagents. From at least the early nineteenth century onwards, these drastic measures were established practice. An example with which Jamieson may have been familiar is the manuscript of the Cambridge Songs (Cambridge University Library Gg.v.35) which contains "Suavissima nunna," a macaronic erotic dialogue dating from the middle of the eleventh century, perhaps the oldest German pastourelle. At some point in the Middle Ages the song was erased, presumably because of its obscene content. Then, in the nineteenth century there was an attempt to read it, using reagents. In consequence the text is covered by a black layer. In 1968 Peter Dronke tackled the poem with ultra-violet light, and established sufficient letters to attempt a reconstruction.[2] Another medieval German lyric which suffered a similar fate in the nineteenth century was Heinrich von Morungen's "Die Räuberin" (*Des Minnesangs Frühling* 130,9), written on an absorbent hair leaf of CC 248, a tenth-century manuscript in the Benedictine monastery of Kremsmünster (Upper Austria). It now resembles a piece of blotting paper that has been treated with two coats of varnish, one light-brown, one almost black.[3] The perpetrator could, to judge from the notes he wrote on the back of an envelope, read more of the text than can be read today, but probably for only a very brief space of time before the acids took effect.

Martin Kaufmann of the Bodleian Library is aware of reagents still being applied in Oxford in the early years of the last century; Susan Reynolds recalls them being used in English archives as late as 1950, in particular by a colleague who favoured the use of fuming acid. To some extent this "unlucky zeal" could be justified by reference to precedent and authority. Wattenbach's *Das Schriftwesen im Mittelalter*, which first appeared in 1871, but was reprinted as late as 1958, recommends the practice, albeit with some reservations as to the possible effect of some acids. It is characteristic of the writing upon the subject that Wattenbach voices uncertainty as to whether even Studemund's preferred solution, "1 Theil Schwefelcyancalium in 15 Theilen Brunnenwasser, mit wenigen Tropfen möglichst condensierter Salzsäure" may not in the long term damage the writing: "Ob nicht doch eine schädliche Nachwirkung eintritt und die Schriftreste völlig vertilgt werden, muß längere Erfahrung lehren."[4] Wattenbach, in self-contradictory fashion, goes on to discuss the question of whether chemical means should be employed at all. Given the advanced state of photography, he feels able to answer the question in the affirmative. Reservations had been voiced for a long time. Friedrich Ebert issued a warning in 1825: reagents were only to be used with great care, particularly gall-apple tincture, used in the Vatican and Verona, which in the course of time blackens the whole surface of the parchment to which it is applied.[5] He recommends as the most effective and least destructive reagent sulphurated potash, which had then long been in use in Wolfenbüttel and Hanover; despite its penetrating smell, it had the additional advantage of helping to cure gout. Ebert goes on to recommend various tinctures, including the Gioberti recipe, perfected by a Turin chemist, which involved coating the parchment with layers of hydrochloric acid and potassium cyanide.[6] Perhaps the most notorious user of reagents was Angelo Mai (1782–1854), who applied them to palimpsests in Milan and Rome. In common with most German editors, Mai does not refer to his use of reagents in the prefaces to his editions, but "in realtà li usò con la massima larghezza."[7] Mai, like so many others, was convinced that his reagents were harmless.

At the end of the nineteenth century, Franz Ehrle surveys the damage and concludes that two categories of manuscripts affected by reagents may be distinguished. The first class have been damaged by the use of gallic acid, which colours parchment brown, or if used in abundance, virtually black. The second class have been affected by the "Gioberti-Tinctur" recommended by

Ebert and used in Paris, which leaves behind a bright or dark blue colour. Both acids eat into the parchment. Ehrle recommends countering corrosion by applying gelatine.[8]

The origins of the use of acids to read faded or invisible ink can be traced back at least as far as the Renaissance. At first the procedure was regarded as belonging to the realm of magic, as for example in Giovanni Battista della Porta's *Magia naturalis*, published in Cologne in 1562. This work has several recipes for writing in and reading invisible ink, involving acids and the juices of fruits. It recommends boiling "galls in wine and with a spunge wipe over the letters, the letters will presently be seen, when they are once wet thus, and be well coloured as they were at first."[9] The beginnings of the long transition from magic to science are visible in works such as Petro Maria Canepari's *De Atramentis* of 1619, which places more emphasis on the practical effect of the recipes in restoring faded script.[10]

The Age of the Enlightenment is characterised by the experiments of Sir Charles Blagden (1748–1820), a distinguished physician, a "careful worker in physical research,"[11] who by patronage became Secretary to the Royal Society in 1784. He was praised by Dr. Johnson as "a delightful fellow," and by Hannah More as "so modest, so sensible." In 1787 Blagden published "Some Observations on ancient inks, with the Proposal of a new Method of recovering the Legibility of decayed Writings."[12] His friend and fellow member of the Royal Society, Thomas Astle (1735–1803), an antiquary and palaeographer who catalogued the Harley manuscripts of the British Library, was keeper of the public records at Westminster, Whitehall and in the Tower, and also possessed a huge private collection. He supplied Blagden with manuscripts dating from the ninth to the fifteenth century. Blagden does not tell us anything of the content of these manuscripts, which is perhaps as well for the peace of mind of the modern scholar.

Blagden's concerns are purely scientific: "On all of these I made experiments with the chemical re-agents which appeared to me best adapted to the purpose; namely, alkalies both simple and phlogisticated, the mineral acids, and infusion of galls. . . . It would be tedious and superfluous to enter into a detail of the particular experiments; as all of them, one instance only excepted, agreed in the general result, to shew, that the ink employed anciently, as far as the above-mentioned MSS extended, was of the same nature as the present: for the letters turned of a reddish or yellowish brown with alkalies, became pale, and were at length obliterated." Blagden is not totally impervious to the damage he is wreaking: "Some degree of effervescence was commonly to be perceived when the acids came in contact with the surface of these old volumes." Nothing daunted, he persists in his attempt to establish how much iron was used in ancient inks; he tries acids on one ink that proves resistant to them, but then establishes that he is in fact working on an early printed book. One experiment leads to another: "Whilst I was considering of the experiments to be made, in order to ascertain the composition of ancient inks, it occurred to me, that perhaps one of the best methods of restoring legibility to decayed writing might be, to join phlogisticated alkali with the remaining calx of iron; because, as the quantity of precipitate formed by these two substances very much exceeds that of iron alone, the bulk of the colouring matter would thereby be greatly augmented." When this fails to work, Blagden "was next induced to try the effect of adding a dilute mineral acid to writing, beside the alkali. This answered fully to my expectations; the letters changing very speedily to a deep blue colour, of great beauty and intensity." Blagden is genuinely troubled as to whether or not alkali should be used: "For the principal inconvenience which occurs in the proposed method of restoring [*sic!*] MSS, is, that the colour frequently spreads, and so much blots the parchment, as to detract greatly from the legibility." At times the aesthete in Blagden triumphs over the scientist: "The sudden evolution of so fine a colour, upon the mere traces of letters, affords an amusing spectacle."

Blagden ultimately decides in favour of the application of alkali, followed by acid applied with a feather, or a blunt stick, and then using blotting paper near the letters: "Care must be taken not to bring the blotting paper in contact with the letters, because the colouring matter is soft whilst wet, and may easily be rubbed off. . . . The acid I have chiefly employed has been the marine; but both the vitriolic and nitrous succeed very well. They should undoubtedly be so far diluted as not to be in danger of corroding the parchment, after which the degree of strength does not seem to be matter of much nicety."

Bladgen is critical of Canepari's method: "The method now commonly practised to restore old writings is by wetting them with an infusion of galls in white wine. This certainly has a great effect; but it is subject, in some degree, to the same inconvenience as the phlogisticated alkali, of staining the substance on which the writing was made." Blagden concludes by recommending further experimentation, but is confident that the method he has evolved is preferable to the application of galls, in that "it produces its effect immediately, and can be confined to those letters only for which such assistance is wanted."

Two OHG manuscripts in particular have been affected by the use of reagents: the *Hildebrandslied* and the *Muspilli*. The damage to the latter is greater by far. The manuscript (Clm. 14098) came to Munich from St. Emmeram; the *Muspilli* is written in that part of the manuscript which contains the pseudo-Augustinian *Sermo de symbolo contra Iudaeos*, on the originally blank endleaves (fols. 61^r, 120^v, 121^{r-v}) and in the lower margins of fols 119^v and 120^r. The now lost beginning and end of the poem were presumably written on the covers which were lost when the manuscript was rebound. Reagents were applied to the end-leaves and have penetrated through to the corners of the leaves of the Latin sermon (see illustration 7). The perpetrator was Bernhard Joseph Docen (1782–1828), who studied the manuscripts in the Bavarian State Library from 1804, an exciting time for the discovery of medieval texts because of the dissolution of the monasteries. Docen never published an edition of the *Muspilli*, although that he had intended to do so is clear from a letter addressed to him by Jacob Grimm, dating from 2 June 1817. Probably at some point prior to this he applied acids to the end-leaves, which were evidently very faded. To judge from his notes, it is doubtful whether he succeeded in reading many additional letters. The damaged portions of the text indicated by his readings are those which are still for the most part illegible today. Using ultra-violet light in 1998, I found myself unable to advance beyond the work of the nineteenth-century editors. Docen's notes were recovered and published by Hofmann in 1866.[13] The study of OHG was in 1817 very much in its infancy, and the pencilled notes and ink comments reveal Docen's uncertainty. Hofmann believed, somewhat over-optimistically, that the readings revealed the state of the manuscript before it was damaged, or at least soon after the reagents were applied. We cannot be certain of this; we can only regret that Docen applied the then customary drastic remedy rather than leaving the task of deciphering the text to later, superior editors. The consequence is that modern editions are composite ones based on Docen's readings, Schmeller's two editions of 1832, the readings of Haupt in the autumn of 1860, and of subsequent scholars, not to mention the huge number of conjectures.[14] All scholars, with the possible exception of Docen, were working with a badly damaged text.

It is hard to imagine that any manuscript has had a more adventurous life than the two leaves of the *Hildebrandslied* (illustrations 8–9). In 1943 the manuscript was taken from Kassel to a bunker in Bad Wildungen for safe-keeping, only to be looted by American soldiers. In November 1945 it was purchased from an American army officer in Philadelphia, by Mr. A. S. W. Rosenbach. In 1954 the second leaf returned to Germany, having been tracked down to the library of St. John's Seminary in Camarillo, California. It had been bought from the Rosenbachs for the Estelle Doheny collection. Searches for the missing leaf led nowhere at first, but then in 1972 it was rediscovered in the Rosenbach Museum, Philadelphia. It was flown back by a special aircraft of the Luftwaffe in 1972, in the company of Helmut Schmidt. The aircraft was, it has to be admitted, commissioned because of Schmidt's talks with the US Treasury, rather than because of the intrinsic value of the *Hildebrandslied*, but, nevertheless, on one momentous day in 1972, Old High German literature appeared on the front page of *The Times*. Yet long before the two leaves were reunited in Kassel, the manuscript had been subjected to considerable maltreat-ment. David McLintock quotes the dictum of his mentor, the postwar scholar J. Knight Bostock: "Some swine has been using reagents."

The manuscript was made known to the modern world by the scholar and librarian Johann Georg von Eckhart (1674–1730). The precise date of the discovery is uncertain, but thought to be *c.* 1715, when Eckhart was working as a librarian in Hanover.[15] The text was first published by Eckhart in 1729 in his *Commentarii de rebus Franciae orientalis*, under the title "FRAGMENTVM FABVLAE ROMANTICAE, Saxonica dialecto Seculo VIII. conscriptae, ex Codice Hasso-Cassellano."[16] It was prefaced by a "Specimen Scripturae," a copperplate "facsimile," prepared in Hanover, of the first fourteen lines of the first leaf. The technique is primitive by modern standards, the engraving probably based, as Wilhelm Grimm thought, upon a freehand drawing: "flüchtig und aus freyer Hand gemacht."[17] The script bears only a superficial resemblance to that of the original. This was, however, the first attempt at a facsimile of an OHG text. In the centuries that followed, the *Hildebrandslied* was to become perhaps the most frequently reproduced text in German literature.

In 1812 the Grimm brothers, Jacob (1785–1863) and Wilhelm (1786–1859), published the first modern edition of the *Hildebrandslied*. Broszinski suggests in his introduction to the excellent facsimile of 1984–85 that the Grimms also accompanied their edition with a facsimile, and Wilhelm Grimm refers to an "Abdruck," but, if the Taylor Institution's copy is intact, the reproduction was restricted to a lithographic attempt at the *d* in the first four lines.[18] In 1813 a Russian cannonball hit the library in Kassel, and this was one factor which inspired the librarian to use the latest techniques to make a facsimile of the *Hildebrandslied* in order to preserve it for posterity. With unmistakable pride he declares that he used reagents at two points (next to lines 10–12, and at the bottom of the second leaf) to clarify the state of the original manuscript. The perpetrator was none other than Wilhelm Grimm. His facsimile was published in 1830 with the title *De Hildebrando antiquissimi carminis teutonici fragmentum*. Grimm describes his facsimile technique in detail: "Mit Hilfe des trefflichen Pariser Pflanzenpapiers verfertigte der Herausg. eine Durchzeichnung des Ganzen, bey welcher er sich keine Mühe verdrießen ließ, und von welcher er glaubt ohne Anmaßung behaupten zu dürfen, daß sie im Stande sey, das Original völlig zu vertreten. Jede Zeile, jeder Buchstabe hat seinen richtigen Platz, kein Strich fehlt."[19] This drawing was then etched by the lithographic institute of Arnold in Kassel. Whilst undoubtedly a triumph of its time, the facsimile, like its many successors, does not, perforce, take into account that many of the words on the first leaf are written over erasures. It shows no sign of the use of reagents at the points Grimm mentions. Perhaps they had yet to stain the text, or Grimm thought it advisable to conceal the damage. However, the word *seggen* in line 1, which was written over an erasure, looks as if it may have been treated with acid. Other Kassel manuscripts, such as the Kassel Glosses, were so treated, either by the Grimms or with their permission.

Christian Wilhelm Michael Grein (1825–77), a successor to Grimm as librarian at Kassel, obtained permission from the library's administration to employ reagents again in 1855. Grein describes his procedure in his 1858 Marburg dissertation: "Nachdem ich nun zuvor die betreffende Stelle mit Wasser sorgfältig von dem anklebenden Schmutz gereinigt hatte, brachte ich Galläpfeltinctur in Anwendung, deren treffliche Wirkung als eines unschädlichen Reagens ich an den halbvermoderten Urkunden zu Bückeburg zu erproben reichlich Gelegenheit gehabt, und ich beobachtete ihre Wirkung auf unser Wort [*sc.* 'wettu'] mehrere Wochen durch zu allen Tageszeiten und unter der verschiedensten Beleuchtung."[20] Grein reproduced a number of letters of the manuscript lithographically, in particular the scribe's experiments with the wynn-rune in the left-hand margin of the first leaf, which had been treated with reagents by Wilhelm Grimm.

Between 1858 and the second edition of Grein's book in 1880 the making of facsimiles was revolutionised by photography. The first of the many photographic reproductions of the *Hildebrandslied* was published by Eduard Sievers (1850–1932) in 1872 and shows clearly the disastrous effects of Grimm's and Grein's "harmless" reagents.[21] By 1880, to judge from the photograph that accompanied Grein's second edition, things had deteriorated still further. Photographs can be deceptive, however, and Grein seems to have been as careless with photography as with reagents. A lot depends on the amount of care taken in the reproduction, and the early colour facsimile printed by Friedrich Vogt (1851–1923) in 1904 indicates that the deterioration was not quite as bad as Grein's reduced photograph suggested.[22] On the other hand, photographs, like lithographic reproductions, can be touched up, and this may have been the case with the Vogt facsimile, which has supernaturally clear contours for its wormholes.

Sievers's and Vogt's photographs show that the *Hildebrandslied* had, presumably under treatment with reagents, acquired a new first line (line 1a). Reagents have subsequently erased some letters of this line and affected letters of the line below it, too (line 1 proper).[23] However it is clear that the first four words of the text, *Ik gihorta dat seggen*, have been written above the first line of the text as reproduced by Grimm, in what would appear to be a different hand. (Hermann Pongs thought it possible that the two hands are identical, or certainly contemporary.)[24]

Emma Danielowski's detailed discussion of the manuscript is accompanied by a reproduction of this new first line in an enlarged photograph. Danielowski takes on trust Wilhelm Grimm's assertion that he reproduced every stroke of the original and concludes that this new first line must therefore have originated, along with other "Glossen," to use her term, after 1850. The purpose of the first gloss, she suggests, is an attempt to read the erasure around *seggen*. If that were so, it would be difficult to explain away some puzzling features. The hand of line 1a, accurately described by Danielowski and Pongs, prefers the open, Merovingian *a* (in both *gihorta* and *dat*) to the closed form that came to dominate in Carolingian minuscule and which is the dominant form in the *Hildebrandslied*, as for example in *gihorta* and *dat* in line 1. "Scribe A" of the *Hildebrandslied* proper, the scribe responsible for the first page and the first seven and a half lines of the second page, fluctuates between Merovingian open *a*, Anglo-Saxon closed *a* and the closed *a* with an ascender preferred by Carolingian minuscule.[25] The older, open *a* occurs only twice, in *ubar* (line 4, word 1) and *uuas* (line 6, word 6). Moreover, the scribe of line 1a has an *r* with an elongated descender in *gihorta*, an insular scribal feature otherwise only found in *garutun* (line 3).

Both scribes are using a script which is in a state of flux, moving toward the preference in Carolingian minuscule for letters of uniformly medial height. We can see the same state of flux in the roughly contemporary Wessobrunn Prayer manuscript. An *r* with an elongated shaft is to be found in **fregin* (line 1) and *pereg* (line 5); open Merovingian *a* is present in *sunna* (line 5), though closed *a* predominates.

Danielowki also argues that the scribe of line 1a has a pronounced cursive tendency, though this is by no means clear from her enlarged photograph, nor from my own examination of the manuscript. Danielowki's conclusions are less satisfactory than her description. Why should a nineteenth-century scholar, in copying the first line of the Hildebrandslied, opt for the more archaic scribal features to be found in the hand of "Scribe A"? It is more likely that more accurate photography, or perhaps the effect of the reagents, has revealed an earlier attempt to record the lay.

This has implications for the way in which we view the recording of the lay. It was done with great care, as an attempt to copy an older, written original. Wilhelm Grimm's theory of two scribes writing down the lay from memory, from the oral tradition, has long been out of fashion. Line 1a reinforces the consensus that the *Hildebrandslied* is far from being a fortuitous survival. Its entering on the front and end leaves of a theological manuscript from the monastery of Fulda, 2^0 Ms. theol. 54, is characteristic of the mode of transmission of many of the smaller OHG texts. It was written on originally blank pages, and such attempts as have been made to link it with the theological contents of the main part of the manuscript are unconvincing. However, at least two people were interested in the preservation of the *Hildebrandslied*. It seems most likely that they were acting in an antiquarian interest — perhaps they were inspired by Charlemagne's desire, as recorded by his biographer Einhard, to preserve literature of the heroic past. In the nature of things, and particularly in view of the nature of the manuscript, we can only speculate concerning the motive of the scribes, but the link with Charlemagne is an appealing one. Imperial and monastic minds, we may say, thought alike.

Recently Peter-Erich Neuser has claimed that the hand of "Scribe A" of the *Hildebrandslied* bears a close resemblance to the Carolingian minuscule of the hand responsible for the first theological text in the main body of the MS, the *Missa contra obloquentes*, although he has not gone so far as to state that it is identical.[26] The two pages of the manuscript which he reproduces, fol. 1ᵛ, "ORATIO ET PRECES CONTRA OBLOQUENTES," and fol. 76r, the final lines of Ecclesiasticus and the Prayer of Solomon, have no great affinities in my view with the hand(s) of the *Hildebrandslied*. Neuser correctly characterises fol. 1v as Carolingian minuscule, and fol. 76r as an insular hand. The dominant characteristic of "Scribe A" of the *Hildebrandslied* is the blend of insular and Carolingian features. There is an open *a* in *superbia* (line 14) on fol. 1v, but otherwise little resemblance in hand or ductus.

As Neuser's analysis shows, both the first leaf of the *Hildebrandslied* (1r) and the first leaf of the *Missa* (1v) have 24 lines, while the bulk of the manuscript pages have 28 lines. Line 1a is thus supernumerary to the ruled lines. The second leaf of the *Hildebrandslied* has 29 lines, like the Latin leaf that precedes it. The evidence suggests that the manuscript is the work of a number of hands very close to one another in time, scribes who had disparate interests — theological, and antiquarian.

One possible scenario is that the scribe of 1a started the job; then "Scribe A," perhaps a younger man, took over. But this is only one possibility of many: the scribe of 1a may have died on the job, wearied of the task, or even been directed away from it by a superior who regarded the recording of the *Hildebrandslied* as a task unworthy of a monk's labours. Far less likely, on both palaeographical and rational grounds, is that the scribe of 1a wrote the words after "Scribe A" had finished his task.

"Scribe A," the younger scribe or scribe with a more fashionable hand, apparently had considerable difficulties with the written source before him. After reproducing *đ* for the first four or five lines, he abandoned this feature. It is not clear to Danielowski, nor to Pongs, whether the *đ* in line 1a has a bar or not. I would have thought probably not, from the facsimiles I have seen, and from looking at the original. (The *đ* is described by Lühr as a Saxonism, an attempt at an orthographic feature from further North, perhaps in harmony with the Saxonising phonology in the lay.[27]) The scribe also had considerable difficulties with the wynn-rune, the *p*-like letter that stands for *w*. Twice the scribe adds an extra, superfluous *u*: *puas*, first leaf, (manuscript) line 22; *puortun*, second leaf, line 7. The latter instance occurs in the part of the poem thought by Grimm to be the work of "Scribe B." The unique acute accent over the rune is not handled consistently, being omitted in *pas* (fol. 1, line 22); *pant* (fol. 2, line 2); *pidar* (fol. 2, line. 6); *pic* (fol. 2, line 10). This error, too, is common to both "Scribe A" and "Scribe B." On the first leaf *uu* occurs where one might expect the rune in *uuet* (l. 10) and *uuas* (l. 19); on the second leaf in *uualtan* (lines 25–26). The rune is not employed after a consonant: *suert* (fol. 1, line 4), *suasat* (fol. 2, line 17), *suertu* (fol. 2, line 18), *huitte* (fol. 2, line 28).

Wilhelm Grimm was the first to argue, on the basis of his observations in preparing the facsimile, that there were two scribes involved in the main body of the text. Van der Kolk's survey of the views on this shows commendable scepticism and emphasises the fact that the script of the second leaf is generally smaller in character; in the end, however, Van der Kolk accepts the consensus that there are at least two hands.[28] The fact that there is more frequent recourse to erasures on the first leaf does not prove that there is a different scribe, only that the scribe is more careful and less confident than is the case with the second leaf. When I examined the original, admittedly hampered by the fact that the leaves were on display in a vitrine, I still hesitated as to whether there is sufficient difference between the two scripts to justify ascribing them to two distinct hands. At the beginning of the ninth line on fol. 2, possibly already after the fold half-way through line 8, the ductus of the script appears to change slightly. The main difference, however, is in size; the letters are generally bigger after line 8, though not as large as in the 24 lines of fol. 1. It seems possible that on fol. 2 the scribe may have written in a more compressed way at first, perhaps sensing that there might not be enough room to complete the task, but then relaxed and reverted to a slightly larger hand. At the beginning of line 9 on fol. 2, the text commences noticeably further into the left-hand margin than in lines 1–8. A new phase of writing begins here, though I am more inclined to believe that the scribe has taken a break, and taken up his task again, probably with a new quill, rather than relinquished the task to another scribe. The more scribes one posits in the recording of such a short text, the more difficult it is to explain the underlying rationale. But the emergence of line 1a shows that, in all probability, at least two scribes attempted to write down the lay.

The reagents applied to the *Hildebrandslied* have both elucidated and obscured the text. Facsimiles have the disadvantage that erasures, water-stains, wormholes and acid marks all tend to show up as dark holes. The most detailed description of the manuscript, and in particular of the erasures made by the scribe(s) is that by Elias von Steinmeyer.[29] Below I list the areas where I thought I could discern the workings of acids and other stains, and collate my observations with those of Steinmeyer. Reading my pencilled notes after looking at the manuscript, I did wonder if I was exaggerating, but a glance at Grein's dark facsimile of 1880 confirmed every blotch.

fol. 1ʳ (first leaf)

line 1a, stretching below into line 1. Steinmeyer: "von einer nicht wesentlich jüngeren Hand."

line 1: *urhettun*; on Grimm's 1830 facsimile the word *seggen* is marked by a dark blotch. While the word is now slightly faded, having been written over an erasure, no blotch suggestive of acid is evident. Either a weaker acid was used, the effects of which have faded, or perhaps the blotch reproduced by Grimm was a watermark which has dried in the course of time.

line 5,1 *ubar*

line 6,1 *gimahalta*. The reagent used on *ubar* has affected all but the first two letters.

lines 8–16 left-hand margin

lines 10–12 right-hand margin. Some letters are visible below the acid here.

line 15 above *gihueit*

line 17 *unpáhsan*, affecting the first two letters   Steinmeyer: "auf Rasur."

line 18 *her raet*. After *he* there is little more than a blotch visible.

line 19 *mines*, affecting the last two letters

line 22 *leop*
line 23 *chud*
line 28 following *habbe* — a dark splodge, Grein's work   Steinmeyer:
"das erste *b* auf Rasur."

fol. 76ᵛ (second leaf):

possibly line 8 *epin*
the last two lines (28–29); and the gloss below, 'christus grece unctus
dicitur latine'.

In many instances it is hard to imagine why acid was used on the first leaf,
given the unproblematic nature of words such as *gimahalta* or *mines*. It seems
probable that acid was spilt accidentally, or that its effects spread.

Steinmeyer limits his comments on damage to a note of erasures, although
he must have seen the impact of the reagents. The tale of woe is corroborated
by the report of the Institut für Buch- und Handschriftenrestaurierung of the
Bayerische Staatsbibliothek in Munich, commissioned by the Murhardtsche
Biblothek in Kassel when the two leaves of the *Hildebrandslied* were reunited
in 1972. An analysis made by the Institut für Makromolekulare Chemie of the
Technische Hochschule Darmstadt noted the damage caused by the application
of chemicals. At those points in the text which reveal considerable discolour-
ing, it is possible that the application of gall-apple tincture was supplemented
by that of an alkaline sulphide.[30] The conclusion was reached that no further
use should be made of such methods. It is to be hoped that the leaves will
henceforth rest in peace.

Notes

[1] Robert Jamieson, *Popular Ballads and Songs*, 2 vols (Edinburgh and London:
Archibald Constable & Co.; Cadell & Davies, and John Murray, 1806), vol. 2, 43.

[2] Peter Dronke, *Medieval Latin and the Rise of European Love-Lyric*, 2nd ed., 2 vols
(Oxford: Clarendon Press, 1968), vol. 2, 353–56. My own efforts, employing a cold
light source, have added little. See the facsimile and transcription in Cyril Edwards,
"Von Archilochos zu Walther von der Vogelweide. Zu den Anfängen der Pastourelle
in Deutschland," in *Lied im deutschen Mittelalter. Überlieferung, Typen, Gebrauch.
Chiemsee-Colloquium 1991*, ed. Cyril Edwards, Ernst Hellgardt and Norbert H. Ott
(Tübingen: Niemeyer, 1996), 1–25 (10–11; 22–24).

[3] See C. W. Edwards, "Die 'Räuberin' Heinrichs von Morungen im Benediktinerstift
Kremsmünster," *PBB* 108 (1986): 206–11; idem, "The Growth of a Song: Heinrich
von Morungen's Robber-Lady (MF 130,9)," *Medium Aevum* 58 (1989): 17–33; *Des
Minnesangs Frühling*, 38th ed., rev. by Hugo Moser and Helmut Tervooren
(Stuttgart: S. Hirzel, 1988), 469–71. The lyric is a fragment only in the sense that it
remains imperfectly legible.

[4] Wilhelm Wattenbach, *Das Schriftwesen im Mittelalter*, 3rd ed. (Leipzig, 1896; repr. Graz: Akademische Druck- und Verlagsanstalt, 1958), 315.

[5] Friedrich Adolph Ebert, *Zur Handschriftenkunde*, 2 vols (Leipzig: Steinacker & Hartknoch, 1825–27), I, 83–85.

[6] See I. D. Reynolds and N. G. Wilson, *Scribes and Scholars: A Guide to the Transmission of Greek and Latin Literature*, 3rd ed. (Oxford: Clarendon Press, 1991), 193–94. I am grateful to Nigel Wilson for drawing my attention to this account.

[7] Sebastiano Timpanaro Jr., "Angelo Mai," *Atene e Roma*, N.S., 1 (1956): 3–34 (6).

[8] Franz Ehrle, "Über die Erhaltung und Ausbesserung alter Handschriften," *Centralbibliothek für Bibliothekswesen* 15 (1898): 17–33. See also Wattenbach, 310.

[9] Giovanni Battista della Porta, *Magiae naturalis* (Cologne: Hannes Birckmann & Werner Richvuin, 1562), lib. II, cap. 12; translated as *Natural Magick in XX Bookes* (London: Thomas Young & Samuel Speed, 1658), bk. 16, ch. ix (351).

[10] Petro Maria Canepari, *De Atramentis* (Venice: Apud Euangelistam Deuchinum, 1619), 179.

[11] *DNB*, vol. 2, 617.

[12] *Philosophical Transactions of the Royal Society of London* 77 (1787): 451–57.

[13] C. Hofmann, "Ueber Docens Abschrift des Muspilli," *Sitzungsberichte der königlichen bayerischen Akademie der Wissenschaften. Philosophisch-philologische Classe* (Munich, 1866), II, 225–35.

[14] See Elias von Steinmeyer, *Die kleineren althochdeutschen Sprachdenkmäler*, 73–74; *MSD*, 264–65. The footnote references to the manuscript in Braune's *Lesebuch* are thus something of an over-simplification. A trace of the *s* in the first word of the first line is still clearly recognisable; the italicisation in the latest, seventeenth edition of the *Lesebuch* (1994) is therefore redundant.

[15] Rosemarie Lühr, *Studien zur Sprache des Hildebrandliedes*, Europäische Hochschulschriften, 2 vols (Frankfurt am Main: Peter Lang, 1982), vol. 1, xix; Gustav Süßmann, *Das Hildebrandlied — gefälscht?* (Staufenberg: Eigenverlag Gustav Süßmann, 1988), 101.

[16] See the reproduction in Gustav Süßmann, *Das Hildebrandlied — gefälscht?*, 19.

[17] Wilhelm Grimm, *GGA* (1830), vol. 1, 48th fascicle: 466.

[18] *Hiltibraht. Das Hildebrandlied. Faksimile der Kasseler Handschrift*, with an introduction by Hartmut Broszinski, 2nd ed. (Kassel: Stauda, 1985), *sine pagina*; Wilhelm Grimm, *loc. cit.*, 465.

[19] Wilhelm Grimm, *loc. cit.*, 466–67.

[20] C. W. M. Grein, *Das Hildebrandslied nach der Handschrift von Neuem herausgegeben, kritisch bearbeitet und erläutert* (Göttingen: Georg H. Wigand, 1858), 28.

[21] *Das Hildebrandlied, die Merseburger Zaubersprüche und das fränkische Taufgelöbnis, mit photographischem Faksimile*, ed. Eduard Sievers (Halle: Verlag der Buchhandlung des Waisenhauses, 1872).

[22] Friedrich Vogt and Max Koch, *Geschichte der deutschen Litteratur von den ältesten Zeiten bis zur Gegenwart*, 2nd rev. ed. (Leipzig and Vienna: Bibliographisches Institut, 1904), between 26–27.

[23] See Emma Danielowski, *Das Hiltibrantlied. Beitrag zur Überlieferungsgeschichte auf paläographischer Grundlage* (Berlin: Mayer & Müller, 1919), 42–44.

[24] Hermann Pongs, *Das Hildebrandslied. Ueberlieferung und Lautstand im Rahmen der althochdeutschen Literatur* (Marburg: W. Hütter, 1913), 5.

[25] Danielowski, *Das Hiltibrantlied*, 17.

[26] Peter-Erich Neuser, "Das karolingische 'Hildebrandslied'. Kodikologische und rezeptionsgeschichtliche Aspekte des 2⁰ Ms. theol. 54 aus Fulda," in *Architectura Poetica. Festschrift für Johannes Rathofer zum 65. Geburtstag*, ed. Ulrich Ernst and Bernhard Sowinski (Cologne: Böhlau, 1990), 1–16.

[27] Lühr, *Studien*, I, 47–54.

[28] Heinrich Van der Kolk, *Das Hildebrandlied. Eine forschungsgeschichtliche Darstellung* (Amsterdam: Scheltma & Holkema, 1967), 4–17.

[29] Steinmeyer, *Die kleineren althochdeutschen Sprachdenkmäler*, 1–8.

[30] Süßmann, *Das Hildebrandlied — gefälscht?*, 28–29.

10: Domstiftsbibliothek Merseburg, Cod. 136, fol. 85ʳ.
The Merseburg Charms.

4: The Merseburg Charms: Contexts and Function

(written in collaboration with Andrea Hodgson)

> "Magic is merely undiscovered science"
> — advertisement for The Macallan whisky

I   Eiris sazun idisi,   sazun hera duoder.
    suma hapt heptidun,   suma heri lezidun.
    suma clubodun   umbi cuoniouuidi:
    insprinc haptbandun,   inuar uigandun .H.

II   P^{h}ol ende uuodan   uuorun zi holza.
    du uuart demo balderes uolon   sin uuoz birenkict.
    thu biguol en sinhtgunt,   sunna era suister;
    thu biguol en friia,   uolla era suister;
    thu biguol en uuodan,   so he uuola conda:
    sose benrenki,   sose bluotrenki,
        sose lidirenki:
    ben zi bena,   bluot zi bluoda,
    lid zi geliden,   sose gelimida sin.

[Once women sat [or: alighted], sat here and there. / Some fettered the prisoner, some hampered the army. / Some picked at fetters: / leap forth from the fetters, escape from the warriors .H. //

P^{h}ol and Wodan went to the wood. / Then Balder's foal sprained its foot. / Then Sinhtgunt charmed it, Sunna her sister; / then Friia charmed it, Volla her sister; / then Wodan charmed it, as he well knew how: / Be it sprain of the bone, be it sprain of the blood, / be it sprain of the limb: / bone to bone, blood to blood, / limb to limbs, be they as stuck together.]

THE STUDY OF EARLY MEDIEVAL TEXTS is bedevilled by a dichotomy largely unknown to the student of modern literature: the gulf between the authorial creation of the text and its earliest extant transmission. In the High Middle Ages, this gulf can be more readily appreciated and taken into account. The surviving manuscripts of, for example, an Arthurian romance, can be related to an archetype which may predate the transmission by as much as a century or more, but the possibility of the reconstruction of the archetype, and of the cultural context of the act of the authorship, remains a viable enterprise. Thus the first German Arthurian romance, Hartmann von Aue's *Erec*, survives in its entirety only in a manuscript of the early sixteenth century, yet it has proved possible to reconstruct the twelfth-century original, and we know of its seminal importance from the evidence of near-contemporary authors such as Gottfried von Straßburg and Wolfram von Eschenbach, not to mention the rest of Hartmann's œuvre. The further back that literature stretches, the more problematic contextualisation becomes. The problems are, however, not evenly spread. Even within the comparatively slender corpus of OHG literature, there are works such as Otfrid's gospel harmony, or the translations of Notker of St Gall, where we can discern a clear relationship between authorial context, function and transmission. With regard to many of the smaller OHG texts, however, the relationship between creation and transmission is obscure. The survival of the vernacular text in its codical context can never be totally fortuitous. On the other hand, there has recently been a temptation to assume too readily that the historical circumstances surrounding the text's transmission may be those that conditioned its authorship. Thus the *Hildebrandslied* has been linked, on the basis of the supposed date of the manuscript, with the politics of Germany in the third decade of the ninth century.[1]

The same open game has been played with regard to the contextualisation of the Merseburg Charms. Susan Fuller decries "the preoccupation of scholars with reconstructing and analysing the 'Urtext' of the Charms," and seeks to find an explanation for why the charms "were committed to writing for a specific purpose ca. 925."[2] This ignores Bischoff's conservative wider dating span of the first two thirds of the tenth century.[3] Fuller wishes to link the writing down of the charms with the wars against the Magyars on the Saxon-Thuringian border, which ceased after 938. The charms reflect "two of the most dominant concerns of the time in Saxony: namely the dread of being captured by the Magyars and the awareness of the urgent need to use horses in warfare" (p. 167). She concludes: "Probably about 924–928, a frightened cleric in Merseburg may have had the Charms dictated to him . . . as defence measures against the Magyar onslaughts." (p. 168).

Such specific contextualisation is more bold than I should wish to attempt. The Second Merseburg Charm is best seen in the context of the other OHG charms intended to heal injuries to horses (Braune § XXXI, 7; 9A; 9B.2), and *bluotrenki* suggests a link with those concerned to stop the excessive flow of blood (Braune § XXXI, 6, 6a, 9B.1). Conceivably the horse-charms were used for injuries to human beings, too; Brian Murdoch cites a warning in Latin attached to a worm-charm which "notes that if it is used on animals the practitioner will lose his skill with men."[4] We need scarcely dwell upon the importance of horses to early medieval society, whether or not the context be one of warfare.

More problematic is the function of the First Merseburg Charm. At first sight it would appear to be a charm for freeing prisoners-of-war, and this function is confirmed by a number of analogues. Among the earliest, adduced by Wallner,[5] is the oft-quoted story of Imma in Bede's *Historia Ecclesiastica*.

During the battle between Ecgfrith and Æthelred in A.D. 679, Imma, a thegn of King Ælfwine, was taken prisoner, but his captors found him impossible to bind, "Nam mox, ut abiere qui uincierant, eadem eius sunt uincula soluta." [For no sooner had those who chained him gone, than his fetters were loosed].[6] Imma's brother, Tunna, a priest, had concluded that Imma was dead. A search for his body led to the finding of a corpse resembling him, which Tunna had buried with due honours. As a result of the many masses which Tunna offered for the absolution of his supposedly dead brother's soul, Imma's fetters were constantly being loosed. Imma's captor is amazed at this and asked "quare ligari non posset, an forte litteras solutorias, de qualibus fabulae ferunt, apud se haberet" [whether he had about him any loosing spells such as are described in stories].

The Anglo-Saxon translation of Bede expands this passage, Imma being asked whether he has knowledge of the loosening runes and had the written sticks with him: "hwæðer he þa alysendlecan rune cuðe and þa stafas mid him awritene hæfde."[7] The story is incorporated into a homily on the efficacy of the mass by Ælfric: "Þa axode se ealdorman þone hæftling, hwæðer he ðurh drycræft oððe ðurh runstafum his bendas tobræce." Page translates: "then the ealdorman asked the captive whether he broke his bonds asunder by means of sorcery or *runstafum*."[8] Bede has the story from some who had it direct from Imma. Clearly, he intends it as a *miraculum* to demonstrate the superiority of the mass over sorcery. His narrative model may have been a story told by Gregory the Great in his Dialogues. Gregory is also dependant on the oral tradition: "Hoc quoque, quod audiuimus, quendam aput hostes in captiuitate positum et in uinculis religatum fuisse, pro quo sua coniux diebus certis sacrificium offerre consueuerat. qui longo post tempore ad coniugem reuersus, quibus diebus eius uincula soluerentur, innotuit, eiusque coniux illos fuisse dies, quibus pro eo offerebat sacrificium, recognouit." [I once heard of a man who had been taken captive and put in chains. His wife had masses offered for him on certain days. When the man returned home after many years he described to his wife the days on which he had been released from chains. She instantly recalled that these were the days on which she had Mass offered for him].[9]

The Anglo-Saxon sources suggest a continuity of fabulae which link the use of loosening spells with runes, and this continuity is further borne out by the later, Icelandic evidence. The *Hávamál* concludes with a collection of magic charms which are attributed by the poet to Odin. A group of these are to aid the speaker in battle and hamper the enemy; here the resemblances to the activities of the *idisi* in the Merseburg charm are unmistakable. Thus the third spell serves to fetter the enemy and blunt the edges of their swords. The fourth reads:

> Þat kann ec it fiórða, ef mér fyrðar bera
>   bǫnd at boglimom:
> svá ec gel,   at ec ganga má,
>   sprettr mér af fótom fiǫturr,
>   enn af hǫndom hapt.

[I know a fourth one if men put / chains upon my limbs; / I can chant so that I can walk away, / fetters spring from my feet, / and bonds from my hands.][10]

In the *Svipdagsmál*, the earliest manuscript of which dates from the second half of the seventeenth century, Svipdag seeks the grave of his mother, Gróa, wakes her from her death-sleep, and has her recite to him some spells which are to aid him in his quest for the hand of the fair Mengloth:

> Þann gel ek þér inn fimta:
> ef þér fjǫturr verðr
> borinn at bóglimum —
> leysigaldr laet ek þér
> fyr legg of kveðinnok støkkr þa láss af limum,
> en af fótum fjǫturr.

[This fifth one I will chant you: / if a chain / is set about your limbs — / I will have a loosing-charm / uttered over your limbs; / and the manacle will then spring from your joints, / and the fetter from your feet.][11]

The parallels in Bede and in the *Hávamál* and *Svipdagsmál* show loosening spells being used to free captives, but need we, with Fuller, assume such a warlike context? It seems more likely, given that the texts are transmitted together with theological material and given the purpose of the second charm, that the first charm was used analogically for a medical function. Elise Riesel attempts to demilitarise the charm.[12] She thinks it probable that sympathetic magic underlies it, and that it could have been applied to some kind of oppressive disease. Riesel considers various possibilities, including that the charm was employed to cure cholic or ease labour pains. Turning to J. G. Frazer's seminal anthropological study, *The Golden Bough*, she finds a parallel in Togoland for the role of a magician in easing childbirth: "When a woman is in hard labour and cannot bring forth, they call in a magician to her aid. He looks at her and says: 'The child is bound in the womb, that is why she cannot be delivered.' . . . For that purpose he orders them to fetch a tough creeper from the forest, and with it he binds the hands and feet of the sufferer on her back. Then he takes a knife and calls out the woman's name, and when she answers he cuts through the creeper with a knife, saying: 'I cut through today thy bonds and thy child's bonds.'"[13]

Both Riesel and Ute Schwab adduce a Latin charm, preserved in a ninth-century manuscript, St. Gall Cod. 751, as an analogue:

> Tres sorores ambulabant;
> una uoluebat.
> alia cernebat,
> tertia soluebat.[14]

[Three sisters were walking; one was thinking. Another was sifting, the third was solving.]

The charm is intended for use against "coli dolor et matricis dolor" [pain in the colon and pain in the womb]. It belongs to an extensive family of charms which involve three virgins or three sisters; the three groups of *idisi* in the First Merseburg Charm clearly belong to this type.[15] More important, however, is the indication of function, taken together with the freeing imagery. Charms for easing childbirth also occur in the Anglo-Saxon leechbooks. A close parallel to the First Merseburg Charm is formed by a charm in the early eleventh-century *Lacnunga*. An Anglo-Saxon rubric: "GIF WIF NE MAEGE BEARN BERAN" [IF A WOMAN IS UNABLE TO BEAR CHILDREN] is followed by a Latin incantation: "Solve iube ter catenis" [Free, order, three times from chains]. Godfrid Storms comments appositely: "Its magical effect is supposedly based on the idea of similarity" — the loosening of chains is likened to the labour process.[16]

Turning to Scandinavia again, we find a link between charms with this labour-easing function, the Valkyries, and runes. In the *Sigrdrífomál* Sigrdrífa, a valkyrie, instructs Sigurd:

> Biargrúnar scaltu kunna,   ef þú biarga vilt
> oc leysa kind frá konom;
> á lófa þær scal rísta   oc of liðo spenna
> oc biðia þá dísir duga.

[Helping-runes you must know if you want to assist / and release children from women; / they shall be cut on the palms and clasped on the joints, / and then the *disir* asked for help.][17]

In the *Fáfnismál* Sigurd asks:

> hveriar ro þær nornir,   er nauðgǫnglar ro
> oc kiósa mœðr frá mǫgom?

[which are those norns who go to those in need / and choose mothers over children in childbirth?][18]

While Valkyries are not normally associated with childbirth, it would appear that a link between a goddess and childbirth is prone to shift from one group of goddesses to another. Riesel argues somewhat over-emphatically against the equation of the *idisi* in the Merseburg charm with the ON *dísir*, first mooted by Jacob Grimm.[19] The interlinking evidence points strongly to an origin for the charm in the Scandinavian belief-system. Perhaps the .H. at the end of the First Merseburg Charm is a "helping-rune" or "birth-rune."[20]

When Grimm published the first analysis of the Merseburg Charms, he felt confident that he could describe them as being "aus der zeit des deutschen

Heidenthums." The manuscript context, however, is indisputably Christian. The manuscript as it is now bound combines leaves of different sizes and different dates.[21] The charms are written on the originally empty fly-leaf of a missal, which comprises the sixth fascicle of Cod. 136 of the Merseburg Dom-stiftsbibliothek (illustration 10). Bischoff finds no resemblance between the hand responsible for them and Fulda hands of the tenth century, such as that of the Fulda sacramentary. He suggests that the hand dates from the first or the second third of the tenth century, but makes no attempt to determine the provenance in view of the lack of comparable material.[22]

Baesecke sought to associate the recording of the charms with the anti-quarian activities of Hrabanus Maurus.[23] Considerable doubt has been cast upon the Renaissance attribution of the recording of a runic alphabet to Hrabanus, and there is no hard evidence of a personal interest on his part in the preservation of pagan Germanic texts.[24] The manner of the charms' preserva-tion, on a fly-leaf, argues against such a motive being behind their recording. Even more speculatively, Leonard Forster saw the Second Merseburg Charm as "ein gelehrt-literarisches Spiel," a learned essay in pseudo-mythology which could only have originated in the hothouse of scholarship that was Fulda.[25]

Steinmeyer suggested a link with Fulda on the basis of the close resem-blance between the prayer which is written below the charms and the text of the tenth-century Sacramentary of Fulda, although he notes that this part of the codex must have emanated in a monastery subordinate to Fulda, rather than in Fulda itself.[26] Andrea Hodgson has examined the tradition informing both the Merseburg prayer and that in the Fulda sacramentary, and her findings are set out below.

The Merseburg text reads:

Omnipotens sempiterne deus quifacis mirabilia magna solus. praetende super famulum tuum .N. et super cunctas congregationes illis commissas spiritum gratie salutaris. et ut in ueritate tibi conplaceant perpetuum eis rorem tue benedictionis infunde .per.

[Almighty and everlasting God, who alone workest great marvels, spread over thy servant N, and over all congregations committed to them the spirit of thy saving grace, and so that they may in truth please thee pour over them the continual dew of thy blessing, through [Jesus Christ our Lord].]

The Fulda text is substantially the same:

MISSA ABBATIS ET CONGREGATIONIS SIBI COMMISSAE.

Omnipotens sempiterne deus, qui facis mirabilia magna solus, pretende super famulum tuum abbatem nostrum et super cunctam congregationem sancti Bonifacii illi commissam spiritum gratiae salutaris, et ut in ueritate tibi complaceant, perpetuum eis rorem tuae benedictionis infunde. P.d.n.[27]

[MASS OF THE ABBOT AND THE CONGREGATION COMMITTED TO HIM.
Almighty and everlasting God, who alone workest great marvels, spread over thy servant our abbot, and over the whole congregation of St Boniface committed to him the spirit of thy saving grace, and so that they may in truth please thee pour over them the continual dew of thy blessing, through (Jesus Christ our Lord).]

Fuller's statement that "This prayer has been abstracted from No. 2148 of the Fulda Sacramentary"[28] is, however, somewhat problematic, in view of the prayer's widespread occurrence in other contexts. In origin, the prayer appears to be from the Gelasian Sacramentary, of Roman provenance and dating from the mid-seventh century. It appears twice in Vatican Reginensis 316, a mid-eighth century manuscript from Chelles, which is the nearest text we have to the original Gelasian. That it was intended for use as a monastic mass prayer is indicated by the rubric accompanying its first occurrence: "Missa in monasterio." The second version falls under the heading "Item orationes ad missas," and has a further rubric indicating the prayer's function:

ITEM ORATIONES AD MISSAS
POST COMMUNIONEM Omnipotens sempiterne deus, qui facis mirabilia magna solus, praetende super hos famulos degentes in hac domo spiritum gratiae salutaris, et ut conplaceant tibi, deus, in veritate tua, perpetuum eis rorem tuae benedictionis effunde; per.[29]

The addition of *in hac domo* suggests monastic use, *domus* probably referring to a small monastery, or a community of canons or canonesses.

The prayer then recurs in the group of texts known as the "eighth-century Gelasians." It is to be found twice in both the Sacramentary of Gellone and the Phillips Sacramentary. The titles "Orationes ad missa in domum" and "Missa in monasterio" in the Sacramentary of Gellone again point to a monastic function.

Though still in use in the ninth century, the "eighth-century Gelasians" probably ceased to be copied after 800. Charlemagne ordered that the Gregorian Sacramentary which he had requested and received from Pope Hadrian, Paul the Deacon acting as his intermediary, was to be used instead.[30] Early in the ninth century Benedict of Aniane added a supplement to this text, known as the Hadrianum, to make it more suitable for Frankish use. This supplement was based primarily on the "eighth-century Gelasians" and again contains our prayer, in a form closer to the tenth-century versions in the Fulda Sacramentary and on the Merseburg leaf:

MISSA PRO ABBATE VEL CONGREGATIONE
Omnipotens sempiterne deus, qui facis mirabilia magna solus, praetende super famulum tuum *ill.* abbatem, vel super cunctam congregationem ilii

commissam spiritum gratiae salutaris, et ut in veritate tibi complaceant, perpetuum (eis) rorem tuae benedictionis infunde. Per.[31]

The inclusion of the words *abbatem* and *congregationem* is anticipated in an eighth-century Gelasian text, the Sacramentary of Angoulême.[32] In the Leofric Missal, a composite manuscript in use at Exeter in the eleventh century, but which is thought to be of early tenth-century origin, the wording is again virtually identical with the Merseburg text.[33]

The Romano-Germanic Pontifical of the mid-tenth century marks an apex in the development of the liturgy. Its text is thought to have originated in Mainz and has been dated to 950–963/964. The prayer here has the title "Orationes et preces pro monachis ad missam," although there is no reference to a *congregatio* or *domus*.[34]

The Fulda text differs from all the others in its specific reference to the founder, St. Boniface. The Merseburg prayer differs from the Fulda version in that a name, .N., is to be substituted for the words *abbbatem nostrum*, and in the fact that it refers to *congregationes* in the plural. This would seem to point away from Fulda. Might the several congregations, taken together with the absence of the abbot, suggest that the Merseburg version of the prayer is referring to a bishop and his lay congregations? *Congregatio* is, to judge from the dictionaries, unlikely to refer to anything other than a monastic community.[35] The rubrics point solidly in the direction of a monastic mass prayer. Carolingian conciliar material uses the term *congregatio* to mean the monastery itself, or the monastic community. Thus the Council of Chalons of 813 reads: "Abbatissa diligenter habeat curam de congregatione sibi commissa et provideat. . . ."[36] The word *congregatio* does not appear to include the laity until the eleventh century.[37] The plural use in the Merseburg text might be thought to argue against a monastic context, but it was not unknown for persons to have the care of more than one monastic community. The picture is complicated by the fact that abbots could simultaneously be bishops; Baturich of Regensburg was both abbot of St. Emmeram and Bishop of Regensburg, while Bishop Haito of Basle was also abbot of Reichenau.

To conclude, it is not beyond the realms of possibility that the Fulda prayer was the immediate source of the Merseburg prayer, but this is only one possibility of many. The divergences imply that it was intended for use in a different monastery or monasteries.

The Fulda monks owned property in the Merseburg area in the tenth century, but the Merseburg tithes were paid to Hersfeld.[38] Perhaps the strongest argument for the Fulda link has been the supposition that there was no monastery in Merseburg until the eleventh century.[39] This supposition rests upon the founding of the monastery of St. Peter by Bishop Werner of Merseburg (1059–93); it is at best an over-simplification. On 12 February 962, Pope John XII sent a bull to Germany: "iubemus, ut Merseburgense monasterium, quod ipse piissimus imperator, qua Ungros prostravit, futurum

Deo devovit, in episcopalem debeatur sedem." [we order that the monastery of Merseburg, because the most pious emperor, in laying low the Huns, vowed to God that it would be so, should be destined for an episcopal see]. The Latin is somewhat obscure, but it is clear that the episcopal see at Merseburg, founded in 968 by the Emperor Otto, was thus based upon a monastery already in existence.[40] The capacity to write and the need for such a liturgical compilation as we find in the Merseburg Charms manuscript was certainly present in the first half of the tenth century in Merseburg.

An attempt to date and locate the charms on a linguistic basis is bedevilled by the lack of comparable sources. The tenth century is poor in vernacular texts, compared with the riches of the ninth and eleventh centuries. Bostock describes the phonology as "Middle German."[41] There are however traits which point to Old Saxon. The pronoun *he* (II, 5) is an essentially Northern form; the enclitic *-en* (II, 3–5) has no obvious parallel. The dative ending *-on* in *folon* is found more readily in Old Saxon, where *-on*, *-an* and *-un* occur seemingly at random in the declension of weak nouns. Where the High German dialects are concerned, one would expect *-en* or *-in*; *-un* and *-on* (*-an*) are late forms, associated in particular with Bavarian.[42] Initial *d-* (II, 1) conflicts with *th-* in subsequent lines; medially this fluctuation may also be present if we accept the emendation *Sinthgunt*. The change from *th* to *d* takes place from south to north in the course of the OHG period, reaching Old Saxon last. In Thuringian and in North Franconian *th* is still dominant in the tenth century.[43] Our text may reflect a synchronous state of flux, or the copying of an older exemplar, perhaps by a scribe from further north, or indeed south. Baesecke characteristically regarded the two charms as being of distinct dialectal origin. He sought, rather unconvincingly, to link the language in which they were copied with Fulda, on the basis of similarities with one of the scribes responsible for the OHG Tatian translation, scribe γ.[44] This is problematic because, first, we are not certain that the 'Tatian' stems from Fulda, and, secondly, because many traits in γ diverge from the language of the charms (*ch* for *k*; occasional *p* for *b*). Moreover, γ is now generally held to be of Alemannic origin.[45] Comparisons with modern dialects, such as Thuringian, are obviously methodologically problematic. On the whole, the language is not incompatible with what one would expect of a text written in the southern part of Saxony in the tenth century. Merseburg in the tenth century was in the south-eastern corner of the duchy of Saxony, on the border of East Frankish territory to the south, and Bavarian territory to the south-east.[46]

Literary history can help us but little when it comes to dating and provenance. It seems unlikely that a text possessing such a heavy reliance on alliteration could have been composed after the mid-ninth century. Both charms, however, combine alliteration with end-rhyme, or at least assonance: "insprinc haptbandun, inuar uigandun"; "sose benrenki, sose bluotrenki, sose lidirenki." This helps to create a climactic effect, as at the end of the Wessobrunn Prayer. If we seek an *ante quem non*, then we flounder. Genzmer holds that the charms must have originated in a time of pure alliterative technique, and suggests a date of composition between 200 B.C. and 500 A.D.[47] Neckel suggests a date of *c.* 700, when the north of Germany was still pagan; he posits songs concerning Baldr which predated the second charm by a century.[48]

Three distinct structural elements in the charms have given rise to a search for parallels, if not sources. A wide range of parallels for the triple "suma" formula in lines 2–3 of the first charm has been adduced. Here it may be no coincidence that the closest resemblances would appear to be in the Poetic Edda. Baesecke points to the fourth strophe of the *Brot af Sigurðarqviðo* ("Fragment of a Poem about Sigurd"):

> Sumir úlf sviðo,   sumir orm sniðo,
> sumir Gothormi   af gera deildo

[Some roasted wolf, some sliced up serpent, some gave Guthorm wolf-meat].[49]

Stanley compares the quadruple formula in strophe 69 of the *Hávamál*:

> sumr er af sonom sæll,
> sumr af frœndom,   sumr af fé œrno,
> sumr af vercom vel.

[one man is blessed with sons, another with kinsmen, another has enough money, another has done great deeds.][50]

Stanley notes similar formulae in Anglo-Saxon poetry and in the Old Saxon *Heliand*.[51] Such formulae are not, however, confined to alliterative poetry. The sinners in the Frankish kingdom of the ninth-century *Ludwigslied* (ll. 17–18) form another trio:

> Sum uuas lugināri,   Sum skāchāri,
> Sum fol lōses

[Some were liars, some robbers, some full of loose living].

It must be doubted whether such anaphoric groupings originated in a single source.

As for the epic introduction to the second charm, the Merseburg version would appear to be the oldest form of the story, and the only evidently pagan version, but here too the analogues persist into the twentieth century and encompass a huge linguistic range. Christiansen's monograph of 1914 has been supplemented by countless subsequent articles.[52]

Thirdly, the parallel between the conjuring formula at the end of the Second Merseburg Charm and that in the Indian *Atharva veda* was first pointed out by Kuhn in 1864, who argued that the charm was of Indo-European origin.[53] The resemblances are striking, but the possibility of polygenesis cannot be excluded. Some variants of the charm combine both the narrative introduction and the conjuring formula. Several have been collected in Scotland, including a version dating from 1643:

> Our Lord to hunting red,
> His *fooll foot* sled;
> Doun he lighted,
> His *fool fot* righted;
> Blod to blod
> Shenew to shenew.[54]

All in all, we are faced with an *embarras de richesse* of analogues, which demonstrate little other than the ease with which they may be adduced. As Stanley concludes: "The fact that very late examples are to be found in England and Scotland demonstrates that such popular material can be produced at any time (until there is a break with the underlying, widely held superstition)."[55]

Little note has been taken among Germanists of the work of Karl Hauck. Hauck attempts to relate the Merseburg charms to gold bracteates, arguing that the latter constitute iconographic parallels to the Second Merseburg Charm dating from the time of the Germanic migrations. The bracteates depict a figure resembling a human being, or perhaps a god, aiding a fallen quadruped. Clusters of these bracteates have been found both in Saxony and Denmark, as well as in Holland, Jutland and Norway. Hauck argues plausibly that the resemblances between the bracteates and the charm constitute evidence of a continuity of Germanic beliefs.[56] In the absence of any identifying inscription, the relationship between the bracteates and the charm is likely to remain speculative, but the bracteates may well be the earliest evidence found on German soil of the thought-world in which the charm originated.

If we are to date the charms prior to the point in the tenth century when they were written down, then it is necessary to ask when the invocation of Norse gods would have become meaningless. Steinhoff would have it that the creation of our text predates the coming of Christianity: "Die Christianisierung Frankens seit Bonifatius liefert einen ungefähren Terminus ante quem."[57] Yet in Saxony a continuity of evidence for pagan beliefs long after the subjugation by Charlemagne is suggested by later sources such as Adam of Bremen and Thietmar of Merseburg (both adduced by Fuller). Thietmar alludes to pagan practices in his Chronicle, in a passage dating from 1017:

Nam habitatores illi raro ad æcclesiam venientes de visitatione custodum nil curant; domesticos colunt deos multumque sibi prodesse eosdem sperantes hiis immolant. Audivi de quodam baculo, in cuius sumitate manus erat unum in se ferreum tenens circulum, quod pastore illius villæ, in quo is fuerat, per omnes domos has singulariter ductus, in primo introitu a portitore suo sic salutaretur: "Vigila, Hennil, vigila!" — sic enim rustica vocabatur lingua —; et epulantes ibi delicate de eiusdem se tueri custodia stulti autumabant. . . .

[For the people living there rarely go to church and care nothing for the visits of their spiritual guardians; they worship household gods and, expecting these same to benefit them greatly, they offer sacrifices to them. I have heard of a staff, at the end of which a hand was fixed holding an iron ring; it was carried by the shepherd of the village from house to house, and its bearer on entering addressed it in the following way: Vigila, Hennil, vigila! — for so it was called in the rustic language. Then the fools feasted indulgently, thinking themselves safe in his protection. . .][58]

Adam of Bremen, who is fully conversant with the names Wodan and Thor, describes the difficulties faced by Bishop Unwan in Hamburg in 1013 because of the dominance of superstition and pagan beliefs.[59] The Christianisation of Saxony was evidently a slow process, and as with the conversion of Scandinavia, "did not proceed at a uniform pace in all levels of society."[60]

The transmission of the charms in Saxony does not necessarily mean, of course, that they are of Saxon origin. In the light of the many links of the charms with the beliefs of the Scandinavian North, the contiguity of Danes and Saxons may be of significance. Denmark lay on the northern border of the duchy of Saxony; it did not, however, become officially Christian until c. 965.[61] The reign of Louis the Pious saw a Danish fief on his borders, in Frisia, though we are uncertain of its territorial extent. Danish rulers such as Harald and Roric embraced Christianity, however superficially.[62] A lesser convert might have become a monk in Saxony, and might have thought it useful to translate a medical charm into his adopted tongue. This is just one of many possibilities of cultural contact which might explain the presence of the Norse gods in the charm. The continuing usefulness of such names in Christian magico-medical practice is attested by the presence of Odin in the Nine Twigs Charm (Dobbie 2) in the early eleventh-century Anglo-Saxon *Lacnunga*.

Two contrasting views exist concerning the reasons underlying the transmission of the charms. The older view of Baesecke, revived by Stuart and Walla, regards the survival of the Merseburg Charms as a more or less freak product of antiquarian interest.[63] Against this, as Brian Murdoch has argued,[64] there are pointers to the essentially functional nature of the surviving charms. The rubrics in the *Lacnunga* make it clear that it is, as its editors entitle it, a "magico-medical commonplace book," probably for use by a monastery leech.[65] The multi-purpose, "encyclopædic formulæ,"[66] which make the charms applicable to as many ills ("sose benrenki . . .") — or colours of horses — or locations — as possible, argue strongly against the antiquarian view, and suggest that it is anachronistic. The codical context of the charms is significant here: whether they occur with other medical texts or as fillers in blank spaces, the Old High German charms tend to be in a different hand from the texts for which the manuscripts were designed. Perhaps we can detect here the hand of the monastery's leech, wishing to pass on his precious knowledge, perhaps fearful that the magic words might fade from memory.

This has implications for the way in which we view the charms in their relation to orthodox religion. It is unlikely that they owe their survival to any systematic distinction between black and white magic. The verdict of the Carolingian Church councils and the penitentials is unanimous. Augustine's distinction between black and white magic was not incorporated into Church law, which states clearly that magical practices, whether they have good or evil intent, are to be eradicated.[67] It might be argued that the condemnations of the Church are derivative and therefore divorced from the reality of contemporary beliefs, but it is clear from the occasional coincidence between the content of the charms and the wording of the condemnations that the Church is conversant with the practices of the people it wishes to reach. To dismiss the charms as "popular religion," and to adduce this as the reason for their tolerance by the Church, is essentially anachronistic. The Church of the ninth and tenth centuries, particularly in newly or partially converted areas such as Saxony, could not afford such a degree of tolerance. The analogy with "Talk of the devil," "Touch wood," with the survival of popular superstition in our own superficially Christian society, is invalid, for, as Valerie Flint writes, "To suggest that we are concerned here mainly, or even partly, with 'pagan survivals' is to put the matter altogether too feebly."[68] The eighth-century *Homilia de sacrilegiis* would have no doubt: whoever indulges in such practices, "non Christianus sed paganus est."[69] The only possible motive for preserving the charms, in the face of the official hostility of the Church, was that they were held to work. It is likely that the hand that wrote them down sometimes did so in fear and trembling.

Notes

[1] Horst Dieter Schlosser, "Die Aufzeichung des *Hildebrandslieds* im historischen Kontext," *GRM* 28 (1978): 217–24.

[2] Susan D. Fuller, "Pagan Charms in Tenth-Century Saxony? The Function of the Merseburg Charms," *Monatshefte* 72 (1980): 162–70 (163).

[3] Bischoff, "Paläographische Fragen," 111.

[4] Brian O. Murdoch, *Old High German Literature*, Twayne's World Authors Series, 688 (Boston: Twayne Publishers, 1983), 50.

[5] Anton Wallner, "Eiris sazun idisi," *ZfdA* 50 (1908): 214–18 (218).

[6] *Bede's Ecclesiastical History of the English people*, ed. and trans. Bertram Colgrave and R. A. B. Mynors, Oxford Medieval Texts (Oxford: Clarendon Press, 1969), 400–05.

[7] Quoted by Ralph W. V. Elliott, *Runes. An Introduction* (Manchester: Manchester UP, 1959; repr. 1980), 67.

[8] R. I. Page, "Anglo-Saxon Runes and Magic," *Journal of the British Archaeological Association*, 3rd. Series, 27 (1964–65): 14–31 (22).

[9] *Gregorii Magni Dialogi*, ed. Umberto Moricca, Fonti per la storia d'Italia, Scrittori Secolo, VI, (Rome: Tipografia del Senato, 1924), IV, 59 (320). The translation is that of Odo John Zimmermann, *Saint Gregory the Great, Dialogues*, The Fathers of the Church, 39 (New York: Fathers of the Church, Inc., 1959), vol. 39, 270. I am indebted to Alan Thacker (Victoria County History) for suggesting the parallel. Perhaps derivative of Bede is a posthumous *miraculum* in the eleventh-century Life of St. Cadoc: "After a very long interval of time, three foreigners bound with iron rings, came from the East to the monastery of the aforesaid Saint, on the day of his solemnity. And while they celebrated mass, those iron bonds, all the people beholding them, broke. Wherefore that this miracle might be known to all, they hung those rings on the altar." (*Lives of the Cambro British Saints, of the fifth and immediately succeeding centuries: from ancient Welsh and Latin MSS. in the British Museum and elsewhere*, ed. Rev. William J. Rees (Llandovery: William Rees, 1853), 373–74 (§ 39). The parallel is adduced in *A History of the English Church and People*, trans. Leo Sherley-Price (Harmondsworth: Penguin, 1955), 339.

[10] *Hávamál*, str. 149. *Edda. Die Lieder des Codex Regius nebst verwandten Denkmälern*, ed. Gustav Neckel, 4th ed., rev. Hans Kuhn (Heidelberg: Carl Winter, 1962), 42; *The Poetic Edda*, trans. Carolyne Larrington (Oxford: Oxford UP, 1996), 35.

[11] *Svipdagsmál*, str. 10. The text and translation are those of P. M. W. Robinson, "An edition of Svipdagsmál" (D. Phil. diss., University of Oxford, 1991), 64. Robinson dates the poem to *c.* 1200–50. He divides the *Svipdagsmál* into two poems: *Gróagaldr*, in which the hero calls up his dead mother for help before undertaking the quest, and *Fjölsvinnsmál*, in which he goes to visit Menglöð.

[12] Elise Riesel, "Der erste Merseburger Zauberspruch," *Deutsches Jahrbuch für Volkskunde* 4 (1958): 53–81.

[13] Riesel, 68–69; James George Frazer, *The Golden Bough: a study in magic and religion*, 3rd. rev. ed, 12 vols (London: Macmillan, 1907–15), vol. 2, 295.

[14] Richard Heim, *Incantamenta magica graeca latina*, Jbb. für Phil. und Päd., Suppl. NF 19 (Leipzig: B. G. Teubner, 1893), 463–576 (559); Riesel, 67; Ute Schwab, "Sizilianische Schnitzel. Marcellus in Fulda und einiges zur Anwendung volks-sprachiger magischer Rezepte," in *Deutsche Literatur und Sprache von 1050–1200. Festschrift für Ursula Hennig zum 65. Geburtstag*, ed. Annegret Fiebig and Hans-Jochen Schiewer (Berlin: Akademie Verlag, 1995), 261–96 (278). I am grateful to Hajo Schiewer for drawing my attention to this article.

[15] See Schwab, 275–80.

[16] Godfrid Storms, *Anglo-Saxon Magic* (The Hague: Nijhoff, 1948), § 63; cf. also § 45.

[17] *Sigrdrífomál*, str. 9, in *Edda*, ed. Neckel/Kuhn, 191; Larrington, 168, and note, 285.

[18] *Fáfnismál*, str. 12, ed. Neckel/Kuhn, 182; Larrington, 159.

[19] Jacob Grimm, "Ueber zwei entdeckte gedichte aus der zeit des deutschen Heidenthums," *Abhandlungen der Berliner Akademie der Wissenschaften,*

philologische und historische Abtheilung, 1842, 1–26 (4–5) (= *Kleinere Schriften*, ed. Karl Müllenhoff, vol. 2 (Berlin: Dümmler, 1865), 1–29.

[20] See chapter 5 below.

[21] The most detailed description is by Steinmeyer, *Die kleineren althochdeutschen Sprachdenkmäler*, 23–26.

[22] Bischoff, "Paläographische Fragen," 104–05; 111.

[23] Georg Baesecke, "Die Karlische Renaissance und das deutsche Schrifttum," *DVJS* 23 (1949): 143–216 (190–206).

[24] See René Derolez, *Runica manuscripta*, Werken uitgegeven door de Faculteit van de Letteren en Wijsbegeerte, Rijksuniversiteit de Gent, 118ᵉ Aflevering (Bruges: De Tempel, 1954), 83; 354.

[25] Leonard Forster, "Zum zweiten Merseburger Zauberspruch," *Archiv für das Studium der neueren Sprachen* 192 (1955–56): 155–59.

[26] Steinmeyer, 25.

[27] *Sacramentarium Fuldense saeculi X: Cod. Theol 321 der K. Universitätsbibliothek zu Göttingen*, Quellen und Abhandlungen zur Geschichte der Abtei und der Diözese Fulda, 9, ed. Gregor Richter and Albert Schönfelder (Fulda, 1912; repr. Farnborough: Saint Michael's Abbey Press, 1983), § 2148 (245).

[28] Fuller (as note 2), 168.

[29] *Liber Sacramentorum Romanae Aeclesiae ordinis anni circuli. (Cod. Vat. Reg. Lat. 316 / Paris Bibl. Nat. 7193, 41/56) (SACRAMENTARIUM GELASIANUM)*, ed. Leo Cunibert Mohlberg, Rerum ecclesiasticarum documenta. Series minor: Subsidia studiorum, 5 (Rome: Herder, 1960), § 1429 (207).

[30] See Giles Brown, "Introduction: The Carolingian Renaissance," in McKitterick, *Carolingian Culture*, 1–51 (22).

[31] *Le Sacramentaire Grégorien: ses principales formes d'après les plus anciens mansucrits*, ed. Jean Deshusses, Spicilegium Friburgense vols 16, 24, 28 (Fribourg: Éditions Universitaires, 1971–82), vol. 16, § 1308 (435).

[32] *Le sacramentaire gélasien d'Angoulême*, ed. Paul Cagin (Angoulême: Société Historique et Archéologique de la Charente, 1919), § 2204 (161).

[33] *The Leofric Missal: as used in the Cathedral of Exeter during the episcopate of its first bishop, A.D. 1050–1072, together with some account of the Red Book of Derby, the Missal of Robert of Jumièges, and a few other early manuscript service books of the English Church*, ed. Frederick Edward Warren (Oxford: Clarendon Press, 1883), 182.

[34] Michel Andrieu, *Les Ordines Romani du haut moyen âge*, 5 vols (Louvain: Spicilegium Sacrum Lovaniense, 1931–61) vol. 1, 504–05; Cyrille Vogel and Reinhard Elze, *Le Pontifical Romano-Germanique du dixième siècle*, Studi e Testi, 226, 2 vols (Vatican: Biblioteca Apostolica Vaticana, 1963), vol. 1, XVI–XVII and 75–76.

[35] Jan Frederik Niermeyer, *Mediae Latinitatis Lexicon minus*, 246; Du Cange, *Glossarium Mediae et Infimae Latinitatis* (Paris: Instituti Regii Franciae Typographi, 1883–87), vol. 2, 504.

[36] MGH, Legum, Sectio II, Conc. II.ii, 284, ch. LIIII.

[37] Niermeyer, *loc. cit.*

[38] Walter Schlesinger, *Kirchengeschichte Sachsens im Mittelalter*, 2 vols (Cologne and Graz: Böhlau, 1962), 1, 33–34.

[39] Fuller, 168.

[40] Schlesinger, 1, 295. Schlesinger suggests *evehatur* for *debeatur*. See the *Urkundenbuch des Hochstifts Merseburg*, ed. Paul Fridolin Kehr, Geschichtsquellen der Provinz Sachsens, vol. 36 (Halle: Hendel, 1899), § 1 (2). Schlesinger suggests "daß die Pfarrgeistlichkeit schon frühzeitig zu kanonischem Leben zusammengeschlossen war." (34).

[41] *Handbook*, 26.

[42] Ludwig Rösel, *Die Gliederung der germanischen Sprachen nach dem Zeugnis ihrer Flexionsformen*, Erlanger Beiträge zur Sprach- und Kunstwissenschaft, 11 (Nuremberg: H. Carl, 1962), 85–86; Wilhelm Braune, *Althochdeutsche Grammatik*, 14th ed., rev. Hans Eggers (Tübingen: Niermeyer, 1987), § 283; § 221, note 3.

[43] Braune, *Althochdeutsche Grammatik*, § 167.

[44] Baesecke, "Die Karlische Renaissance," 190–91. See also the more cautious analysis of Ferdinand Wrede, "Zu den Merseburger Zaubersprüchen," *Sitzungsberichte der Preussischen Akademie der Wissenschaften* (Berlin, 1923), 85–90.

[45] See *Handbook*, 161–62.

[46] See the maps at the back of *Widukind von Corvey: Res gestae Saxonicae. Die Sachsengeschichte*, ed. and trans. Ekkehart Rotter and Bernd Schneidmüller (Stuttgart: Reclam, 1981).

[47] Felix Genzmer, "Da signed Krist — thû biguol'en Wuodan," *Arv* 5 (1949): 37–68 (62).

[48] Gustav Neckel, *Die Überlieferungen vom Gotte Balder* (Dortmund: F. W. Ruhfus, 1920), 245.

[49] Baesecke, "Die Karlische Renaissance," 192; *Edda*, ed. Neckel/Kuhn, 198; Larrington, *Poetic Edda*, 174.

[50] Eric G. Stanley, "Alliterative Ornament and Alliterative Rhythmical Discourse in Old High German and Old Frisian Compared with Similar Manifestations in Old English," *PBB* 106 (1984): 184–217 (201); *Edda*, ed. Neckel/Kuhn, 27; Larrington, 23.

[51] Stanley, 199–201.

[52] See Reidar Th. Christiansen, *Die finnischen und nordischen Varianten des zweiten Merseburgerspruches*, Folklore Fellows Communications, 18 (Hamina: Suomalaisen tiedeakatemian kustantama, 1914); Stanley, 202–03.

[53] A. Kuhn, "Indische und germanische segenssprüche," *Zeitschrift für vergleichende Sprachforschung* 13 (1864): 49–74 and 113–57 (51–63; 151–55).

[54] Stanley, 202, quoting J.G. Dalyell, *The Darker Superstitions of Scotland* (Edinburgh: Waugh & Innes, 1834), 27. Another version was collected on the Hebridean island of South Uist at the turn of the century: "First, the Lord's Prayer at the beginning and at the close of the charm: — 'Christ went out at early morn. / He saw horse's bones broken and scattered; / He put bone to bone, and marrow to marrow; / He put sinew to sinew, and flesh to flesh, and blood to blood, / And as He

repaired that, may you mend this!'" — Malcolm MacPhail, "Folklore from the Hebrides. IV," *Folk-Lore* 11 (1900): 439–50 (449). For further versions see Rolf Ködderitsch, "Der 2. Merseburger Zauberspruch und seine Parallelen," *Zeitschrift für Celtische Philologie* 33 (1974): 45–57.

[55] Stanley, *loc. cit.*

[56] Karl Hauck, *Goldbrakteaten aus Sievern. Spätantike Amulett-Bilder der 'Dania Saxonica' und die Sachsen—'Origo' bei Widukind*, Münstersche Mittelalter-Schriften, 1 (Munich: W. Fink, 1970); idem, "Völkerwanderungszeitliche Bilddarstellungen des zweiten Merseburger Spruchs als Zugang zu Heiligtum und Opfer," in *Vorgeschichtliche Heiligtümer und Opferplätze in Mittel- und Nordeuropa*, Abhandlungen der Akademie der Wissenschaften in Göttingen, Philologisch-Historische Klasse III.74 (Göttingen, 1970), 297–319.

[57] Hans-Hugo Steinhoff, "Merseburger Zaubersprüche," *Verfasserlexikon*, vol. 6 (1987), col. 416.

[58] Fuller, 165–66; *Die Chronik des Bischofs Thietmar von Merseburg*, MGH SS. rer.germ. IX, ed. Robert Holtzmann, 2nd ed. (Berlin: Weidmannsche Buchhandlung, 1965), 482–83. Siebs interpreted Hennil as Wodan in his capacity as god of light, but his argument is unconvincing. See Theodor Siebs, "Beiträge zur deutschen mythologie. I. Der todesgott ahd. Henno Wôtan = Mercurius," *ZfdPh* 24 (1892): 146–57 (148).

[59] Adam von Bremen, *Bischofsgeschichte der Hamburger Kirche*, in *Quellen des 9. und 11. Jahrhunderts zur Geschichte der Hamburgischen Kirche und des Reiches*, ed. Rudolf Buchner et al., 5th ed. (Darmstadt: Wissenschaftliche Buchgesellschaft, 1978), 284.

[60] *The Christianization of Scandinavia. Report of a Symposium held at Kungälv, Sweden, 4–9 August 1985*, ed. Birgit Sawyer, Peter Sawyer and Ian Wood (Alingsås: Viktoria Bokförlag, 1987), 11.

[61] *The Christianization of Scandinavia*, 22.

[62] Walther Vogel, *Die Normannen und das fränkische Reich bis zur Gründung der Normandie, 779–911*, Heidelberger Abhandlungen zur mittleren und neueren Geschichte, H. 14 (Heidelberg: C. Winter, 1906), 45; 59–60; 194.

[63] Baesecke (as note 23); Heather Stuart and F. Walla, "Die Überlieferung der mittelalterlichen Segen," *ZfdA* 116 (1987): 53–79.

[64] Brian Murdoch, "Peri Hieres Nousou: Approaches to the Old High German Medical Charms," in *"mit regulu bithuungan." Neue Arbeiten zur althochdeutschen Poesie und Sprache*, GAG, 500, ed. John L. Flood and David N. Yeandle (Göppingen: Kümmerle, 1989), 142–59.

[65] *Lacnunga: an Anglo-Saxon magico-medical commonplace book*, ed. John Henry Grafton Grattan and Charles Singer, Publications of the Wellcome Historical Medical Museum, NS 3 (London: Geoffrey Cumberlege, 1952).

[66] The term derives from Heather Stuart, "A Critical Edition of some Anglo-Saxon Charms and Incantations" (Diss. Flinders University of South Australia, 1973), 223.

[67] For fuller discussion of this problem, see A. A. Barb, "The Survival of the Magic

Arts," in *The Conflict between Paganism and Christianity in the Fourth Century*, ed. Arnaldo Momigliano (Oxford: Clarendon Press, 1963), 100–25; Valerie I. J. Flint, *The Rise of Magic in Early Medieval Europe* (Oxford: Clarendon Press, 1993), passim.

[68] Flint, 69.

[69] *Eine Augustin fälschlich beigelegte Homilia de Sacrilegiis. Aus einer Einsiedeler Handschrift des achten Jahrhunderts herausgegeben und mit kritischen und sachlichen Anmerkungen, sowie mit einer Abhandlung begleitet*, ed. Carl Paul Caspari (Christiania: Jacob Dybwad, 1886), 11.

5: The Merseburg Charms: Conjectures

Odin, however, had no such difficulty in knowing what was going on. The accounts had "Thor" written all over them in letters much too big for anyone other than another god to see.
— Douglas Adams, *The Long Dark Tea-Time of the Soul*

CONJECTURE HAS BECOME something of a dying art in the study of Old High German. This is not intrinsically a retrograde step, for its excessive application bedevilled much early scholarship. Scholars now possess, perhaps, a greater awareness of their uncertainties concerning OHG lexis and morphology, and have become more restrained, daunted by a slender corpus as well as by the dialectally and generically isolated nature of many of the texts. The Second Merseburg Charm, however, is not only open to conjecture, but positively invites it, as its most problematic word, the first word P^hol, is written in a way which suggests uncertainty on the part of the scribe vis-à-vis his exemplar. As a journey to Merseburg confirmed, the superscript h is written in the same hand as the rest of the text of the charms, suggesting an afterthought on the part of the same scribe.[1] The obvious inference is that what the scribe found before him was in some way problematic; conceivably, the first letter of his exemplar was no ordinary *P*.

Theories concerning P^hol are legion.[2] Jacob Grimm, to whom the charms were passed on their discovery in 1841, argued for a Germanic god with the name Pol, substantiating his theory with reference to English and German place-names.[3] The etymology of these is highly problematic, given the neighbouring Germanic roots **pola*, NHG "Pfuhl," English "pool," and **pakslo*, NHG "Pfahl," English "pole" and "pale." To Grimm we also owe the thesis that Pol and Balder are the same god, "nach den Regeln einer guten Erzählung"; as the first line mentions only two travellers, P^hol and Uuodan, one would not expect a third major character to be introduced in the second line. Against this, it may be pointed out that the presence of two — or perhaps four — goddesses, also presumably participants in the journey, is not mentioned until lines 3–4. Grimm held that Balder and Phol might be dual names of the same god, suggesting as a parallel Phoebus and Apollo. This led to the theory that P^hol might be a corruption of Apollo, who might, on the basis of the *interpretatio romana*, have been equated with Balder. In successive editions of Grimm's *Deutsche Mythologie*, the god Pol or Phol became the basis for a whole host of etymologies, but, as Bostock pragmatically observed, "no god or goddess *Pol*, or *Phol* or *Vol* is known."[4]

The form *Pol* occurs in an Anglo-Saxon charm in a manuscript now in Corpus Christi College, Cambridge, the purpose of which is the retrieval of lost property, such as a stolen horse. Here the word is clearly a contraction of Paulus, the incantation invoking the saints: "Petur, Pol, Patric, Pilip, Marie, Bricȝit, Felic."[5] The charm has no other point of resemblance to the Second Merseburg Charm. Arguing from the preponderance of (later) Christian charms that the Merseburg charms must also be Christian in origin, Christiansen, following Bugge, held that Pol is a corruption of Paulus, who occasionally, but not often, occurs in later Scandinavian variants of the charm.[6] Pol also occurs in a dozen North German charms collected in the nineteenth century, the purpose of which is to cure boils, warts ("Adel"), stitches and other minor ailments. These charms were analysed by Adolf Spamer, who distinguishes in these quatrains between Pol as a person:

> De Adel un de Pol
> dei güngen beid to Schol
> de Pol gewünn,
> de Adel verswünn

and as a place:

> Der Adel und die Mond,
> Die gingen beide ze Pohl;
> Der Adel, der vergeht,
> Die Mond, die besteht.

Pol is interpreted by Spamer as denoting a pool of manure, renowned for its therapeutic qualities. Neither form nor content of these rhymes suggests any link with the Merseburg text other than the phonological similarity of the proper names, and Spamer has to admit that he can find no evidence for manure being applied to broken or sprained limbs, which the Merseburg charm clearly aims to cure.[7]

Siegfried Gutenbrunner has had two bites at the cherry, combining etymological with mythological and anthropological approaches. In 1943 he argued that the P^h was manifestly corrupt. The exemplar might have had w, so that *Phol* was originally OHG *wuol*, OS *wôl* ("ruin, defeat, plague,") or *Hol*, OHG *hôl*, *hôla*, "rupture." In 1965, Gutenbrunner chose to accept **Vol* or *Pol*, and argued for a derivation from Indo-Germanic **pē(l)-*, meaning a milk-pail, referring to the custom of snakes being given a bowl of milk, when they were recognised as household spirits.[8]

For Grimm the superscript *h* could be satisfactorily explained as a consequence of the second sound shift, inserted by the scribe in accordance with his dialect — an assertion which disregarded the problem of the text's linguistic provenance.[9] Later scholars took the superscript *h* to be integral to the text's exemplar, the common explanation being that it is essential for this line, like all the other lines of the narrative, as opposed to the conjuring part of the text, to alliterate in accordance with the conventions reconstructed for OHG alliterative verse: *Phol* : *vuorun*. Here, too, there must be some uncertainty. While we know from the charm itself that *Volla* can alliterate with *Friia*, there is no evidence in the admittedly small corpus of OHG alliterative verse for *f* or *v* alliterating with *ph*. If, however, one assumes that P^h is an alternative spelling of *f*, then a new range of interpretations becomes feasible. Dennis Green, following Genzmer, looked to the Old Norse pantheon for help, and suggested that *Fol might be a male equivalent of the goddess Volla in the fourth line of the charm.[10] Another suggestion made by Grimm was that Phol might be cognate with MHG *vâlant* [devil]. This led Warnatsch to combine the first two words of the text, Wodan becoming the (otherwise unattested) demon *Volende*.[11] Even more imaginatively, Krogmann read his combination of the two words as *vollenti* (< *vollhendi*), an attribute referring to Wodan's magic powers — "full-handed," therefore "helpful."[12] Wadstein reconstructed *Folente*, "foaling," therefore "on horseback."[13] The plural verb *uuorun* would seem to militate against reading *Phol ende* as an adjective before *uuodan*. Steller, and more recently, Rosenfeld, have argued that Phol means "foal," Steller on the basis of a mythological interpretation of the horse as a god of death, Rosenfeld less obscurely but anachronistically on the basis of the NHG formula "Roß und Reiter," which enabled him to find a solution as to why a horse should be given precedence over a god.[14]

Genzmer maintained that the unusual spelling, *ph*, is derived from Latin orthography, as a third alternative to *f* and *u* (*Uolla*). But if Phol is the foal, why should the scribe choose to spell the same sound in the same word in two such radically different ways, in the space of two lines? The hand is neat and practised. The scribe had plenty of parchment space available, and presumably the tools to make an erasure if necessary. The occurrence of superscript letters in OHG and OS orthography is rare, and offers no grapheme comparable with P^h.

In the charm there are three gods who would seem to be readily identifiable from Scandinavian mythology, Uuodan (Óðinn), balder (Baldr), and Friia (Freyja). Again inspired by Grimm, a whole school of thought has argued that *balder* is not a god but an appellative noun meaning "chieftain" or "lord," and has identified the resulting lord of the gods either as P(h)ol, or as Wodan.[15] The evidence for *balder* with this connotation is uncertain; the word does not occur elsewhere in OHG, and the ON and OE evidence has been the subject of much dispute. Nowhere is Óðinn referred to in this way. Almost as slight, admittedly, is the evidence for a cult of Balder outside Scandinavia. When the Utrecht inscription was discovered in 1929, this new evidence for Balder was treated with suspicion. *Baldruo* in the inscription, like *balder* in the charm, was held to signify "chieftain," rather than being the name of a god.[16]

The equation of Volla with Freyja's servant Fulla seems eminently reasonable, yielding a fourth identifiable goddess. Sunna, presumably a sun-goddesss, may correspond to Sól, daughter of Mundilfæri, one of the Æsir in *Gylfaginning* and in *Skaldskaparmal*. Sinhtgunt is not attested elsewhere, and remains a problem scarcely second to P^{h}ol. It seems reasonable to base an approach to the gods in the charm on such gods as we can identify in the Old Norse pantheon, and to reintroduce the precedence argument: which god might conceivably precede Óðinn? Such a naïve approach is, of course, open to an objection on the grounds of syllogism, such as that levelled against the presence of the god Balder by Green: "the too facile assumption that, because the word *balder* occurs here in the context of a group of gods, it must therefore itself be the name of a god."[17] Against this a formal argument may be adduced: the Second Merseburg Charm works, like the First, in clearly discernible groups of the magic number three. This is most evident in the conjuring section, with its encyclopædic, triply applicable formula, followed by the triple juxtaposition of sundered bones, limbs or blood-vessels.[18] It is debatable whether we have, in the second part of the narrative section, five deities or three. The problem is the absence of a copulative conjunction. The unusualness of asyndeton in OHG syntax would seem to favour four goddesses rather than two, but the triadic structure of the charm argues for two goddesses, identified by reference to their sisters. Even if there are four goddesses, there remain only three distinct attempts to work magic by conjuring. If we then look back to the first part of the charm, the numerical symbolism is singularly wanting, unless we posit three gods in the first two lines.[19] Schirokauer, indeed, sought four, arguing that *Balder* was the name of the god in his human form, *Balderesvolo* his name in the animal or totem form, and *Phol* the name of the combined animal and totem forms.[20]

The only god in the Norse pantheon who holds a standing comparable with that of Óðinn is Þórr. When the two gods occur in conjunction, Þórr is customarily followed by Óðinn. This sequence obtains both on their Scandinavian home ground and in Germany, both in Christian contexts, when the pagan gods are renounced, and in contexts where "pagan" magic is being practised.

To take the pagan contexts first, there have been two main periods when texts of a magical nature were collected. The first was in the sixteenth and seventeenth centuries, when the transcripts of witch-trials preserved many charms. In Iceland, there was an average of one witch-trial a year between 1554 and 1720; as might be expected in a country with an age-old tradition of feminism, only nine out 125 witches tried were women.[21] Davíðsson's study of Icelandic magic as revealed by these trials shows runes and other magic signs to be an integral part of late medieval Icelandic witchcraft; these runes on occasion denoted the names of the Asir. In 1664 the schoolmaster of Skálholt found a tattered book of magic in the bed of two pupils, aged 19 and 20. He handed the book over to his bishop, who duly consigned it to the flames, "was ein großer Schade ist."[22] Thirteen pupils were revealed to have been involved in the conspiracy, but only the two ringleaders were expelled and, like Rosencrantz and Guildenstern, sent to England. One of the pair died there, but the other survived and returned to Iceland after a few years, his youthful misdemeanours apparently forgotten. Fortunately for us, the bishop, before burning the book, made a detailed list of its contents, which included three charms invoking Þórr and Óðinn, as a pair. The two names occur in the same fixed order.[23]

The folklorists of the late nineteenth and early twentieth centuries were responsible for the collection of a huge number of charms. Foremost among these was Reidar Christiansen, who tracked down hundreds of variants of the Second Merseburg Charm.[24] One Norwegian variant was collected from the oral tradition by Christiansen himself, in Svelvik on the Kristianfjorde on 27 August 1913.[25] His informant told him that the charm worked best if one spoke it over brandy, smeared some over the sick limb, and then drank the rest. The charm apparently usually took some two to four days to work, but was generally successful.

In a Norwegian charm collected c. 1880, the aim is to bring the speaker luck in the throwing of dice. The dice have to be buried for three nights north of the churchyard, then kept hidden under the altar-cloth through three services, and then a charm is to be spoken over them, invoking Thor and Odin. After the dice have been thrown, a second incantation is spoken, invoking Enoch, Elias, Frigg, Freya, Thor, Odin and the Virgin Mary.[26] A Swedish charm invokes Odin, Freya and Fylle.[27] Another trilogy, Oden, Thore, Fregga, occurs in a charm against ulcers.[28] Christiansen sees all such groups of three as derivative of the Holy Trinity, with Fregge as a substitution for the Virgin Mary.[29] Similarly, when the Finnish thunder-god Ukko occurs in some charms, Christiansen regards Ukko as a "zufällige Substitution."[30]

An essentially anachronistic thesis permeates Christiansen's massive study. Characteristic of the "Finnish school," inspired by Kaarle Krohn,[31] it argues backwards from the majority of later, overtly Christian charms to claim that all charms are Christian in origin. In the Second Merseburg Charm pagan deities have thus been substituted for the original Christian names to avoid the taint of blasphemy. The only hard evidence for the deliberate substitution of pagan names for Christian ones derives from a female informant in 1880.[32] It seems doubtful whether this thought-process could function in a society only recently converted from paganism, such as that of tenth-century Saxony. The context of the charms' transmission, among liturgical texts, argues against the substitution theory, too, for the Frankish Baptismal Vow, bound together in the same manuscript as the Merseburg Charms, specifically asks the catechumen to renounce pagan gods and practices: "den gotum thie im heidene man zi geldom enti zi gotum habent" [those gods to whom heathen men sacrifice as gods].

The substitution theory shows the dangers which are inherent in employing later analogous material as evidence. The occurrence of Thor and Odin as a pair in late charms does not, of course, mean that they must be there in the earliest of the charms. There is, however, some evidence which is closer in time to the writing down of the Merseburg charms. The Frankish Baptismal Vow is the only other vernacular text in the Merseburg manuscript. It belongs to the first section of the manuscript, a priest's manual for the understanding and practice of mass and baptism ritual, which occupies fols. 1–21. The script of this part of the codex is described by Bischoff as "deutsch-angelsächsich"; he assigns it to the second or third decade of the ninth century.[33] The Frankish Vow has a Low German equivalent, the Saxon Baptismal Vow, dating from the end of the eighth century, the time of the conquest and conversion of the Saxons. The Saxon Baptismal Vow is preceded by the celebrated *Indiculus superstitionum*, our richest source for pagan magic in the Carolingian period, which condemns *incantationes* among other pagan practices, and has been linked with the councils of 743–744.[34] The Saxon vow is more specific in what it asks the catechumen to renounce: "respondet: end ec forsacho allum dioboles uuercum and uuordum, Thunaer ende Uuoden ende Saxnote ende allum them unholdum the hira genotas sint" [let him respond: and I forsake all the Devil's works and words, Thor and Woden and Saxnot and all the demons which are their companions]. This would appear to be the sole source for Saxnot, presumably the local god of the Saxons; significantly, he follows Thor and Woden in their customary order. It seems that the Saxons, like their Scandinavian neighbours, were highly polytheistic. Ian Woods cites a story from the *Vita* of the missionary Anscar (865–876). Arriving in Birka, Anscar found a multitude confused by a very great error, in consequence of the eloquence of a pagan who had just come from a convention of the local gods. These were much offended at the way that sacrifices and worship had fallen off in consequence of the cult of a god who taught against them, and their message was: "If you desire any further gods and we do not suffice for you, we unanimously accept into our company Eric, sometime your monarch, that he may be one of our number."[35] It may be that some of the more obscure deities in the Second Merseburg Charm enjoyed a similarly tenuous deification.

A second piece of evidence stems from the 780s, from a poem-epistle of Paul the Deacon, part of the three-way verse correspondence between Paul, Peter of Pisa, and Charlemagne, which involves a series of obscure riddles. Peter of Pisa gives Paul the Deacon the choice of three alternatives: being bound in chains, lying in prison, or converting the wild Sigfrid, king of the Danes. Paul directs his reply to Charlemagne, to whom he is full of gratitude for the release of his brother. He has no need of fetters or a prison, being subjugated by his love for his king and lord. His ignorance of the language would make him an unfitting missionary to the hairy Dane. The task of baptising Sigfrid will be the divine mission of Charlemagne. If Sigfrid is not converted, he will be bound in chains, and his gods will be of no help to him: "nec illi auxilio Thonar et Waten erunt." Neff dates this verse letter to 783.[36] Peter Godman envisages the correspondence as emanating from a circle of poets who travelled with Charlemagne from court to court.[37]

At some point the naming of gods from the Scandinavian pantheon in the attribution of cults to neighbouring peoples would appear to have become a cliché. Perhaps this is the case when Orderic Vitalis, writing *c.* 1125 about events in 1069, describes the Lithuanian allies of Swein, king of Denmark, as a "populosissima natio . . . quæ gentilitatis adhuc errore detenta uerum Deum nesciebat; sed ignorantiæ muscipulis illaqueata Guodenen et Thurum Freamque aliosque falsos deos immo dæmones colebat" [a teeming race . . . which was still blinded by heathen error and did not know the true God; ensnared by ignorance the people worshipped Wodin, Thor, Freya, and other false gods, or rather demons].[38] But in the 780s Charlemagne's interest in the conquest and conversion of the Saxons and Danes was at its height, and there is no reason why one of his most learned courtiers should not have been well acquainted with the beliefs of his adversaries. Paul the Deacon's interest in the Scandinavian pantheon is further borne out by his account in the eighth chapter of his *Historia Langobardorum* of the etymology of the name *Langobard*: Frea counselled the women of the Winnili to take down their hair and arrange it upon their faces like a beard, and appear in this manner to Godan at sunrise, having promised victory in the war between the Wandals and the Winnili to whoever he first saw at daybreak.[39]

When Christian and pagan cultures enter into conflict in medieval Iceland, the pairing of Þórr and Óðinn recurs, in a manner strikingly reminiscent of the Saxon Baptismal Vow. Arrow-Odd is willing to embrace Christianity, and proclaims his readiness to renounce sacrifices to Þórr, Óðinn, or other idols.[40]

Þórr, as we have seen, commonly occurs in the later Scandinavian charms. He would also seem to be present in the OHG charm *Contra caducum morbum* (Braune § XXXI, 8) which survives in two late manuscripts, in Bavarian dialect in the eleventh century, and in Rhenish Franconian in a twelfth-century Paris manuscript. The Paris text begins with a Latin prescription for a course of action in treating epilepsy:

> Contra caducum morbum. / Accede ad infirmum iacentem. et a sinistro / vsque ad dextrum latus spacians, sicque super eum stans dic ter: Donerdutigo. / dietewigo. . .

> [Against the falling sickness. / Approach the prone invalid, and walking from his left side / to his right, stand above him and say three times: Thunderer (?). / Eternal One (?)]

The text that follows is composite and highly problematic. The Latin rubric is absent in the Munich manuscript, except for 'pro cadente morbo' in the first line. In the Munich text *Doner* is built into the syntax of the first sentence and becomes the adversary of the Devil:

> Doner dutiger p*ro* cadente mor*bo* / diet mahtiger stuont uf der / adamez prucche . . .

> [Thunderer for the falling sickness. / Mighty one (?) stood upon / Adam's bridge . . .]

diet and *dutiger* would appear to be cognates of OHG *diot, diutisc* [people, popular], suggesting perhaps that Doner is a god of the local populace. The obvious explanation for the presence of Doner is that both versions of the charm begin by apostrophising the god. Grienberger's suggestion that Doner is in fact John, one of the Boanerges, the "sons of thunder," as James and John are called in Mark 3.17, is less than convincing. It has been suggested that the apostrophic formula represents a survival of an alliterative hymn in praise of Donar.[41] If P^{h}ol in the Second Merseburg Charm is in fact Thor, then we would possess two OHG charms which begin with Donar. It would seem that only conjecture can restore to the Second Merseburg Charm something of its original thunder.

David McLintock has raised in discussion two major objections to the Thor conjecture. The first objection is linguistic in essence. As the forms in the Saxon Baptismal Vow, in the verse-epistle of Paulus Diaconus and in the charm *Contra caducum morbum* show, *Donar* in a German context has two syllables with a medial nasal consonant. In contrast, the ON cognate, *Þórr*, is thought to have lost its nasal in the Viking Age.[42] Anglo-Saxon has a wide variety of forms, both with and without the medial nasal: *dunor, Þunor, Þúr, Dor, Dur.* Thus 'Thursday' is variously *Dunres-dæg* and *Þurres-dæg*.[43] We have too little evidence to ascertain whether the god invariably had a nasal in Old Saxon. If the Merseburg charms are Scandinavian in origin — or if their mythology is Scandinavian — then the absent nasal is less of a problem, although one might then expect a double final consonant as in *Þórr*. That the gods in the second charm are Germanised to some extent is clear from the forms *uuodan* and *balderes*, and may explain *sunna*, if she derives from Sól. If P^{h}ol is Thor, then the form might suggest that the charm originated in Scandinavia rather than Saxony. The German scribe's failure to recognise the name of a god with which he was doubtless familiar may perhaps be explained by the fact that he was confronted not only with a name for Donar which lacked a nasal, but with an unfamiliar rune, as I shall argue below.[44]

A more significant objection raised by McLintock is the problem of alliteration. If Phol is Thor in disguise, then even the doubtful *ph* : *u* alliteration in the first line is lost. Stanley has argued for a distinction between strict adherence to alliterative metre, found in longer texts such as *Beowulf* and the *Muspilli*, and the "kind of very loose rhythmical discourse to which the Old English metrical charms mainly belong."[45] Turning to the Merseburg charms, he regards these as also belonging to the looser tradition. Thus, even in the first line of the Second Merseburg Charm, we find "the finite verb [*vuorun*] taking precedence of the noun *holz* in the adverbial phrase *zi holza*," and the second line is deficient in that "the first noun, the proper name *Balderes*, should alliterate, not the second noun *uolon*. The third line has double alliteration in the second half, which in Old English would be irregular." Stanley acknowledges that the deficient alliteration may be a consequence of transmission and concludes with admirable caution: "I am reinforced in my inability to decide where in the borderland between irregular alliterative verse and rhythmical alliterative prose the Old High German texts should be ranked." The Merseburg charms combine alliteration with rhyme — and conceivably "rhythmical alliterative prose" — in a manner similar to the Wessobrunn Prayer. We may assume such poetic licence is typical of the transition period in German verse in the ninth century, when the older alliterative metre begins to yield to end-rhyme as the dominant form. One might feel tempted to amend, with Joseph Wilson,[46] *holza* to *walde*, on the grounds that a scribe might easily confuse the two words, but this would yield the impermissible alliterative pattern *xaax*. In any case, if the charm we have before us is a translation or adaptation from a Scandinavian source, defective metre is all the more understandable.

The obvious inference from the superscript *h* in *P^{h}ol* is that what the scribe found before him was in some way problematic. It is conceivable that the first letter of the text was originally not *P*, but the thorn-rune *Þ*. Perhaps the same letter troubled the scribe in *Sinhtgunt*, which is generally amended to *Sinthgunt*. The scribe does seem to suffer from slight dyslexia, as evinced also by *birenkict*, where the *c* is clearly redundant. The Second Charm also shows a discrepancy between *th* and *d* in initial position: *du, demo* in line 2, *thu* in lines 3–5. The shift from *th* to *d* was generally completed in OHG by *c.* 900. The simplest explanation of the discrepancy would be that it is a consequence of scribal or dialect mix. The three occurrences of *th* may, however, reflect an older stratum of the charm, and may perhaps be further reflections of the thorn-rune.

The OHG charms survive for the most part in nooks and crannies of manuscripts. The typical codical contexts in which they are found are preceding or, more commonly, following unassociated theological material, or, as in the case of the Trier charms (Braune XXXI, § 9B), Latin medical texts. Frequently they occur at the end of a section of a manuscript or in space that was originally left blank. Not infrequently, Latin and OHG or OS charms occur side-by-side in this "filler" function (for example, Braune XXXI § 2; 4a; 7; 8; 9). It may be that the exemplar of the Merseburg charms survived in a similarly tenuous fashion, before they were copied onto a blank page in that part of the liturgical compilation in which they now survive. If in the exemplar the first line of the second charm had been cut or had faded because it was at the top of a piece of parchment, so that only the lower half of its letters was legible, then it is easy to imagine how *Pol* might result from *Thor*. The thorn-rune, deprived of its top, as in the seventh-century Istaby stone, a three-dimensional equivalent, might have been taken for a majuscule *P*.[47] The superscript *h* may indicate a residual awareness on the part of the scribe that what he had before him was no ordinary *P*, but a graphy representing an aspirated sound. And the bottom of an *r* in the scribe's exemplar might have been misread as the bottom of an *l*.

In this context it may be significant that the most problematic line of the First Merseburg Charm is also its first line. *Eiris* is generally taken to be a scribal corruption of **einis* [once]. *hera duoder* remains extremely problematic. "Here and there" is at best an informed guess, as *duoder* is not attested elsewhere. Gerhard Eis suggested that *duoder* might be a corruption of *muoder*, with the second *d* affecting the initial *m*; he saw the charm as reflecting the cult of the *matrones*, for which there is evidence in Celtic survivals, as for example at Bath.[48] The odd scribal behaviour might again be the consequence of dyslexia. Perhaps with regard to the first charm, too, the scribe had before him a first line which was in part illegible. The charms may have originally been written in the upper margins of two facing pages, or on odd scraps of parchment. The latter could themselves be used for magico-medical purposes, immersed in potions, the power of the spoken word extending to the written word. Thus a recipe in one of the Leechbooks prescribes that the parchment on which the charm is written be incorporated into the ointment; charms could even be written down on paper and eaten, so strong was the belief in the power of the magic letters.[49]

It is not inherently unlikely that we should find a rune in an OHG text. In the course of the ninth century, however, the sporadic use of runes in Germany points to increasing unfamiliarity on the part of scribes. The evidence indeed suggests that runes never established themselves as an orthographic system in German manuscripts — as opposed to Germanic inscriptions. The star-rune in the *Wessobrunn Prayer* is used inconsistently, making way for the grapheme *ga* in *ganada* and *galaupa* in the "prose part" of the prayer. The scribe's unfamiliarity with the rune is also clear from when he first attempts to employ it, in the glosses on fol. 63ʳ of the manuscript (clm. 22053); here an erasure is followed by a star-rune with a horizontal rather than a vertical stroke. Like the star-rune, the wynn-rune in the *Hildebrandslied* is thought to derive from Anglo-Saxon scribal practice. Here too, the continental scribe betrays his unfamiliarity with the rune. In line 9 the scribe corrects a *p* into the wynn-rune; in line 27 and in line 40 the function of the rune, to represent *w*, is clearly misunderstood, for the scribe follows the rune with a superfluous *u*. The diacritic mark over most of the wynn-runes remains unexplained.[50] The Basle Recipes of *c.* 800 similarly employ the thorn-rune and other insular scribal features without understanding their function.[51] Most problematic of all the ninth-century German texts that employ runes is the St Gall *Abecedarium Nordmannicum*, another text whose present appearance suggests it was treated with reagents in the nineteenth century. The *Abecedarium* offers a comparison between two runic alphabets, but the rune-names are so problematic that no consensus prevails even as to what language is being employed. The Merseburg Charms may contain further evidence of a late and misunderstood attempt to incorporate runes into Carolingian minuscule.

An obvious reason for the presence of runes in the text of a charm might seem to be the magic powers felt to be inherent in the runes. Here, however, we encounter an area of heated controversy. In the early part of the twentieth century scholars such as Sigmund Feist were happy to conclude that wherever runes were found there was magic afoot.[52] Post-war scholarship has been more sceptical. Lucien Musset and Ray Page follow the lead of the Danish scholar, Anders Baeksted: "nous croyons que l'obsession magique de beaucoup de runologues s'explique plus par la psychologie des savants que par le contenu intrinsique des inscriptions."[53] What is at issue here is not whether the runic alphabet originally had a magic function, but whether runes may have been employed for magic purposes in charms. Here even Page, who regards his "method of putting forward the evidence" as "inimical to the theory of rune-magic," concedes that runes occur in some Anglo-Saxon charms, even if "the magical quality of the runes compared with other alphabets is not striking."[54]

In both Anglo-Saxon and Old Icelandic contexts, there is, as we have seen, evidence for the scratching of runes on bark or sticks for magic effect. In the one Anglo-Saxon charm which mentions Woden, the Nine Herbs Charm, Woden strikes the serpent, so that it flies into nine fragments, by the use of nine *wuldortanas* [glory-twigs]. These are generally interpreted, with Godfrid Storms, as "nine runes, that is, nine twigs with the initial letters in runes of the the plants representing the power inherent in them."[55] In strophe 36 of *Skírnismál*, three runes are scratched, presumably on a twig, as part of a curse. In the *Sigrdrífomál* (str. 11), the would-be healer is instructed to scratch *limrúnar* [limb-runes] on the bark of a tree. As we have seen, several of the analogues of the First Merseburg Charm point to an association with runes.[56]

Few attempts have been made to explain the capital H which is written at the end of the first charm.[57] It has been suggested that the three strokes comprising the H are a further reference to the magic number three. Or the H might be an initial standing for the person who is to employ the charm, or who is to receive the benefit of it. In the Latin prayer which follows in a different hand, the .N. — for *nomen* — performs this function, and .N. is common in charms to denote the patient. However, the cross-bar of the H is clearly horizontal. Might this too be a runic survival? The late Professor Michael Barnes of University College London, consulted on this possibility, wrote in reply: "The three forms of H are non-distinctive variants and all occur in pre-AD 700 Scandinavian inscriptions. The angle at which the cross stave slopes can also vary from very steep to almost horizontal. The symbol at the end of the first Merseburg charm could therefore well be the H rune. On the other hand, H went out of use in Scandinavian runic writing before or around AD 800. The Anglo-Saxon and continental Germanic tradition used a symbol with two cross staves." If, then, the H is a rune, it would derive from the Scandinavian alphabet, and the exemplar of the text would date from before *c.* 800.

A number of runic inscriptions from Scandinavia, ranging in date from the first to the sixth century A.D., end with an isolated H; others incorporate the rune-name *hagl* or *hagal(l)*, "hail."[58] In the Anglo-Saxon riddles in the Exeter Book, single runes, separated by points in similar fashion to the Merseburg H, are used in acrostic puzzles; there is an .H. in Riddle 24.[59] The .*N.* which stands for *nomen* in the Latin blessing written beneath the charm is separated by points in markedly similar fashion, the first point being slightly lower than the second. It seems probable that the H between the Merseburg charms is an abbreviation, in which case it may perhaps refer to one of the appellatives of Óðinn, as in the *Hávamál*, the Sayings of the High One. Wodan is present in the second charm, and the first charm has clear affinities with one of those Óðinn knows in the *Hávamál*. Another candidate might be the local god Hennil, referred to by Thietmar of Merseburg. The H-rune itself does not appear to have any readily identifiable magic function. The rune-name is thought by extension to refer to mean "ruin," "sudden disaster," although Elliott believes it refers primarily to "damaging natural forces."[60] Perhaps in the Merseburg text it refers to the disasters which the charms were intended to avert.

If Pʰol is Thor, what implication does this have for the narrative part of the charm? The argument adduced by Grimm, and often rehearsed subsequently, is that Phol must be identical with either Wodan or Balder, for otherwise he would be a mere bystander who plays no further part in events. Thus Steinhoff argues that Phol would have no function in the text, if he were not the owner of the horse.[61] This rather depends upon what we assume to be the purpose of the journey. Here we are dependant upon the thirteenth-century retelling of the Norse myths in the Prose Edda. One would not in principle expect the epic introduction of a tenth-century charm to tally exactly with a story contained in Snorri's compendium. The narrative parts of the early medieval charms are often clearly *ad hoc* inventions, probably on the part of the individual leach or healing-woman, which work on the basis of analogy. While some of the epic introductions, such as the widespread story of Peter sitting on a rock with toothache, can be traced to apocryphal sources, others are apocryphal to the point of absurdity: Christ healing a fish whose gills have burst (Braune XXXI, § 9A), or, in the Lorsch Bee Charm, the Virgin Mary quelling a swarm of bees. Yet the Second Merseburg Charm, when compared with the later evidence, reveals "des similitudes frappantes . . . avec les phénomènes nordiques."[62] In *Gylfaginning* Snorri describes how the gods hold their court of justice by the great ash-tree Yggdrasil: "Hvern dag ríða Æsir þangat upp um Bifrǫst . . . Hestar Ásanna heita svá: Sleipnir er baztr — hann á Óðinn, hann hefir átta fœtr . . . Baldrs hestr var brendr með honum. En Þórr gengr til dómsins ok veðr ár." [Every day the Æsir ride there up over Bifrost . . . The names of the Æsir's horses are as follows: best is Sleipnir, he is Odin's, he has eight legs . . . Baldr's horse was burned with him. And Thór walks to the court and wades rivers]. Snorri is drawing on the account in *Grímnismál*, where Thor is described as wading through the waters, while the other gods ride to Yggdrasil:

Kǫrmt oc Ǫrmt   oc Kerlaugar tvær,
þær scal Þórr vaða,
hverian dag,   er hann dœma ferr
at asci Yggdrasils,
þvíat ásbrú   brenn ǫll loga,
heilog vǫtn hlóa.

Glaðr oc Gyllir,   Glær oc Sceiðbrimir,
Silfrintoppr oc Sinir,
Gísl oc Falhófnir,   Gulltoppr oc Léttfeti,
þeim ríða æsir ióm,
dag hvern,   er þeir dœma fara
at asci Yggdrasils.

[Kormt and Ormt and the two Kerlaugar, / these Thor must wade / every day, when he goes to sit as judge / at the ash of Yggdrasil, / for the bridge of the Æsir burns with all flames, / the sacred waters boil.

Glad and Golden, Glassy and Skeidbrímir, / Silvertuft and Sinir, / Brilliant and Hidden-hoof, Goldtuft and Lightfoot, / these horses the Æsir ride / every day, when they ride to sit as judges, / at the ash of Yggdrasil.][63]

If the context of the Merseburg charm is an assembly of the gods, then Thor's presence is essential.

Thor's customary method of locomotion is on foot, or in his goat-pulled chariot. An injury to a horse would therefore be of no great concern to Thor, nor is it likely that a sprain to one of the eight legs of Wodan's steed, Sleipnir, would prove such a disaster as to require the combined efforts of several gods to cure it. Moreover, if the injured horse belonged to Wodan, why should he bother to enlist the aid of the other deities, being so skilled in magic himself — "so he uuola conda?" Such collaborative concern on the part of the Æsir is manifested most clearly in the *Edda* when Baldr is slain by mistletoe. In the Second Merseburg Charm, it seems probable that Balder is again the object of their interest. It is, moreover, at least poetically appropriate for the young god Balder to ride a foal. The alliteration calls for cognates of the word "foal" in a great number of the charm's variants; the Germanic word *folon* appears to refer to a horse which is young, but already rideable.[64] The association of Balder with a horse is emphasised again by Snorri when he describes how Balder's horse and harness form part of the god's funeral-pyre. Genzmer argues that Balder corresponds to Freyr, the best of the riders among the Vanir,[65] and it may therefore be significant that Freyr's horse is called Blóðughófi, "Bloody-hoof."[66] The evidence is circumstantial, but it supports the most literal reading of the charm, that it was Balder's horse which suffered the injury. Neckel's theory that the injury to the foal is a premonition of Balder's death remains an attractive explanation, suggesting that the charm takes as its poetic basis a pre-existent myth.[67]

Among the other Æsir whom Snorri describes as riding to the daily assembly are Freyja: "En er hon ferr, þá ekr hon kǫttum tveim ok sitr í reið" [when she goes on a journey sits in a chariot drawn by two cats]; Fulla, a virgin "[h]on berr eski Friggjar ok gætir skóklæða hennar ok veit launráð með henni." [carries Frigg's casket and looks after her footwear and shares her secrets]; and Sól, the sun-goddess.[68] Sinhtgunt is conspicuously absent, but if the form of the name in the charm is a corruption, it may be based upon Sigyn, the wife of Loki, though it has to be said that she is unlikely to desire to aid Balder, her husband's enemy. Other, more remote possibilities might be Sjöfn, the goddess of love, or Syn, the guardian of the door of the hall.

zi holza varan in the charm's first line would thus have its origin in the journey to Yggdrasil, the sacred ash-tree at the centre of the cosmos. OHG *holz* frequently refers to a group of trees, or a wood, as in the Lorsch Bee Charm: "zi holce ni fluc du." *holz* and *uuald* seem to be virtually synonymous in the tenth century.[69] The suggestion that the gods in the charm constitute a hunting-party seems less likely. This is not supported by a mythological analogue, but only by two interdependent occurrences of *ze holze varn* in MHG texts.[70] The most curious omission which emerges from a comparison of the Second Merseburg Charm with Snorri's account of the assembly of the gods is the apparent absence in the former of Thor.

Notes

[1] I am grateful to my former employers, Goldsmiths' College, University of London, to the Humboldt Universität Berlin, and the British Council for funding my journey to Merseburg in 1985, and to the librarian of the Cathedral Chapter for his assistance.

[2] The literature concerning the charms is barely superable, and these notes have no pretension to be a complete bibliography. The following are the main bibliographical sources I have consulted: Ehrismann, *Geschichte*, I, 100–04; *Handbook*, 26–37; Groseclose and Murdoch, *Die kleineren althochdeutschen poetischen Denkmäler*, 50–53; Hans-Hugo Steinhoff's article on the "Merseburger Zaubersprüche," in *Verfasserlexikon*, vol. 6 (1987), cols. 410–18; on-line searches conducted by Marilyn Jones, formerly of Goldsmiths' College. The major theories are excellently summarised in the *Handbook*, and by Adolf Spamer, "P(h)ol ende Uuodan. Zum zweiten Merseburger Spruch," *Deutsches Jahrbuch für Volkskunde* 3 (1957): 347–65.

[3] Jacob Grimm, "Ueber zwei entdeckte gedichte aus der zeit des deutschen Heidenthums," *Philologische und historische Abhandlungen der Königlichen Akademie der Wissenschaften zu Berlin* (Berlin, 1842), 1–24.

[4] *Handbook*, 33.

[5] MS. Corpus Christi Cambridge 41, quoted by Heather Stuart, "A Critical Edition of some Anglo-Saxon Charms and Incantations," vol. 2, 358 (§ XIV); cf. Storms, *Anglo-Saxon Magic*, §12 (206).

[6] Reidar Th. Christiansen, *Die finnischen und nordischen Varianten des zweiten*

Merseburgerspruches, 6; 211; Sophus Bugge, *Studier over de nordiske Gude- og Heltesagns Oprindelse* (Christiania: Gad, 1881–89), 548.

[7] Spamer, "P(h)ol ende Uuodan," 359.

[8] Siegfried Gutenbrunner, "Der zweite Merseburger Spruch im Lichte nordischer Überlieferungen," *ZfdA* 80 (1943): 1–5; idem, "Ritennamen — Kultnamen — Mythennamen der Götter," in *Namenforschung. Festschrift für Adolf Bach zum 75. Geburtstag*, ed. Rudolf Schützeichel and Matthias Zender (Heidelberg: C. Winter, 1965), 17–31.

[9] Grimm, "Über zwei entdeckte gedichte," 12.

[10] Felix Genzmer, "Die Götter des zweiten 'Merseburger Zauberspruches'," *Arkiv för nordisk filologi* 63 (1948): 55–72; Dennis E. Green, *The Carolingian Lord. Semantic studies on four Old High German words: balder, frô, truhtin, hêrro* (Cambridge: Cambridge UP, 1965), 12.

[11] Grimm, "Über zwei entdeckte gedichte," 15; Otto Warnatsch, "Phol und der 2. Merseburger Zauberspruch," *ZfdPh* 64 (1939): 148–55.

[12] Willy Krogmann, "Phol im Merseburger Pferdesegen," *ZfdPh* 71 (1951/52): 152–62.

[13] Elis Wadstein, "Zum zweiten Merseburger Zauberspruch," *Stud. Neophil.* 12 (1939/40): 205–09.

[14] Walther Steller, "'Phol ende Wodan'," in *Volkskundliche Studien. Festschrift Friedrich Schmidt-Ott zum siebzigsten Geburtstage dargebracht* (Berlin: de Gruyter, 1930), 61–71; Hellmut Rosenfeld, "*Phol ende Wuodan vuorun zi holza*. Baldermythe oder Fohlenzauber?," *PBB* (Tübingen) 95 (1973): 1–12.

[15] See Green, *The Carolingian Lord*, 15ff.; Hans Kuhn, "Es gibt kein balder 'Herr'," in *Erbe der Vergangenheit: germanistische Beiträge. Fs. für Karl Helm zum 80. Geburtstag, 19. Mai 1951* (Tübingen: M. Niemeyer, 1951), 37–45.

[16] See Siegfried Gutenbrunner, *Die germanischen Götternamen in antiken Inschriften* (Halle/Saale: M. Niemeyer, 1936), 22; 63; 210; Green, *The Carolingian Lord*, 12–13; K. Schier, "Balder," in *Reallexikon der germanischen Altertumskunde*, ed. Johannes Hoops, 2nd ed., rev. Heinrich Beck et al. (Berlin: W. de Gruyter, 1977), vol. 1, 2–7.

[17] Green, *The Carolingian Lord*, 15.

[18] The third alternative is suggested by H. B. Willson, "'bluotrenki'," *MLR* 52 (1957): 233–35.

[19] Kenneth Northcott, "An Interpretation of the Second Merseburg Charm," *MLR* 54 (1959): 45–50.

[20] Arno Schirokauer, "Der Zweite Merseburger Zauberspruch," in *Corona. Studies in Celebration of the Eightieth Birthday of Samuel Singer*, ed. Arno Schirokauer and Wolfgang Paulsen (Durham, NC: Duke UP, 1941), 116–41.

[21] Ólafur Davíðsson, "Isländische Zauberzeichen und Zauberbücher," *Zeitschrift des Vereins für Volkskunde* 13 (1903): 150–67; 267–79 (150ff.).

[22] Ibid., 270.

[23] Ibid., 268.

[24] Christiansen, *Die finnischen und nordischen Varianten* (as note 6).

[25] Ibid., 37.

[26] Ibid., 46.

[27] Ibid., 54.

[28] Ibid., 55.

[29] Ibid., 56.

[30] Ibid., 121. Whether Thor lurks in the background here is questionable, as Hans Fromm doubts the equation of Ukko and Thor, suggesting rather that Oðinn and Ukko are to be identified. See Hans Fromm, "Lemminkäinen und Baldr," in *Märchen. Mythos. Dichtung. Festschrift zum 90. Geburtstag Friedrich van der Leyens am 19. August 1963*, ed. Hugo Kuhn (Munich: Beck, 1965), 287–302 (296).

[31] Kaarle Krohn, "Wo und wann entstanden die finnischen zauberlieder?," *Finnischugrische Forschungen* 1 (1901): 147–81, especially 148–49.

[32] Christiansen, *Die finnischen und nordischen Varianten*, 46; A. Bang, *Norske hexe-formularer og magiske opskrifter* (Christiania: J. Dybwad, 1901), § 40; cf. Walther Preusler, "Zum zweiten Merseburger Spruch," in *Beiträge zur Deutschkunde. Festschrift Theodor Siebs zum 60. Geburtstag*, ed. Helmut de Boor (Emden: Davids, 1922), 39–45.

[33] On the date of the two vows, see Bischoff, "Paläographische Studien," 109–11.

[34] Alain Dierkens, "Superstitions, christianisme et paganisme à la fin de l'époque mérovingienne. A propos de l'Indiculus superstitionum et paganiarum," in *Magie, sorcellerie, parapsychologie*, ed. Hervé Hasquin (Brussels: Université de Bruxelles, 1984), 9–26. I am indebted to Jinty Nelson for this reference.

[35] *Rimbert, Vita Anskarii*, ed. and trans. Werner Trillmilch, in *Quellen des 9. und 11. Jahrhunderts zur Geschichte der Hamburgischen Kirche und des Reiches*, ed. Werner Trillmilch and Rudolf Buchner, 5th ed. (Darmstadt: Wissenschaftliche Buchgesellschaft, 1978), cap. 26. I am indebted to Ian Wood for this reference.

[36] *Die Gedichte des Paulus Diaconus*, ed. Karl Neff, Quellen und Untersuchungen zur lateinischen Philologie des Mittelalters, III, iv (Munich: C. H. Beck, 1908), 98–105 (Letter XXII, line 36).

[37] Peter Godman, *Poetry of the Carolingian Renaissance* (London: Duckworth, 1985), 5–10.

[38] *The Ecclesiastical History of Orderic Vitalis*, ed. and trans. Marjorie Chibnall, Oxford Medieval Texts, 6 vols (Oxford: Clarendon Press, 1969–80), vol. 2, 226–27. I am indebted to Steve Church for this reference. The coupling continues in the folk mind, as perceived by the scholar. Thomas Hardy, reconstructing the Ancient British culture of Wessex in 1878, charts the history of the beacon on Rainbarrow: "The flames from funeral piles long ago kindled there had shone down upon the lowlands as these were shining now. Festival fires to Thor and Woden had followed on the same ground and duly had their day. Indeed, it is pretty well known that such blazes as this the heathmen were now enjoying are rather the lineal descendants from jumbled Druidical rites and Saxon ceremonies than the invention of popular feeling about Gunpowder Plot." (*The Return of the Native*, 1878; repr. New York: The New American Library, Inc., 1959, 23.)

[39] Paul the Deacon, *History of the Langobards*, trans. William Dudley Foulke (Philadelphia: Department of history, University of Pennsylvania, PA, 1907), 16–19, and Appendix II, 326–28.

[40] *Arrow-Odd*, in *Seven Viking Romances*, trans. Hermann Pálsson and Paul Edwards (Harmondsworth: Penguin, 1985), 72.

[41] Hans-Hugo Steinhoff, "Contra caducum morbum," in *Verfasserlexikon*, vol.2 (1980), cols. 8–9; Th. von Grienberger, "Althochdeutsche Texterklärungen," *PBB* 45 (1921): 212–15; Georg Baesecke, "Contra caducum morbum," *PBB* 62 (1938): 456–60.

[42] Adolf Noreen, *Altisländische und Altnorwegische Grammatik*, Altnordische Grammatik, 1, 3rd rev. ed. (Halle: M. Niemeyer, 1903), §§ 108,1; 289,3. The loss of Germanic *w* in Oðinn is dated by Noreen to the pre-literary period (§ 227,1).

[43] Joseph Bosworth and T. Northcote Toller, *An Anglo-Saxon Dictionary* (Oxford: Oxford UP, 1964), 1076; Supplement, 730–31.

[44] The problem of the scribe's failure to recognise the name *Thor* was raised by John Gillingham at the Institute of Historical Research's Earlier Medieval Seminar.

[45] Eric Stanley, "Alliterative Ornament," 203–04; 213.

[46] Joseph B. Wilson, "A Conjecture on the Opening of the Second Merseburg Charm," in *Studies in German in Memory of Andrew Louis*, ed. James E. Copeland and Robert Ludwig Kahn, Rice University Studies, vol. 55, no. 3 (Houston, TX: William March Rice University, 1969), 241–50.

[47] Elliott, *Runes. An Introduction*, fig. 29.

[48] Gerhard Eis, "Deutung des ersten Merseburger Zauberspruchs," *FuF* 32 (1958): 27–39; repr. in Eis, *Altdeutsche Zaubersprüche* (Berlin: W. de Gruyter, 1964), 58–66.

[49] Storms, *Anglo-Saxon Magic*, § 33; cf. Friedrich Pfister, *Deutsches Volkstum in Glauben und Aberglauben* (Berlin and Leipzig: W. de Gruyter, 1936), 67.

[50] Cf. *Handbook*, 74. In discussion, David McLintock has pointed out that the diacritic seems to be without parallel in Anglo-Saxon scribal practice.

[51] *Handbook*, 116.

[52] Sigmund Feist, "Runen und Zauberwesen im germanischen Altertum," *Arkiv för nordisk Filologi* 35 (1919): 243–87: "Der ursprünglich denkende Mensch aller Völker und Zeiten erblickt magische Wirkungsmöglichkeiten und Zusammenhänge, die der nüchternen Objektivität der höher Gebildeten vollkommen unverständlich sind." (284).

[53] Lucien Musset, *Introduction à la runologie*, Bibliothèque de la philologie germanique, 20 (Paris: Aubier-Montaigne, 1965), 142; Ray Page, "Anglo-Saxon Runes and Magic," *Journal of the British Archaeological Association*, 3rd series, 27 (1964–65): 14–31.

[54] Page, "Anglo-Saxon Runes and Magic," 30; 25.

[55] Storms, *Anglo-Saxon Magic*, 270; cf. Page, "Anglo-Saxon Runes and Magic," 25.

[56] See chapter 4 above.

[57] See J. K. Bostock, "H," *MLR* 48 (1953): 328.

[58] See Wolfgang Krause and Herbert Jankuhn, *Die Runeninschriften im älteren Futhark*, Abhandlungen der Akademie der Wissenschaften in Göttingen. Philologisch-historische Klasse, Dritte Folge, Nr. 65 (Göttingen, 1966): 56; 147; 258–59; Stephen E. Flowers, *Runes and Magic. Magical Formulaic Elements in the Older Runic Tradition*, American University Studies Series, I: Germanic Languages and Literature, vol. 53 (New York: Peter Lang, 1986), 231; 245; 256; 276.

[59] *The Exeter Book of Old English Poetry, with introductory chapters by R. W. Chambers, Max Förster and Robin Flower* (Exeter: P. Lund, Humphries & co., 1933), fols. 106ᵇ, 123ᵇ, 125ᵃ.

[60] Helmut Arntz, *Handbuch der Runenkunde* (Halle/Saale: M. Niemeyer, 1944), 203–04; Elliott, *Runes*, 55.

[61] Hans-Hugo Steinhoff, "Merseburger Zaubersprüche," in *Verfasserlexikon*, vol. 6 (1987), col. 413: "die Einführung Phols wäre funktionslos, wenn es nicht um sein Pferd ginge."

[62] Jean Paul Allard and Jean Haudry, "Du Second Charme de Mersebourg au Viatique de Weingarten," *Études Indo-Européennes* 14 (1985): 33–53 (51).

[63] Snorri Sturluson, *Edda: Prologue and Gylfaginning*, ed. Anthony Faulkes (Oxford & New York: Clarendon Press; Oxford UP, 1982), 17; Snorri Sturluson, *Edda*, trans. Anthony Faulkes (London & Melbourne: Dent, 1987), 17–18; *Grímnismál*, strophes 29–30, *Edda*, ed. Neckel/ Kuhn, 63; *The Poetic Edda*, trans. Larrington, 56.

[64] "Der verrenkte Fuß hat das Fohlen mit der magischen Kraft des Stabreims herbeigerufen und zäh weiter festgehalten . . . das altgermanische Wort *folon* bedeutet nicht, wie unser 'Fohlen' ein noch nicht erwachsenes, sondern das junge, auch das reitfähige und schon gerittene Pferd. Bis zum zweijährigen 'Fohlen' wird im Hunnenschlachtliede das Reiterheer aufgeboten." (Felix Genzmer, "Da signed Krist — thû biguol'en Wuodan," 67).

[65] Ibid., 42; cf. *Lokasenna*, str. 37.

[66] Genzmer, "Da signed Krist," 43, referring to *Kálfsvisa*, str. 1, *Den Norsk-Islandske Skjaldedigtning* ed. Finnur Jónsson, 4 vols (Copenhagen and Christiania: Gyldendal, 1908) A, I, 650.

[67] Gustav Neckel, *Die Überlieferungen vom Gotte Balder*, 243–45.

[68] *Edda*, ed. Faulkes, 25, 29; trans. Faulkes, 29, 31.

[69] See Karl-Heinz Borck, "Zur Bedeutung der Wörter *holz, wald, forst* und *witu* im Althochdeutschen," in *Festschrift für Jost Trier zu seinem 60. Geburtstag am 15. Dezember 1954*, ed. Benno von Wiese and Karl Heinz Borck (Meisenheim/Glan: Westkulturverlag, 1954), 456–76 (especially 464–65).

[70] David Dalby, *Lexicon of the Medieval German Hunt* (Berlin: W. de Gruyter, 1965), 92–93.

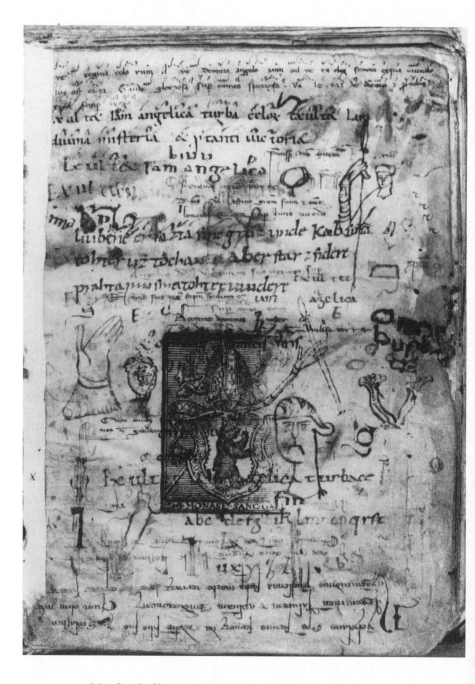

11: St. Gall, Cod. 30, fol. 1. The St. Gall Lampoon.

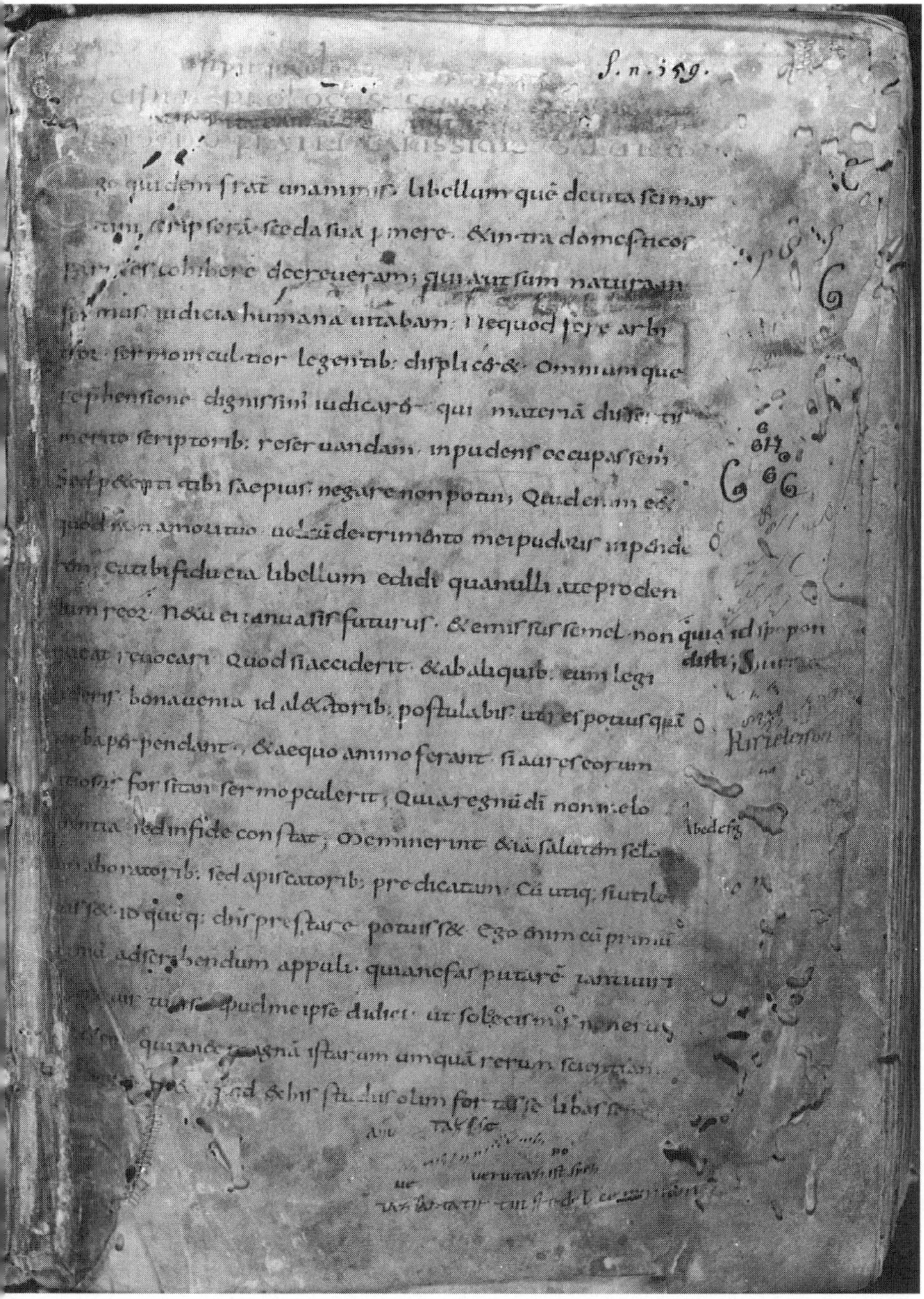

12: St. Gall, Cod. 105, fol. 1. St. Gall Spottverse.

13: *Brussels, Bibliothèque Royale de Belgique, MS. 8862, fol. 15ᵛ.*
Hirsch und Hinde.

6: The Beginnings of the German Lyric[1]

Come write me down, ye powers above,
the man that first created love

— from a folksong
sung by the Coppers of Rottingdean, Sussex

PARADOXICALLY, the beginnings of the German lyric are better attested by indirect than by direct evidence. The surviving corpus is tiny; this despite the wealth of generic terminology, of references and allusions, which scholarship has gleaned from the glosses, the legislation of the Carolingian Church and its missionary literature, and from later, Middle High German sources. For Gustav Ehrismann the reason for this is clear: the OHG period was one of transition, forming a bridge between a pre-literary and a literary culture. The typology constructed by Ehrismann identifies an extraordinarily wide range of lyric genres: songs were sung at weddings, at burials, to invoke magic, at sea, in battle, to accompany dances.[2] As is clear from the wealth of parallels Ehrismann adduces from other Germanic languages, in particular Old Norse and Anglo-Saxon, the terms preserved in the OHG glosses are no mere *ad hoc* formulations.[3]

The most controversial generic term, attested both in the glosses and in Charlemagne's capitulary of 789, is *uuinileot*. Ehrismann devotes a whole section to the discussion of the term, and it has been the subject of several studies.[4] It is worthy of note that there are two sections of the capitulary of 789 which are concerned with nuns or abbesses:

De monasteriis minutis ubi nonnanes sine regula sedent, volumus ut in unum locum congregatio fiat regularis, et episcopus praevideat ubi fieri possint. Et ut nulla abbatissa foras monasterio exire non praesumat sine nostra iussione nec sibi subditas facere permittat; et earum claustra sint bene fermata, et nullatenus ibi winileodos scribere vel mittere praesumant: et de pallore earum propter sanguinis minuationem.[5]

[As for small monasteries where nuns reside without a rule, we desire that a congregation according to the rule be held in one place, and that the bishop should provide a place where these meetings may occur be possible. And that no abbess presume to go outside the doors of the monastery without our permission, nor permit those subject to her to do so; and that their cloisters be well secured, and that they by no means presume to write or send *winileodos*. . . .]

The forbidding of the writing or sending of *winileodos* is thus built into a more general prohibition limiting nuns to their own closed world. A further prohibition (paragraph 31) relates to other secular entertainments:

> Ut episcopi et abbates et abbatissae cupplas canum non habeant nec falcones nec accipitres nec ioculatores.

[That the bishops, abbots and abbessess shall have neither couples of dogs, nor falcons, nor hawks, nor gleemen.]

Taking the two prohibitions together, the probability is that the *winileodos* constituted a secular pastime, which, like hunting and the employment of minstrels, was deemed inappropriate for those in holy orders. The glosses equate *winileodos* with *barbara carmina* or *plebeios psalmos, cantica rustica et inepta*.[6] Despite compounds such as *huorwiniscaft* [whorish amours], or the admission in the Bamberg Confession: "Ich bin sculdig . . . in huorlieden" [I am guilty of (singing) whores' songs,] there has been considerable reluctance to view *winileodos* in an erotic light.[7] *Preislieder*, songs in praise of a secular ruler such as the *Ludwigslied*, are one possibility with which scholars have toyed; de Smet thought the *winileodos* might be songs of greeting or benediction addressed to relatives or friends.[8] It seems inherently unlikely that Charlemagne's prohibition should relate to songs of such harmless, albeit secular content.

It was above all poetry of erotic content which was regarded as dangerous to the peace of mind of nuns in the early Middle Ages. Two MHG references to *wineliedel*, in the lyrics of the thirteenth-century poet Neidhart von Reuental, confirm the erotic connotation. Beyschlag interprets the term as alluding to a sub-literary genre of erotic and provocative nature.[9] This emerges clearly from Neidhart's *Winterlied* 34, in which he proclaims his jealousy of a peasant who surpasses him in dancing, singing, and above all in picking roses, *deflorare*, the central motif of the pastourelle:

> Der mir hie bevor in mînen anger wuot
> und dar inne rôsen zeinem kranze brach
> unde in hôher wîse sîniu wineliedel sanc,
> der beswârte nie sô sêre mir den muot
> als ein dinc, daz ich von Willekinde sach.
> do'r den krumben reien an ir wîzen hende spranc,
> dô swanc er den vuoz,
> des mîn vreude swinden muoz.
> er und Gätzeman gewinnet nimmer mînen gruoz.
>
>   WL 34, VI.

[He who previously waded in my meadow, / picking roses there for a garland / and sang in high melody his *wineliedel* — / he never depressed me as much / as one thing I saw Willekind doing, / when he danced the crooked circle with her white hand in his; / he swang his foot, / causing my happiness to disappear. / He and Gätzeman will never again gain my greeting.]

Two obvious interconnected reasons suggest themselves for the slender corpus of lyrics that survives from the OHG period: firstly, the primarily oral nature of popular culture, and secondly the inimical attitude of the Carolingian Church to this culture, as exemplified by Charlemagne's capitulary. The deliberations that follow will focus upon the surviving traces of the love-lyric, and the relationship between the survivals and the prohibitions of the Church. The love-lyrics may be seen as playing an exemplary role in the conflict between religious and secular culture in the early Middle Ages.

Otfrid von Weißenburg, in the second of the three dedications which preface his *Liber Evangeliorum*, the Latin dedication *Ad Liutbertum*, to Liutbert, Archbishop of Mainz, concerns himself with the problem of the relationship between women and popular culture. He distinguishes between three kinds of poetry: the vernacular *sonus inutilium rerum* of his lay contemporaries which offends the ears of the virtuous; the classical literature of *gentilium vates*; and his own poetic endeavours, the translation of the gospel into German. It is only the first of these three categories at which he directs his opprobrium. He has been inspired by one woman in particular, the estimable *matrona* Judith, who, like his fellow-brothers, objects to the disturbing effect of the *laicorum cantus . . . obscenus*. Medieval Latin *obscenus* has a wide semantic range, and may be no more specific than a general pejorative here, as is suggested by Gisela Vollmann-Profe's translation: "das anstößige Gesinge der Laien."[10]

Otfrid's invective belongs to what Michael Richter describes as "a common vocabulary of condemnation."[11] Richter's studies of the condemnations of the ninth century, in particular of the synod of 813, lead to him the conclusion: "There is no indication that the performance of barbarian culture was unusually prominent in the period under discussion. What was unusual was the effort to reduce its accustomed place in society. There are good indications that it was difficult to combat this culture because it was so firmly established, because it was so widely shared, because it was tradition." Obviously, any absolute quantification of oral culture is out of the question. The vocabulary of invective does, however, permit a certain degree of qualitative analysis. At the Mainz council of 813 clerics and monks are told to abstain from secular dealings in similar wording to the *winileodos* capitulary. They are forbidden gambling, gluttony and drunkenness, forbidden to hunt with dogs and birds, and must not "turpis verbi vel facti ioculatorem esse" [be a jester of disgraceful word or deed; *MGH Concil.* II, I, p. 264]. Two aspects of "barbarian" culture are identified here: lascivious deeds and words. The latter are described as *carmina, cantilenae, cantica*, often occurring in the same context as *ioca*, with mimic performance, but by no means always. The adjectives which occur most frequently are *obscenus* and *turpis*: "et histrionum sive scurronum et turpium seu obscenorum iocorum insolentiam non solo ipsi respuant, verum etiam fidelibibus respuenda percenseant" [and not only should they themselves spit out the insolence of actors and jesters and shameful filthy jokes, but should consider them to be rejected by the faithful; *MGH Concil.* II, I, 276]. Richter traces these terms back to late antiquity, but the vocabulary is constantly varied in a manner that suggests contemporary, Carolingian interest, a concern with an everyday problem. Jonas of Orleans (*c.* 820) describes banquets graced with "histrionum saltatione, et obscena jocatione, et turpiloquiis, et scurrilitatibus" [the dancing of actors, and obscene joking, and lewd talk, and coarse buffoonery; *PL* 106, I,20, col. 164]. A Bavarian capitulary of *c.* 800 expressly forbids "inlecebroso cantico" [seductive songs; *MGH Capit.* 112, c. 34].[12] Similarly, a letter directed by the bishops to Louis the Pious warns against "obscenis turpibusque canticis" (*MGH, Capit.* II, p.45). All in all, a genre of "dirty" or "lecherous" songs does seem to emerge.

That such warnings bore fruit is borne out not merely *ex vacuo.* The almost total absence of early vernacular lyric in written record is suggestive, but not in itself conclusive. The hostile attitude of the Church also took the form of censorship. We can see this at work in the manuscript of the *Carmina Canta-brigiensia,* written towards the end of the OHG period. In his preface to the recent edition of the *Cambridge Songs,* Jan Ziolkowski offers an unusual picture of the early medieval censor at work. Saint Majolus, abbot of Cluny 964–994, is accorded high praise by his biographer, Syrus of Cluny, because he erased with a sharp knife matter he considered superfluous, as if it were deadly poison.[13] Such censorship is directed at secular material in general, but in particular at writings concerned with love:

> quae vero superflua, de amore scilicet rerumque saecularium cura, haec quasi venenata radebat et mortifera, his calvitium inducebat, haec unguium more ferro acutissimo desecabat.

> [Those which were unnecessary — that is to say, which were about love and concern for secular matters — he erased as if they were poisoned and lethal; he reduced them to smooth baldness and scratched them away with a very sharp metal tool, in the manner of fingernails.]

The manuscript of the Cambridge Songs (Cambridge University Library, Gg. v. 35) contains texts of German origin, written down by an English hand of the middle of the eleventh century; from the twelfth century onwards, if not before, the manuscript was in Canterbury. The section containing the songs includes both secular and religious lyrics. The German emperors from 930 to 1050 are the subject of no less than seven songs,[14] one of these being the macaronic, Latin-OHG *De Heinrico* (CC 19).

The Cambridge Songs are of interest not merely because some of them have been censored, but also because they attest a lively interest in nuns. *De Heinrico* is followed by *Est unus locus Homburh dictus* (CC 20), a Latin comic narrative set in Thuringia.[15] With somewhat crude humour this *Schwank* describes how a wolf attacks a pregnant ass belonging to the convent, causing the nuns to panic. *Emicat o quanta pietate Cecilia sancta* (CC 26), on the other hand, describes the exemplary life of the nuns in the convent of St Cecilia in Cologne. The two lyrics that follow on fols. 438^{v}–39^{r} form a stark contrast, and attracted the attention of the medieval censor. Four of the six love-lyrics in the manuscript have been mutilated by his knife. Presumably this censorship took place in England, though in the nature of things we cannot determine at what date. The first two songs are *Iam dulcis amica* (CC 27) and *Suavissima nunna* (CC 28). The latter is a macaronic lyric with a nun as the object of a male's passion; its opening, a seduction attempt set in a *locus amoenus*, suggests at least an affinity with the genre of the pastourelle.[16] William Paden also regards *Iam dulcis amica*, which is clearly influenced by the Song of Songs, as an antecedent of the medieval pastourelle.[17] In the latter instance the erasures seem to vary in intensity. The right-hand column, which contains the last four strophes of the lyric, has suffered most from the knife. These strophes describe the erotic climax of the song, and it has been possible to reconstruct them by drawing upon the parallel versions in the Vienna and Paris manuscripts. Immediately beneath *Iam dulcis amica* is to be found the beginning of *Suavissima nunna*; here the legibility of the text has been further affected by its being treated with reagents.

Of the four love-lyrics it is CC 39 which has suffered most from the knife. The introductory majuscule *V* is perhaps, in the light of the opening of *Iam dulcis amica* and *Veni dilectissime* (CC 49), to be reconstructed as the initial letter of *veni* or *venite* [come]. The first word of the second line ends in *nna*, and a vertical stroke is clearly recognisable before these letters. Strecker was of the view that there was not sufficient space for the word *nunna*,[18] but elsewhere on the same leaf the letters beneath the majuscule at the beginning of a strophe are written very close together. The beginning of the second strophe would seem to contain the central motif of the pastourelle, *deflorare*. Ziolkowski reads:

Nosti flores <carpere>, serta pulchra texere

[You can pick flowers, plait beautiful garlands][19]

The last word in the penultimate line is *studium*. The subject of the lyric would appear to be the conflict between the *vita contemplativa* and *amor*, as in *Suavissima nunna*, and in the penultimate strophe of the Vienna version of *Iam dulcis amica*:

Karissima, noli tardare,
studeamus nos nunc amare!
Sine te non potero vivere;
iam decet amorem perficere.

[Dearest, do not delay! / Let us now apply ourselves to love! / Without you I cannot live; / It beseems us now to consummate our love.]

The song that follows, set in the springtime, *Levis exsurgit zephirus* (CC 40), contains no amorous encounter and was therefore safe from the censor's knife. Only in the last half-line is there a hint of an unfulfilled love-relationship: "nam mea languet anima" [for my heart is ailing].

The censor also disregarded *O admirabile Veneris idolum* (CC 48), a highly controversial lyric which has attracted much critical attention.[20] The chief bone of contention is whether this is a lyric of homosexual or heterosexual love. Perhaps it was precisely the oblique nature of the lyric, the uncertainty as to who is being apostrophised by whom, which spared it from the censor's knife. The eroticism is heavily veiled in classical allusions, less apparent in the other lyrics. The last line reads: "ut cerua rugio cum fugit hinnulus." [I cry out like a hind when a fawn takes flight]. Here too, the Song of Songs may have influenced the imagery: "Be, my Beloved, / like a gazelle, / a young stag, / on the mountains of the covenant." (2. 8).[21] The same anthropomorphic image is, however, also to be found in the OHG lyric *Hirsch und Hinde*, to be discussed below, which has no evident biblical influence.

The final poem in the collection, CC 49, has been viciously erased. Ziolkowski attempts the following partial reconstruction:

> Ven<i>, d<ilectissim>e,
> et a et o,
> gratam me <in>uisere,
> et a et o et a et o!
> in languore pereo.
> <et a> et <o> —
> <uenerem de>sidero,
> <et a et o et a> et o!. . .
> Veni . . . 1 . . . h..
> <et a> *et* <o>. . . . . .
> Si cum clave veneris,
> <et a et o>,
> <mo>x intrare poteris,
> et a et o et a et o!

[Come, dearest love, / with ah! and oh! / to visit me — I will please you./ with ah! and oh! and ah! and oh! / I am dying with desire, / with ah! and oh! / How I long for love! / with ah! and oh! and ah! and oh! / Come . . . / with ah! and oh! . . . / If you come with the key, / with ah! and oh! / You will soon be able to enter, / with ah! and oh! and ah! and oh!]

The lyric is evidently spoken by the female persona, and the image of the key in the final lines points forward over a century and more to the Tegernsee love-letter (Clm. 19411, fol. 114ᵛ), which ends with the lyric *Du bist mîn, ich bin dîn*. Until 1977 this was the first lyric in the standard anthology of MHG love-poetry, *Des Minnesangs Frühling*.

> Du pist min ih bin din.
> des solt du gewis sin.
> du bist beslossen
> in minem herzen.
> verlorn ist daz sluzzellin.
> du mŏst och immer dar inne sin.

[You are mine, I am yours. / Of that you may be certain. / You are locked / in my heart: / the little key is lost, / and you must remain therein forever.]

The Tegernsee manuscript dates from the third quarter of the twelfth century, but the relationship between this and the earliest phase of MHG love-lyric is problematic. Kühnel's study has questioned whether *Du bist mîn* may rightly be included in an anthology of *Minnesang*.[22] Somewhat polemically he concludes that the German lines in the letter do not amount to an independent poem, whether it be a folksong quoted by the female author to conclude a letter from a nun, or a woman's-voice lyric composed by her in *ad hoc* fashion. The content, he argues, reflects in summary that of the preceding, the prose part of the letter; in formal terms the lines constitute, in his view, rhymed prose.[23]

The Tegernsee love-lyric differs from the majority of lyrics in *Des Minnesangs Frühling* in that it quite clearly stems from a monastic context. The vexed question of whether the lines are rhymed prose need not concern us here. More significant is that these lines are voiced by a nun. The consensus, as expressed by Kühnel, is that the Tegernsee letters are a fictitious corres-pondence between a monk and a nun, that the woman's voice is, as would seem to obtain for all the other "Frauenstrophen" in the early phase of *Minnesang*, a figment of the male imagination.

Kühnel's argument that the Tegernsee letters are no more than rhetorical exercises is not altogether convincing. The degree of reality that lies behind the letters can scarcely be determined with certainty. The manuscript records a correspondence between a monk and a nun in a single hand. In the Cambridge Songs the feelings attributed to a nun would appear to have their origin in the male psyche, and this may be the case in the Tegernsee letters too. On the other hand, the Latin *Carmina Ratisponensia* of the early twelfth century would appear to be a record of a genuine correspondence between male tutors and their female pupils in a nunnery.[24] The case history of Abelard and Heloise will always colour the medievalist's view of such correspondence. Looking backwards to the ninth century, Charlemagne's capitulary directs itself against the possibility that real nuns might entertain authentic feelings of such an amorous nature. The employment of the OHG term *winileot* in the capitulary does not, of course, necessarily imply that such lyrics were in the vernacular tongue.[25]

Walther von der Vogelweide (*fl. c.* 1190–c. 1230) laments that women are incapable of drawing proper distinctions between men on a moral basis.[26] The nun in the Tegernsee letters, prompted by the advice of her monastic *amicus*, is in no such dilemma. Knights, *milites*, are for her no fitting sex-objects — they are *portenta*, monsters,[27] anticipating the *ungetan*, the monster who de-flowers the maiden in the macaronic pastourelle *Ich was ein chint so wolgetan* (*Carmina Burana* 185).[28] Men in general are to be treated with caution, and in particular their spears (again anticipating *CB* 185, *cuspide erecta.*) Monks, however, present far less danger than the *milites*. The oldest MHG love-lyric is thus directed by a nun (however fictitious) at a monk (however fictitious). The censorship prescribed by the Carolingian capitulary, seen at work in the manuscript of the Cambridge Songs, collapses in Tegernsee in the third quarter of the twelfth century.

But did anything slip through the net in the OHG period? We may disre-gard here the late evidence of the Kölbigk dance-song, which can only be re-constructed tentatively from eleventh-century Latin annals and even later sources,[29] and the occurrence of isolated German words suggestive of love-lyric in the late eleventh-century *Ruodlieb*. The Cambridge Songs apart, there are only three survivals which may be regarded, however loosely, as belonging to the category of the love-lyric. In an essay that appeared in 1992, Ute Schwab published facsimiles of all three of these survivals, enabling scholars to take a new look at the texts in their codical context.[30] All three texts occur with neumes attached to them, or at least in their vicinity.

The *Liubene* lines, the St Gall Lampoon (St. Gall, Cod. 30; illustration 11), have only a tangential claim to consideration in the context of the love-lyric:

> liubene ersazta sine gruz
> unde kab sina tohter uz
> to cham aber starzfidere
> prahta imo sina tohter uuidere.[31]

[Liubene brewed his root-beer / and gave away his daughter; / Starzfidere came back again, / returned to him his daughter.]

The name *starzfidere* [tail-feather] may have obscene connotations; perhaps its bearer was promiscuous, perhaps he was impotent. The lampoon apparently refers to a marriage-rite, but the marriage has clearly gone wrong. One can best imagine it as being performed on a stag-night (although the latter term, if not the occasion, would appear to be a nineteenth-century American invention). The lack of parallels, be it in legal texts or literature, makes the lyric extremely difficult to interpret. The mode of transmission cannot help here, as this first, originally blank leaf of the manuscript may best be described as a dog's dinner, a hodge-podge of scribblings, drawings and neumed fragments. The first line of the lampoon has neumes written above it, in a hand as crude as the script itself. Perhaps, as later in the *Codex Buranus* and in the Kremsmünster Walther von der Vogelweide manuscript (Codex Cremifanensis 127), the neumes served as an aide-mémoire for the performance of the whole song. The hand would seem to date from *c*. 900. If, as seems likely, the neumes are contemporary, then this must be the oldest German secular lyric to survive together with a melody, although the neumes are no less difficult to interpret than the text.

On the first leaf of St. Gall, Cod. 105, in the bottom margin (illustration 12), two lines of OHG are written in Alemannic dialect of the tenth century:

ue ueru taz.ist.spiz
taz santa tir tin fredel ce minnon[32]

[*ue ueru* that is [a] spear / your beloved sent you it as a love-gift]

Here too there is little context to help the interpreter. Above the first line there are again neumes, but the distance between the cluster of notes and the words makes it difficult to say with certainty that the neumes relate to the text. Moreover, the neumes do not extend to the end of the first line. It is, however, possible that the melisma indicated in the neumes was part of the melody for the lines, which, while they do not rhyme, have a marked trochaic rhythm. In the right-hand margin of the same leaf there is a neumed *Kirieleison*. Text and music were again clearly intimately linked in the minds of the scribes.

The meaning of *ueru* has led to some debate. Sonderegger asks whether the first *ue* means "alas," or is a failed attempt to write the complete word that follows.[33] If the neumes do relate to the text, then the repetition of the first syllable might relate to the melisma. Sonderegger interprets *ueru* as the first person present indicative of the OHG weak verb *we(r)ren* [I forbid, I defend]. Haubrichs, on the other hand, sees it as a Romance word.[34] The link with *spiz* supports this interpretation. Both medieval Latin *ueru* and OHG *spiz* are employed to refer to a wide range of pointed objects. *ueru* can mean "a spike to fasten a statue" or "an obelus"; "a spit for roasting meat," or "the spit-like point of a weapon," or even "a spiked railing."[35] OHG *spiz* can denote "(Brat)spieß; Häkchen, Schrägstrich; oberes Ende, Spitze, Dorn, Horn, Palisade; Anhöhe, Gipfel."[36] It would appear that the lines are a kind of extended gloss, developed into an erotic play on words.

Given such limited context as we have, an originally blank area of parchment employed for scribal dabblings, perhaps the most likely interpretation is that both the Latin and OHG words refer to an obelus, a scribal mark indicating "a spurious, corrupt or doubtful word."[37] The scribe's sense of humour works from a gloss to an erotic pun in rhythmic prose.

The person who has given the love-gift, the *fredel* in the second line, must be male.[38] Both *fredel* and *minnon* anticipate the vocabulary of early *Minnesang*, some two centuries later. The recipient of the gift is presumably female, there being no obvious basis for a homoerotic interpretation. Perhaps the lines owe their origin to an exchange between two nuns, two literate females? Or the female recipient may be a figment of a male scribe's imagination. Wolfgang Meid, in an essay on Gaulish inscriptions, suggests that the lines might originally have been carved on a pointed object such as a spinning whorl, which served to bear a lover's message to his girl-friend.[39] In the discussion that followed when this essay was presented as a paper in Bavaria, female participants suggested that *spiz* might refer to a dildo.

Perhaps the introduction of a discourse deriving from a different discipline may further our understanding. *minnon* implies that the pointed object is a love-token. In psycho-analytical theory love-tokens belong to the sphere of fetishism: "Perhaps the most frequent normal fetishistic phenomenon of adulthood is the love-token, or memento, which enhances the courtship love-play and may find its place as a preferred, but not a necessary, contribution to the foreplay of intercourse."[40] The fetishistic object, when fetishism takes the form of a perversion, "may be some other body part, or some article of clothing, or even a seemingly impersonal object. In this latter instance however, the fetish is found to be a symbolic substitute for a body part."[41]

It comes as no great historiographic surprise that there is a school of thought which claims that "fetishism, as we understand it today, seems to have first appeared in Europe in the eighteenth century and then *crystallized* as a distinct sexual phenomenon in the second half of the nineteenth century."[42] Similar statements are frequently made — particularly by early modern historians — with regard to other aspects of *mentalité*, such as the sense of individual personality, the feeling for nature, scepticism, or the concept of childhood.[43] As Valerie Steele points out, fetishism is also to be observed in nonhuman primates.[44] It would be churlish to deny the possibility of its occurrence amongst medieval human primates.

The last part of this essay is concerned with the lines known as *Hirsch und Hinde*, written in a hand of the late tenth century, in the upper margin of fol. 15^v of MS. 8862 of the Bibliothèque Royale de Belgique in Brussels (illustration 13). These lines, too, may originate from the Bodensee area; the neumes point in that direction, and the phonology does not contradict the suggestion of Alemannic origin. Ute Schwab is rightly of the view that the three lines of this lyric are no fragment. The early phases of the lyric in many languages tend to be characterised by such minimalist survivals.[45] The manuscript transmission differs, however, from that of the two documents preserved in St Gall. The OHG text is, again, preserved in a margin and accorded neumes, but the text would appear to be in a direct relationship to a Latin song. The OHG text is written as a single line (a subscript point indicating erasure of the first *e* in *Hierez*):

Hierez run&a hintun in daz ora uildu noh hinta.

It is readily divisible into three lines of verse, with assonance rather than rhyme, and marked alliteration:

> Hirez runeta
> hintun in daz ora:
> uildu noh hinta?

[The hart whispered / into the hind's ear: / d'you want more, hind?]

A neumed OHG line prefaces a Latin line, which comprises the first strophe of the song of St. Peter, *Solve lingua moras*. The melody assigned to the OHG lines is in all essentials identical with that of the Latin strophe, only diverging because of the differing number of syllables at the end of the first line, and again in the neumes for the last two words. The musicologist David Hiley writes: "*Solve lingua moras* is undoubtedly strophic as far as the music is concerned. The small variations from strophe to strophe are unexceptional. And it is clear enough that the same basic melody (with slight adjustments, also unexceptional) is intended for *hirez runeta*."[46]

The hand of *Hirsch und Hinde* is identical with that of *Solve lingua moras*, but the content has no evident point of contact. What was the scribe's motivation? Why did s/he incorporate such an evidently secular lyric into a religious context? Was it purely on the basis of a melodic resemblance? Ute Schwab attempts to solve the problem by means of a complex, wide-ranging argument. Adducing the Kölbigk dance-song and the Abbots Bromley Horn Dance, she attempts to prove that *Hirsch und Hinde* is the first German *Reigenlied*, round-dance or carol. She suggests that an originally erotic lyric lost its erotic import and became incorporated into a song of St. Peter, which may also have been accompanied by a dance. Thus *wildu noh?* [D'you want more?] — or, emended, *wildu mih?*[47] [D'you want me?] — becomes an invitation to the dance, or to continue dancing, rather than an expression of sexual insatiability, be it on the female or male part.[48]

Schwab adduces more than sufficient evidence to demonstrate that dances and rites associated with stags took place in the Middle Ages. *runeta* points, however, to a furtive proceeding rather than an open invitation to a dance. OHG *runen* generally means "to whisper in secret,"[49] and is often associated with magic, as in the charm *Ad equum erręhet* (Braune XXXI, 7). The healing magician is advised by Our Lord:

> "Nu ziuhez da bi fiere,
> tu rune imo in daz ora,
> drit ez an den cesewen fuoz:
> so wirt imo des erręheten buoz."

["Lead it over there by the fire, / whisper into its ear, / step on its right foot / — that way it will be cured of the sprain."][50]

In the case of *Hirsch und Hinde*, the whispering is most likely to be that of lover to lover, as is suggested by the eleventh-century marginalium adduced as a parallel by Bischoff: "Columba columbae talia immurmuravit" [The dove murmured such things to the dove].[51]

Murmurare would be the natural sound made by male to female dove. Stags, however, are not noted for whispering; it is at this point that the anthropomorphic metaphor which is the basis of *Hirsch und Hinde* breaks down. The anthropomorphic concept, the equation of man and deer, informs the many parallels adduced by Schwab. The concept can take on various forms, relating to divergent spheres of life, be it religion, magic, or sex.

Schwab points to the important role played by the stag in both Christian and pagan religions. In Celtic religion, the god Cernunnos is only once attested by name, in the context of the depiction on the monument of the Nautae Parisiaci of the head and shoulders of a bearded man who has the ears and antlers of a stag. The statue dates from the time of the Emperor Tiberius (A.D. 14–37), but the link with the horned god in the cave drawing of Val Camonica, dating perhaps from the fifth century B.C., seems undeniable.[52]

As Schwab's study shows, the motif informing *Hirsch und Hinde* invites the interpreter to digress, to embark upon excursus, and what follows is a similar hunt. There will be no attempt here at an exhaustive catalogue of stag metaphors. The bias is towards such employment of the metaphor as may support an erotic interpretation of *Hirsch und Hinde*.

1. A first parallel lies halfway between magic and eroticism. It is to be found in the often enigmatic *Vita Merlini* of Geoffrey of Monmouth, a Latin poem which clearly draws upon Celtic sources.[53] The hermit and seer Merlin, living in isolation in the forest, sees that his wife Guendolena has been promised to another man at the court of the Cumbrian king Rodarch. Mounted on a stag, he rides to the wedding. Once there he wrenches off the stag's antlers and throws them at the bridegroom's head, killing him instantly. No hind is present here, but the association between the stag and sexual potency is unmistakable.

2. More overtly still, the same imagery is employed in a late medieval Welsh englyn attributed to Dafydd ap Gwilym, *Ceirw'm Ymgydio* (Deer Coupling):

> Doe gwelais cyd â gwialen — o gorn,
>   ac arno naw cangen;
> gŵr balch ag og ar ei ben
> a gwraig foel o'r graig felen.

[Yesterday I saw copulation with a rod of horn, / with nine branches on it; / a proud man with a harrow on his head / and a bald woman from the yellow rock.][54]

3. Hinds as the object of a hunt, with erotic sub-meaning, are to be found in fourteenth-century England, in *Sir Gawain and the Green Knight*. The hunting excursions of Gawayn's host and the attempts at seduction of his hostess, the "gay lady," are subtly interwoven. Stags are exempt from the hunt:

> Thay let the herttes haf the gate, with the hyghe hedes,
> The breme bukkes also with hor brode paumes;
> For the fre lorde hade defende in fermysoun tyme
> That ther schulde no mon meve to the male dere.
>
> (lines 1154–1157)[55]

It is only the female deer which are the object of the hunter:

> The hindes were halden in with 'hay!' and 'war!'
> The does dryven with gret dyn to the depe slades.
>
> (lines 1158–1159)

The narrator explicitly contrasts the fortunes of the two protagonists, Gawain and his host:

> Thus laykes this lorde by lynde-wodes eves,
> And Gawayn the god mon in gay bed lyges.
>
> (lines 1178–1179)

4. The Welsh contemporary of the *Gawain*-poet, Dafydd ap Gwilym, displays a richesse of animal and nature imagery that puts to shame the cliché, still to be found occasionally among historians, that the Middle Ages lacked appreciation of nature. Not even in Stifter, in Thomas Hardy, in D. H. Lawrence, is such an intense sense of the affinity between man and his natural environment to be found. In the poem *Y Carw* (The Roebuck), the lover sends the "sharp-antlered, leaper of the height" as a messenger to his beloved, Dyddgu. The emissary is to bring him back a kiss, his horns and hooves evading the wiles of the "false Jealous One," the *jaloux*. The personnel derives from the European pastourelle and *alba*, but the imagery is Dafydd's own.[56] Here we find only the stag, the vehicle of male eroticism, but in *Y Breuddwyd* (A Dream), the poet dreams on:

> Beyond the clearing I perceived
> a white doe — I enjoyed the hunt —
> the pack of greyhounds were in [hot] pursuit
> following her — their excitement was just —

[she] sought the wooded hillside, across an entire ridge,
over two spurs and a ridge,
and back again across the mountain spurs:
[her] course of equal swiftness with a stag,
[but] having been tamed, she came
for my protection, distressed as I was.
[I felt] two naked nostrils: I awoke
a ravenous man — and in the hut I was.[57]

Like Walther von der Vogelweide (L. 94,11), Dafydd goes in search of a crone, a wise woman, to explain his dream to him. Naturally enough, she explains that the white doe is the lady he has loved, who will eventually find her way to him.

A third poem of Dafydd ap Gwilym, *Cyrchu Lleian* (Wooing the Nuns)[58] employs a human rather than an animal messenger, but deserves mention here to remind us of how justified the writer of the Tegernsee love-letters was to warn his *amica*, the nun, of the wiles of the nobility. Dafydd sends his emissary to the convent, seeking to induce a nun, "the chantress from the choir," or even the abbess, to meet him in the wood.

5. Returning to Germany, and to a different genre, the narrative allegory of love, the *Minnerede*, the same imagery is to be found in a poem preserved in a Nuremberg manuscript of the fifteenth century, now in Munich (Cgm. 439). The poem describes how a huntsman falls in love with a hind in the winter:

> In mir selbs Ich do sprach
> Do ich das tier erst an sach
> Das Ich In aller meiner zeit
> In disem lande weit
> Schöner hinden nie het gesehen.
>
> fol. 141a[59]

[I then said to myself / when I first beheld the deer / that in all my life / far and wide in this country / I never beheld a more beautiful hind.]

As Walter Blank observes,[60] the hind is described according to the conventional pattern of a *descriptio* of a beautiful heroine, from her eyes down to her feet. The anthropomorphic model again obtains, and extends to the identification of the male narrator with the stag:

> Mag der hirß auch leitt entpfan
> Nein nein es tar nit hinan
> Des tiers schonheit
> Vertreibet Jm alles sein leit.   142a

[Even if the stag experiences suffering, / No, no, it will have no effect. / The deer's beauty / will drive away all his sorrow.]

The huntsman has no does at his disposal, nor has he laid a trap to catch the hind. Nevertheless he pursues her. The hind in her flight breaks off a twig:

> Das reyß ich aufhub
> Das hefftet Ich auf meinen hudt.
>
> 143a

[I picked up the twig / and fastened it to my hat.]

But the hapless huntsman loses even this token:

> Ein ast sich do pog
> Den hut er mir abzog
> Vnd auch von dem hute mein
> Das hinden reyßlein.
>
> 143b

[An overhanging branch / removed my hat / and with it from my hat / the little twig of the hind.]

The huntsman encounters three allegorical maidens, Fidelity, Repentance and Honour, who afford him some consolation. Next he meets an old man, called True Counsel, who suggests that he should hunt with falcons and greyhounds, and thus endeavour to forget the hind. Such diversions lead to no success, and the huntsman again asks True Counsel for advice. The plot twists in the direction of Oscar Wilde:

> Sit du nit von der hinden magst lan
> So magst du einen guten maler han
> Vnd solt dir das schone wilde
> Lassen malen ein loblich pilde
> Vnd ergetz dich damitte.
>
> 146b

[Since you cannot abandon the hind, / then you may take a good painter, / and shall have the beautiful beast / painted, a goodly picture made of her, / and derive your satisfaction from that.]

The huntsman follows this advice, and this time it proves successful. This enigmatic poem ends in a pious wish:

> So pin ich meines leides beraubt
> Damit entpfilhe Ich die edel hinde
> Maria der himel konigynne
> Die bescher Jr nach Jres hertzen ger
> Vnd behüt sie vor aller schwer.
>
> 147b

[Thus I am deprived of my sorrow, / and herewith I commend the noble hind / to Mary, the Queen of Heaven. / Let her confer her heart's desire upon her / and protect her from all suffering.]

6. The obvious artist to depict such a beautiful hind in fifteenth-century Germany was the Master of the Medieval Housebook, or, as he is sometimes known, the Master of the Amsterdam Cabinet. Two of the "Genre Scenes," taking up two double pages (fols. 22b–23a; 23b–24a), depict a hunt.[61] On the first double page the Master portrays a noble company in pursuit of game. In contrast to *Sir Gawain and the Green Knight*, the target is a single stag, whereas the does seek refuge under the trees. The rear part of the hunting expedition consists of three mounted pairs of lovers, whose concentration on the stag-hunt is less than total. The next leaf of the *Housebook*, in pointed contrast, is concerned with the "Pursuit of Lesser Game." Two sets of lovers have already paired off; other, single women are pursuing menfolk in the rural surrounds of a castle. The left-hand page has at its centre a lady holding a symbolic birdcage in her hand.

7. Hart and hind continued to serve as a source of anthropomorphic erotic imagery into the twentieth century. In 1909 Cecil Sharp collected a song from Robert Kinchin of Ilmington, entitled *The Keeper*, which found its way into school songbooks:

> O the keeper he a shooting goes
> And all amongst his bucks and does
> And O for to shoot at the barren doe
> She's amongst the leaves of the green O [. . .]
>
> The first doe that he shot at he missed
> And the second doe he trimmed he kissed
> And the third ran away in a young man's heart
> She's amongst the leaves of the green O.
>
> The fourth doe then she crossed the plain
> The keeper fetched her back again
> O and he tickled her in a merry vein
> She's amongst the leaves of the green O.
>
> The fifth doe then she crossed the brook
> The keeper fetched her back with his long hook
> And what he done at her you must go and look
> For she's amongst the leaves of the green O.[62]

The last strophe suffered censorship when folksong came to be taught in junior schools, perpetuating a tradition initiated by Sharp's fellow-collector Sabine Baring-Gould. Baring-Gould, anthropologist, novelist, medievalist and

parson, published the song in 1890, but with drastic alterations: "I have been compelled to rewrite most of the song, which in the original is very gross."[63]
8. The English folksong's German counterpart, 'Ein Jäger aus Kurpfalz', suffered a similar fate in German schools, with the omission of the third strophe:

> Wohl zwischen beide Bein',
> da muß der Hirsch geschossen, geschossen sein. . . .[64]

The theme of the erotic hunt is of course universal, by no means restricted to medieval Europe, and the role of the stag and the doe in that broader framework might and no doubt will be further explored. Returning to our starting-point, there remains the question of why a motif of such evident erotic purport came to preface a Latin religious text. The form of the marginalia in the Brussels manuscript is unique in terms of the transmission of OHG texts. The OHG line precedes a Latin line; the sequence of Latin strophes then follows from one margin to the next, from top margin to side margin clockwise, from fols. 15ᵛ–16ʳ, and then continuing in the two margins of fols. 74ᵛ–75ʳ. Clearly the texts must have been copied from one or more older sources. But what did the source(s) look like? It is not necessarily the case that *Hirsch und Hinde* occupied the same position of precedence over the Latin in the source as obtains in the Brussels manuscript. Conceivably the OHG text was a marginalium in the exemplar too, written perhaps above the Latin text in an upper margin by a different hand. The intention of the original scribe may have been to indicate an analogy in the melody. The integration of the OHG text into the seeming unity preserved in the Brussels manuscript may have been the error of a later scribe.

Where the melody is concerned, the possibility of a contrafactum has to be considered. Which tune imitated which? Given our virtually total ignorance of how a vernacular folk melody would have sounded at the time, the easy way out for the scholar is to assume that the tune to the vernacular lyric was based upon that of the Latin religious sequence. The argument is irretrievably circular.

It was a precondition for the writing down of the earliest traces of the German lyric that the scribal context, if not the authorship, was monastic. If only for the sake of symmetry, nuns were for the monastic writer the obvious sex-objects. The Church could not but be aware of this danger. Both explicitly, in the *winileodos* capitulary and similar proclamations, and implicitly, by suppression and censorship, the Church took steps to oppose the recording of love-lyrics. Until the twelfth century such few fish as slipped through the net tended to be written in Latin, rather than in the vernacular. Otfrid's preface *Ad Liutbertum* illustrates the dominant attitude to the vernacular in Carolingian times: only if it served the needs of the Church could the vernacular be tolerated on the written page. The early traces of the lyric are to be ranked with the *Hildebrandslied* and the charms, as fortunate survivals of vernacular texts which lacked the official backing of the Church. Charlemagne's biographer Einhard records Charlemagne's interest in vernacular poetry — difficult as it is to determine the precise nature of what Einhard meant by "barbara et antiquissima carmina." A more characteristic early medieval attitude to vernacular poetry is that of Thegan, the biographer of Charlemagne's son, Louis the Pious: "Poetica carmina gentilia quae in iuventate didicerat, respuit, nec legere, nec audire, nec docere voluit." [He rejected secular poetic songs which he had learned in his youth, and did not want to read, hear or teach them].[65]

Notes

[1] An earlier version of this essay appeared as *"winileodos*? Zu Nonnen, Zensur und den Spuren der althochdeutschen Liebeslyrik," in *Theodisca. Beiträge zur althochdeutschen und altniederdeutschen Sprache und Literatur in der Kultur des frühen Mittelalters: eine internationale Fachtagung in Schönmühl bei Penzberg vom 13. bis zum 17. März 1997*, ed. Wolfgang Haubrichs et al., Ergänzungsbände zum Reallexikon der Germanischen Altertumskunde, 22 (Berlin: W. de Gruyter, 2000), 189–206.

[2] Gustav Ehrismann, *Geschichte der deutschen Literatur bis zum Ausgang des Mittelalters*, vol. 1, 13–62; Wolfgang Haubrichs, *Geschichte der deutschen Literatur von den Anfängen bis zum Beginn der Neuzeit. Band I: Von den Anfängen zum hohen Mittelalter. Teil 1: Die Anfänge: Versuche volkssprachiger Schriftlichkeit im frühen Mittelalter (ca. 700–1050/60)* (Frankfurt am Main & Tübingen: Athenaeum; Niemeyer, 1988), 89–104; the word-field *liod* is discussed by Hans Schwarz, "Ahd. Liod und sein sprachliches Feld," *PBB* (Halle) 75 (1952): 321–68.

[3] Cf. Stefan Sonderegger: "Man wird diese Zeugnisse nicht überschätzen wollen, doch erfolgte ihre volkssprachliche Nennung sicher aus dem Empfinden heraus, es handle sich um Formen dichterischer Gestaltung." — Stefan Sonderegger and Harald Burger, *Kurzer Grundriß der germanischen Philologie bis 1500*, ed. Ludwig Erich Schmitt, vol. 2, *Literaturgeschichte* (Berlin: de Gruyter, 1971), 360.

[4] Cf. P. B. Wessels, "Zur Wesensbestimmung des Winelieds," *Neophilologus* 41 (1957): 19–25; Cornelis Soeteman, "Venus apud Germanos," *Neophilologus* 45 (1961): 45–54; Gilbert de Smet, "Die *winileot* in Karls Edikt von 789," in *Studien zur deutschen Literatur und Sprache des Mittelalters. Festschrift für Hugo Moser zum 65. Geburtstag*, ed. Werner Besch et al. (Berlin: E. Schmidt, 1974), 1–7.

[5] *MGH Legum Sectio II. Capitularia Regum Francorum*, I, 62–64, (§§ 19; 31). The final clause, lacking a verb, must relate to the medicinal bleeding of the nuns, but is incomprehensible as it stands, suggesting faulty copying.

[6] See Soeteman, "Venus apud Germanos," 53.

[7] For example, Soeteman: "Die . . . *winileodos* als regelrechte Liebeslieder zu deuten, fehlt jede sprachliche Berechtigung, synchronisch wie etymologisch." (*loc. cit.*). Have love-songs ever been "regelrecht"?

[8] De Smet, "Die *winileot*," 7.

[9] *Die Lieder Neidharts*, ed. Siegfried Beyschlag (Darmstadt: Wissenschaftliche Buchgesellschaft, 1975), 62,33 and 96,14, and commentary, 758–59.

[10] *Otfrid von Weißenburg: Evangelienbuch*, ed. and trans. Gisela Vollmann-Profe (Stuttgart: Reclam, 1987), 17.

[11] Michael Richter, *The Formation of the Medieval West. Studies in the Oral Culture of the Barbarians* (Dublin: Four Courts Press, 1994), 127; 144–45.

[12] Quotations in this section are as in Richter, *The Formation of the Medieval West*.

[13] *The Cambridge Songs (Carmina Cantabrigiensia)*, ed. Jan M. Ziolkowski, Garland library of medieval literature, Series A, 66 (New York and London: Garland, 1994), xxix; *Vita Sancti Maioli*, 2,4, *PL* 137, 755D.

[14] See Ziolkowski, *The Cambridge Songs*, xxxii.

[15] See *Die Cambridger Lieder*, ed. Karl Strecker, MGH, Scriptora rerum germanicarum in usum scholarum, 40 (Berlin: Weidmann, 1926), 60.

[16] Cyril Edwards, "Von Archilochos zu Walther von der Vogelweide. Zu den Anfängen der Pastourelle in Deutschland," in *Lied im deutschen Mittelalter. Überlieferung, Typen, Gebrauch. Chiemsee-Colloquium 1991*, ed. Cyril Edwards, Ernst Hellgardt and Norbert H. Ott (Tübingen: Niemeyer, 1996), 1–25 (plate at 10–11).

[17] William Doremus Paden, *The Medieval Pastourelle*, Garland library of medieval literature. Series A, vols 34–35 (New York; London: Garland, 1987), I, 8–10.

[18] Strecker, *Die Cambridger Lieder*, 94.

[19] The translations from the Cambridge Songs are those of Ziolkowksi (as note 13).

[20] See Benedikt K. Vollmann, "'O admirabile Veneris idolum' (Carmina Cantabrigiensia 48) — ein Mädchenlied?," in *Festschrift für Paul Klopsch*, ed. Udo Kindermann, Wolfgang Maaz and Fritz Wagner, GAG, 492 (Göppingen: Alfred Kümmerle, 1988), 532–43.

[21] Cf. "Make haste, my beloved, / And be thou like to a roe or to a young hart / Upon the mountains of spices." (Song of Songs, 8. 14); Ziolkowski, *The Cambridge Songs*, 309.

[22] Jürgen Kühnel, *Dû bist mîn, ih bin dîn. Die lateinischen Liebes (und Freundschafts-) Briefe des clm. 19411. Abbildungen, Text und Übersetzung*, GAG, 52 (Göppingen: Alfred Kümmerle, 1977).

[23] Kühnel, *Dû bist mîn*, 32–33.

[24] *Carmina Ratisponensia*, ed. Anke Paravicini, Editiones Heidelbergenses, 20 (Heidelberg: Carl Winter, 1979); see Nikolaus Henkel, "Carmina Ratisponensia," in *Ratisbona sacra: das Bistum Regensburg im Mittelalter*, exhibition catalogue (Munich/Zurich, 1989), 161–62.

[25] Nikolaus Henkel, in correspondence.

[26] *Walther von der Vogelweide. Leich, Lieder, Sangsprüche*, ed. Karl Lachmann, 14th ed., rev. Christoph Cormeau with contributions by Thomas Bein and Horst Brunner (Berlin and New York: de Gruyter, 1996), L. 48, 29ff.

[27] Liebesbrief, IV, 1, 77ff, ed. Kühnel, *Dû bist mîn*, 76.

138THE BEGINNINGS OF THE GERMAN LYRIC

[28] *Carmina Burana. Die Lieder der Benediktbeurer Handschrift. Zweisprachige Ausgabe*, ed. A. Hilka, O. Schumann, B. Bischoff, trans. Carl Fischer and Hugo Kuhn, 3rd ed. (Munich: Deutscher Taschenbuch Verlag), 548–52.

[29] Ehrismann, *Geschichte der deutschen Literatur*, vol. 1, 248–51.

[30] Ute Schwab, "Das althochdeutsche Lied 'Hirsch und Hinde' in seiner lateinischen Umgebung," in *Latein und Volkssprache im deutschen Mittelalter 100–1500*, ed. Nikolaus Henkel and Nigel Palmer (Tübingen: Niemeyer, 1992), 74–122.

[31] Stefan Sonderegger, *Althochdeutsch in St. Gallen. Ergebnisse und Probleme der althochdeutschen Sprachüberlieferung in St. Gallen vom 8. bis ins 12. Jahrhundert* (St. Gall; Sigmaringen: Verlag Osterschweiz; Tan-thorberke-Verlag, 1970), 73.

[32] Sonderegger, *Althochdeutsch*, 75.

[33] Sonderegger, *Althochdeutsch*, 75.

[34] Haubrichs, *Geschichte der deutschen Literatur von den Anfängen bis zum Beginn der Neuzeit*, 96.

[35] Alexander Souter, *A Glossary of Later Latin to 600 A.D.* (Oxford: Clarendon Press, 1949), 440; *Oxford Latin Dictionary*.

[36] Jochen Splett, *Althochdeutsches Wörterbuch: Analyse der Wortfamilienstrukturen des Althochdeutschen, zugleich Grundlegung einer zukünftigen Strukturgeschichte des deutschen Wortschatzes* (Berlin and New York: de Gruyter, 1993); see also John C. Wells, *Althochdeutsches Glossenwörterbuch, einschließlich des von Prof. Dr. Taylor Starck† begonnenen Glossenindexes* (Heidelberg: C. Winter, 1990); Gerhard Köbler, *Wörterbuch des althochdeutschen Sprachschatzes* (Paderborn: F. Schöningh, 1993).

[37] *Shorter Oxford Dictionary*.

[38] An innovative approach is undertaken by Karl A. Wipf, *Althochdeutsche poetische Texte. Althochdeutsch/Neuhochdeutsch* (Stuttgart: Reclam, 1992). Wipf includes the lines in his section on magic (64), and translates: "Ich halte ab, was spitz ist! Dies sandte dir dein Feund (deine Liebste, Braut?) aus Liebe." He sees the lines as a charm whereby a woman wishes to protect her lover from death in battle (273).

[39] Wolfgang Meid, "Gallisch oder Lateinisch? Soziolinguistische und andere Bemerkungen zu populären gallo-lateinischen Inschriften," in *Principat*, 29, II. *Sprache und Literatur*, ed. Wolfgang Haase (Berlin and New York: Walter de Gruyter, 1983), 1019–44 (1043–44). I am grateful to Kurt Gärtner for the reference.

[40] Phyllis Greenacre, "Fetishism," in *Sexual Deviation*, ed. Ismond Rosen, 2nd ed. (Oxford & New York: Oxford UP, 1979), 79–108 (80).

[41] Greenacre, "Fetishism," 81.

[42] Valerie Steele, *Fetish. Fashion, Sex and Power* (Oxford & New York: Oxford UP, 1996), 22.

[43] It would be otiose to document the vast literature relating to *mentalité*, but on the concept of childhood, see Linda M. Paterson, "Sources Féminines et le 'Sentiment de l'Enfance' dans certains textes médicaux et didactiques du XIIe au XIVe siècle," in *Histoire et Littérature au Moyen Âge. Actes du Colloque du Centre d'Études Médiévales de l'Université de Picardie (Amiens 20–24 mars 1985)*, ed. Danielle Buschinger, GAG, 546 (Göppingen: Kümmerle, 1991), 381–88.

[44] Steele, *Fetish*, 25.

[45] Cf. *Vox feminae: studies in medieval woman's songs*, ed. John F. Plummer, Studies in medieval culture, 15 (Kalamazoo, MI.: Medieval Institute Publications, Western Michigan University, 1981).

[46] David Hiley (Regensburg), in correspondence. It remains open to question as to whether the neumes are of St. Gall provenance. John Caldwell (Oxford) points to resemblances to the neumes in Bamberg lit. 6, from St. Emmeram.

[47] Schwab, "Das althochdeutsche Lied," 101.

[48] As Schwab recognises, her attempt to deny the poem its erotic content follows in the footsteps of Ehrismann (*Geschichte*, vol. 1, 243–44). Cf. Brian Murdoch, *Old High German Literature*, 109.

[49] Rudolf Schützeichel, *Althochdeutsches Wörterbuch* (Tübingen: Niemeyer, 1969), 155.

[50] Braune, *Lesebuch*, § XXXI, 7.

[51] Bischoff, "Paläographische Fragen," 120, note 106; cf. Schwab, "Das althochdeutsche Lied," 90, note 46.

[52] Schwab, "Das althochdeutsche Lied," 95. Cf. Bernhard Maier, *Lexikon der keltischen Religion und Kultur* (Stuttgart: Alfred Kröner, 1994), 74–75; 325.

[53] *Geoffrey of Monmouth: Life of Merlin: Vita Merlini*, ed. and trans. Basil Clarke (Cardiff: U of Wales P [for] the Language and Literature Committee of the Board of Celtic Studies, 1973).

[54] *Canu Maswedd yr Oesoedd Canol. Medieval Welsh Erotic Poetry*, ed. and trans. Dafydd Johnston (Cardiff: Gwasg Gomer, Llandysul, 1991), 110–11.

[55] *Pearl; Cleanness; Patience; Sir Gawain and the Green Knight*, ed. A. C. Cawley and J. J. Anderson (London and Melbourne: Dent, 1983).

[56] *Dafydd ap Gwilym: A Selection of Poems*, ed. and trans. Rachel Bromwich (Harmondsworth: Penguin, 1985), § 27.

[57] Bromwich, *Dafydd ap Gwilym*, § 31, lines 13–24.

[58] Bromwich, *Dafydd ap Gwilym*, § 19.

[59] *Fastnachtspiele aus dem fünfzehnten Jahrhundert*, ed. Adelbert von Keller, Bibliothek des litterarischen Vereins in Stuttgart, XXVIII–XXX (Stuttgart: Litterarischer Verein, 1853), III, 1392ff. The text is quoted according to the manuscript, now in the Bayerische Staatsbibliothek.

[60] *Verfasserlexikon*, vol. 10, col. 246.

[61] Reproduced in *Livelier than Life — the Master of the Amsterdam Cabinet or the Housebook Master, ca. 1470–1500*, ed. J. P. Filedt Kok (Amsterdam: Rijksmuseum, 1985), 227. Cf. the facsimile edition, *The Medieval Housebook*, ed. Christoph Graf zu Waldburg Wolfegg (Munich: Prestel-Verlag, 1997).

[62] James Reeves, *The Idiom of the People* (London: Heinemann, 1958; repr. Mercury Books, 1962), 138. The long hook is reminiscent of the "lange Stange" with which Werther fetches down pears for Lotte (Am 28. August, Erstes Buch, *Die Leiden des jungen Werther*).

[63] Reeves, *The Idiom of the People*, 139.

[64] The text and melody date from the eighteenth century; see Ernst Klusen, *Deutsche Lieder. Texte und Melodien* (Frankfurt: Insel Verlag, 1980), 102; 825.

[65] *MGH SS* II, 595; quoted by Richter, *The Formation of the Medieval West*, 136. For an overview of attitudes to the vernacular see also Patrick Wormald, "Bede, 'Beowulf' and the Conversion of the Anglo-Saxon Aristocracy," 32–95 (especially 45).

14: Österreichische Nationalbibliothek, Cod. Vind. 15.013,
Fragment A4. The OHG Lullaby.

7: The Strange Case of the Old High German Lullaby

> Ich a moder treuly,
> That can hire credel kepe,
> Is wone to lullen lovely
> And singen hire child aslepe.
>
> — Middle English lullaby

THE GENRE OF THE LULLABY, while never pivotal in the history of literature, would appear to have ancient origins; it certainly relates to a universal custom.[1] The third satire of Persius, dating from the first century A.D., refers in derogatory fashion to *lallare*: "cur non potius . . . iratus mammae lallare recusas?" [Why do you not rather refuse the lulling of your nurse?][2] It is not clear whether *lallare* here amounts to a reference to an actual lullaby, or whether the verb merely denotes soporific sounds. Galen, writing in the second century A.D., recommends the practice of singing lullabies on the grounds that children have a natural inclination towards music.[3]

There is an Old Irish poem which may be a lullaby:

> Cride hé dairi cnó
> ócán é pócán dó.[4]

[A heart is he; a nut of oak. / A young thing [he] is — a kiss for him.]

Like the OHG *Hirsch und Hinde*, the poem is preserved as one continuous line, and, as may also be the case with *Hirsch und Hinde*, it owes its survival to its metrical form. It is preserved in the fifteenth-century Book of Ballymote, but the poem itself may date back as far as the ninth or tenth century. It serves as an example to illustrate a dissertation on Old Irish metrics, which Rudolf Thurneysen dates to *c*. 1060 AD.[5] Whether the object of affection is a child or a lover is open to speculation. Like so many early vernacular lyrics, *Cride hé* may be a love-lyric in the woman's voice. *ócán* may denote a man younger than the female speaker, as in the twelfth-century woman's-voice lyrics of Meinloh von Sevelingen, where the object of affection is "einen kindeschen man,"[6] or in the English folksong *Still Growing*:

> The trees they grow so high and the leaves they grow so green.
> The day is past and gone, my love, that you and I have seen.
> It's a cold winter's night, my love, when I must bide alone,
> For my bonny lad is young but a-growing. . . .

'O father, dearest father, you've done to me much wrong.
You've tied me to a boy when you know he is too young.'
'O daughter, dearest daughter, if you'll wait a little while,
A lady you shall be, while he's growing. . . .'[7]

The Old Welsh *Pais Dinodan*, on the other hand, clearly refers to a mother-child relationship, though whether the poem had the function of a lullaby is doubtful. The mother, speaking to her child, says:

The mantle of Dinogat is of many colours, of many colours.
From the skins of martens I made it.
When thy father went a-hunting
With spear on shoulder and cudgel in hand
He would call his big dogs,
Giff gaff: Catch, catch! Fetch, fetch!

In his coracle, he would spear a fish,
Striking suddenly like a lion.
When thy father went up the mountain
He would bring back a roebuck, a wild boar, a stag,
A spotted grouse from the mountain,
A fish from the walls of Derwennydd.
As many as thy father caught with his spear,
Wild pigs, and foxes, and —
None would escape, except those with wings.[8]

The poem is entered at the end of a section of the *Book of Aneirin*, copied from the compiler's second source, and its lack of thematic link with the preceding texts makes it difficult to date. The manuscript of the *Book of Aneirin* dates from the thirteenth century, but the poem is thought to be much earlier in date.

In the late twelfth and early thirteenth centuries more evidence accrues. In the Occitan chanson de geste *Daurel et Beton* a nurse sings a melody to a child.[9] There is a reference to the practice of singing lullabies in a love-song of Wolfram von Eschenbach. Wolfram imagines birds singing lullabies to their offspring in the springtime:

vogel die hellen und die besten:
al des meigen zît si wegent mit gesange ir kint.[10]

[Birds, the bright and best: / all through the Maytime they cradle their offspring with song.]

This anthropomorphic image is complemented by the songs of Neidhart von Reuental, thought to be a slightly younger contemporary of Wolfram. In

Neidhart's songs the female protagonist is in danger, for the first time in the German lyric, of becoming a mother. The girl's mother, in turn, warns her:

> wil dû mit im gein Riuwental, dâ bringet er dich hin:
> alsô kan sîn treiros dich verkoufen.
> er beginnt dich slahen, stôzen, roufen
> und müezen doch zwô wiegen bî dir loufen.[11]

[if you want to go with him to Riuwental, he'll take you there: / his trident will sell you dearly. / He'll start beating you, pushing you, bashing you / and, come what may, there'll be two cradles rocking at your side.]

Neidhart's lyric proffers the cradle without the song. However, at this point in the second quarter of the thirteenth century, there are intimations that courtly love is about to collapse like a defective condom, as pregnancy, child-birth and child-rearing make their incursions upon the German love-lyric. Neidhart's contemporary, Gottfried von Neifen, builds a lullaby into a refrain in a song which expresses, with extraordinary vividness, a psychological conflict: the resentment of the girl who has turned mother against her will, — and, at the same time, the love she bears her child. Such a degree of psychological realism is rare in the medieval lyric:

> Sol ich disen sumer lanc
> bekumbert sîn mit kinden,
> sô wær ich vil lieber tôt.
> des ist mir mîn fröide kranc.
> sol ich niht zer linden
> reigen, owê dirre nôt!
> wigen wagen, gigen gagen,
> wenne wil ez tagen?
> minne minne, trûte minne, swîc, ich wil dich wagen.

> Amme, nim daz kindelîn
> daz ez niht enweine,
> alse liep als ich dir sî.
> ringe mir die swære mîn:
> dû maht mich aleine
> mîner sorgen machen frî.
> wigen wagen, etc.[12]

[If I am to be troubled this whole summer / with children, / I'd much rather be dead. / That is why my joy is enfeebled. / If I'm not to dance the round / at the lime-tree, oh, what a shame! / *wigen wagen, gigen gagen,* / when will day come? / Love, love, dear love, be silent, I will cradle you./

Nurse, take the baby, / stop it crying, / as I am dear to you. / Make my trouble easier to bear: / you alone can / free me of worry. / *wigen, wagen,* etc.]

The nonsense words in the refrain, based on MHG *wige,* "cradle," and perhaps *gîge,* "fiddle," point to a lullaby underlying the text. This is confirmed by *Der Sælden Hort,* an anonymous south-west German work of the late thirteenth century. The author imagines the Christ child being cradled:

> du solt es heben unde legen,
> samft wiegen und wegen.
> sing: "ninna, ninna, wægelin! . . ."[13]

[you must lift it up and lay it down, / gently cradle and rock it. / Sing: "ninna, ninna, little cradle! . . .]

Lullabies grow thick and fast in the European literature of the fourteenth and fifteenth centuries. Two factors may have contributed to this: the cult of the Virgin Mary, and the rise of medieval drama. Many lullabies occur in the context of vernacular Christmas plays, both in Germany and in England. The carol *Joseph lieber nefe mein* is attributed to the Monk of Salzburg. The fifteenth-century rubric makes it clear that the song was sung to accompany Joseph's cradling of the Christ Child in a Christmas play. The melody is a contrafactum of the Latin cantus *Resonet in laudibus:*

> Und so man das kindel wiegt über das Resonet in laudibus hebt unnser vraw an ze singen in ainer person Yoseph lieber neve mein So antwurt in der andern person Yoseph Geren liebe muem mein Darnach singet der kor dy andern vers in aines dyenner weis.[14]

[And when the child is cradled during the *Resonet in laudibus,* Our Lady begins to sing, solo, "Joseph, my dear kinsman." Then Joseph responds, also solo, "Gladly, my dear kinswoman." Then the choir sings the other lines, taking the part of a servant.]

The genres of the carol and the lullaby are closely associated, with the key word *wiegen* present in the first two strophes of the carol's text:

> Joseph lieber nefe mein
> hilff mir wiegen mein kindelein
> das got müeß dein loner sein
> in hymelreich der meide kint Maria

[Joseph, dear kinsman mine, / help me rock my baby, / may God reward you for it / in Heaven — the maiden Mary's child]

Gerne liebe mueme mein
ich hilff dir wiegen dein kindelein
das got müeß mein loner sein
in hymelreich du raine maid Maria

[Gladly, dear kinswoman mine, / I'll help you rock your baby, / may God
reward me for it / in Heaven, you pure maiden Mary]

The custom of cradling survived into the nineteenth century, and Mozart
employed the melody of *Joseph lieber nefe mein* in his *Galimathias musicum*.
In England, the liquid *l* in 'lollay,' 'lullay,' corresponds to the German *w*.
Mak's wife in *The Second Shepherd's Play* is fully aware of the requisite
behaviour if parents are to pass a lamb off as a baby:

UXOR: Harken ay when they call; they will come onone.
Com and make redy all and syng by thyn oone;
Syng 'lullay' thou shall, for I must grone,
And cry outt by the wall on Mary and Iohn,
For sore.
Syng 'lullay' on fast
When thou heris at the last;
And bot I play a fals cast,
Trust me no more.[15]

So well-established are the wording and the custom in early fourteenth-
century England that they can form the basis of parody. The earliest attested
English lullaby is the "adult lullaby" in MS Harley 913, whose theme is the
analogy between the vulnerability of the weeping child and man's passage
through the "weping dale":

Lollay, lollay, little child, why wepestou so sore?
Nedest mostou wepe — it was iyarked thee yore
Ever to lib in sorrow, and sich and mourne evere,
As thine eldren did ere this, whil hi alives were.
Lollay, lollay, little child, child, lollay, lullow,
Into uncuth world icommen so ertou . . .

Lollay, lollay, little child, child, lollay, lollay,
With sorow thou com into this world, with sorow shalt wend away . . .[16]

With this exception, "all other ME lullabies concern the Christ-child."[17] The
earliest attested melody for an English lullaby would appear to be that for
Lullay, lullay: Als I lay on Yoolis night, which has the refrain:

Lullay, lullay, lay, lay lullay:
mi deerë moder, [sing] lullay.[18]

Perhaps the best-known medieval English lullaby is appended to *The Shearmen and Tailors' Play* of the Coventry Cycle, in a sixteenth-century hand. The grisly context is the Massacre of the Innocents, and the song is to be sung by the mothers of Bethlehem. Its refrain runs:

> Lully lulla, thow litell tine child,
> By, by, lully lullay, thow littell tyne child,
> By, by, lully lullay![19]

The refrain's key word "Lullay" was not, however, limited to lullabies, but found its way into a version of the *Corpus Christi Carol*: "Lully, lulley, lully, lulley."[20]

What all these early lullabies have in common is that they are literary arte-facts, art-song rather than folksong. No early folk lullaby survives in its entirety, though the allusions and the refrains with their lulling sounds suggest a thriving sub-literary genre.

In Germany, the refrains of folk lullabies collected in the modern period show an extraordinary continuity with the medieval evidence: "Nini nani Wiagali," "Wiegewage, wiegewage," "Gautscha gautscha wiega waga."[21] The orality of the genre, and its quintessentially maternal nature, are perhaps suffi-cient explanation for the paucity of examples from the early Middle Ages. Most women who could write in the Middle Ages might be said to have had a vocational antipathy towards motherhood; it was scarcely to be expected of them that they should write down lullabies.

The middle of the nineteenth century was a time of intense activity and growth in the new discipline of medieval German studies. Particularly in the area of Old High German, new manuscripts, new texts, new genres, were constantly being discovered. This evolutionary stage was characterised by a patriotically inspired desire to relate the small corpus of early texts to the pagan Germanic past. Germany had shed the shackles of the French Empire and was seeking a new identity as a nation. Nationalism and the search for paganity were, somewhat anomalously, wedded. In 1841 the Merseburg Charms were discovered, texts suggesting belief in Nordic deities on Germanic soil, fuelling Jacob Grimm's researches into Germanic mythology. It is characteristic of the period that when in 1858 the Trier charm *Incantacio contra equorum egritudinem*, invoking Christ and St Stephen, was discovered, Theodor von Karajan sought to explain it in pagan terms, substituting Woden for Christ.[22] In 1866 Franz Pfeiffer expounded the Lorsch Bee Charm; an (anonymous) colleague who suspected the charm might not be authentic warned him against taking on the task: "Warum also dieses Misstrauen? Es zeugt von keinen gesunden Zuständen in unserer jungen Wissenschaft, die vor der Zeit schon alt und grämlich geworden ist."[23] The excitement of discovery frequently fell foul of an atmosphere of distrust and antagonism.

One discovery in particular attracted both intense interest and suspicion. In 1858 Jacob Grimm, by then in his seventies, ailing and suffering from weak eyesight, described it as "der wunderbarste fund, der gemacht werden konnte."[24] He was referring to the Old High German lullaby, discovered by the Austrian scholar Georg Zappert in September 1852. It was one of fourteen parchment binding fragments (now Österreichische Nationalbibliothek, Cod. Vind. 15.013, formerly Suppl. 1668) which he had found in the spine of a paper manuscript written in the 1430s. One fragment in particular had caught the attention of Zappert, because of the line of Hebrew script above the OHG words. In August 1858 he finally succeeded in purchasing the manuscript from an unidentified Viennese library, and publication followed in Vienna that year.[25] But even before this first cursory essay suspicion had reared its ugly head, as a second letter from Grimm to Pfeiffer reveals: "Zapperts commentar zum alten spruch ist noch nicht erschienen; wenn ihn etwas verdächtigt, so sind es die hebräischen wörter. warum muste er gerade auf diese seltsamkeit stoszen?"[26]

The strip of parchment (Fragment A4; illustration 14) has five lines of Old High German written upon it; the line of Hebrew above them is a string of apparently unconnected words, which perhaps originally formed part of a glossary. The following transcription of the OHG text is based upon the original manuscript. The letter *o* at the end of the first line is only partially visible. The division of the words has been rationalised; as is the case with many early OHG texts, it is erratic in the original.

Tocha ſla ſlumo uueinon ſarlaze ſ tri‥uua uu‥rit craftlich*o*
themo uuolfa uurgianthemo ſlafe ſ unza morg‧n‥ man‥ ſ trut
ſunilo o ſtra ſtelit chinde honacegir ſuoz‧u hera pr‧ch‧t chind^v
pluomun plobun rotiu zanfana ſentit morgane ueizu ſ^{c}af
cle‧niu unta <.>ino<.>g herra hurt hor ſca a ſca harta‧

Three words in the OHG text are "glossed" by Hebrew words. Below *Tocha* stands the word *Dodi*, "my beloved"; below *Ostra* the word *Esther*, below *Zanfana* the name *Zipora*, the wife of Moses. The other unique feature consists in the sporadic traces of what appears to be a Hebrew vocalisation system in the words *tri‧uua, uu‧rit, man‥ ſ, ſuoz‧u, pr‧ch‧t, chind^v* and *cle‧niu*. The lullaby was treated on its discovery in much the same manner as other recently discovered OHG texts. The assumption was that the transmitted text was faulty, that an editing process was necessary in order to reconstruct the *Ur-*lullaby. Zappert himself supplied a "corrected" text, provided with accents denoting vowel length and indications of the alliterative pattern in italics:

1. Tocha *s*lafês *s*liumo (A)
   uueinon *s*ar lazzês.
3. Triuua *uu*erit kraftlicho (B)
   themo *uu*olfa *uu*rgiantemo.

> 5. slafês unz za morgane (C)
> manes trût sunilo.
> 7. Ostârâ stellit chinde (D)
> honak egir suozziu.
> 9. Hera prichit chinde (E)
> pluomun plobun rotun.
> 11. Zanfana sentit morgane (F)
> ueiziu scaf kleiniu,
> 13. unta Einouga, herra hurt! (G)
> horska aska harta.

Zappert also proffered the first translation:

> 1 Docke, mögest du schlafen schleunig,
> Weinen gleich mögest du lassen.
> 3 Triwa wehrt kräftig
> Dem Wolf dem würgenden.
> 5 Mögest du schlafen bis zum Morgen
> Mannes trautes Söhnlein.
> 7 Ostara stellt dem Kinde
> Honig, Eier süsse.
> 9 Hera bricht dem Kinde
> Blumen blaue rothe.
> 11 Tanfana sendet morgen
> Weisse schafe kleine,
> 13 Und Wuotan, herra hurt!
> Rasche Speere harte.

Zappert's translation was refined by Pfeiffer, who had corresponded with Jacob Grimm on the subject. One major problem was the last line, where Zappert had interpreted *Herra hurt!* as a battle-cry. Grimm suggested that *hurt* derived form OHG *hûran, meaning *conducere, locare*. It followed that *herra* was an error for *herro*, "lord," a noun preceded by the adjective *einoug[a]*. Thus the last line meant: "And the one-eyed lord will soon give [or: send you] hard spears."[27] Pfeiffer and Grimm took *honakegir* as a compound, so that line 8 meant "sweet honey-eggs," and they understood the lambs to be plump, "feist," rather than "white."

Jacob Grimm, right up to his death on 20 September 1863, had intended to publish a defence of the lullaby, according to the account of his correspondent, Pfeiffer. The latter wrote a passionate 43-page defence in 1866. Of those scholars who were not of Austrian nationality, Grimm stood out from the beginning because of his enthusiastic advocacy of the lullaby. Otherwise the tendency was for the sceptical Prussians to mass ranks against the credulous Austrians.

Zappert's stock stood high in Vienna. He was born in Hungary in 1806, the son of prosperous Jewish parents. Initially he studied medicine in Vienna, but in 1829 converted to Catholicism and began to study theology. Two years later, however, a severe illness deprived him almost entirely of his hearing, and from that point onwards he adopted the life of a private scholar. Among his many publications is an innovative study of body language in medieval literature, *Über den Ausdruck des geistigen Schmerzes im Mittelalter* (1849). Zappert's scholarship was essentially comparative in nature, and his essays tend to be bogged down in minutiæ, but Pfeiffer's characterisation of his work is unduly harsh: "unruhig und umgeordnet wie sein ganzes Wesen und Schaffen war, tragen auch seine Arbeiten nur zu deutliche Spuren dieser Art an sich und über ein planloses unlogisches Aneinanderreihen von wichtigen und mehr noch unwichtigen Notizen erhebt sich keine derselben."[28] Pfeiffer goes on to describe him as "misstrauisch, schweigsam und verschlossen." The only remark in the course of the controversy which might be described as anti-Semitic fell from the lips of Jacob Grimm, who in a letter to von Karajan described Zappert as possessing "die bescheidene jüdische Zudringlichkeit, aber für gewissenhaft und ehrlich hielt ich seine geschmacklosen Compilationen dennoch."[29]

Zappert died on 22 November 1859. His will states that his death was the result of a heart disease that had lasted some years.[30] The will also records his bequest of his books to his illiterate housekeeper, which provoked some indignant reaction. As with Attila the Hun, the hard facts concerning Zappert's death were soon forgotten in the interests of a good story. Thus even the *Biographisches Lexikon des Kaiserthums Österreich* recorded: "Er starb im besten Mannesalter von erst 53 Jahren, nachdem er seinen Tod drei Tage vorher auf die Minute vorausgesagt. Uebrigens sollen ähnliche Fälle von eingetroffenen Todesahnungen bei mehreren Gliedern dieser Familie vorgekommen sein."[31] Still more romantically, the poet and bibliophile Karl Wolfskehl (1869–1948) wrote: "Ein Sturm der Entrüstung, bis in die Tagesblätter hinein, fegte durch die wissenschaftliche Welt. Zappert, als Betrüger gebrandmarkt, erschoss sich."[32]

It does indeed seem probable that the events of Zappert's last years hastened his death. One controversial "discovery" followed another, most of them published in the Vienna *Sitzungsberichte*: the fragment of a *liber dativus*, the description of which is accompanied by some excellent source material concerning the life of the wandering minstrel; a Latin conversation primer intended for the schooling of Emperor Maximilian I.[33] In 1856, two years before his publication of the lullaby, he published an article concerning another find, the "ältesten Plan Wiens," a crude sketch on a parchment flyleaf reused to bind a later manuscript. Let us stay with the lullaby. What was the basis for questioning its authenticity?

The criteria which have been adduced may be categorised as follows: (i) codicological; (ii) palæographic and orthographic; (iii) linguistic; (iv) metrical; (v) thematic, primarily mythological.

(i) Codicological

Wilhelm Müller was troubled by the fact that Zappert did not reveal the provenance of the manuscript, Cod. 14.269, for which the lullaby served as one of several binding fragments.[34] The manuscript was sold to the Nationalbibliothek by Zappert in 1858. Now rebound, it contains Heinrich Hembuche von Langenstein's *Erkenntnis der Sünden* and other theological texts. Pfeiffer described its provenance in 1866 as an open secret, involving a monastery whose librarian dealt negligently with the treasures in his care, and whose name neither Zappert nor Pfeiffer felt at liberty to reveal.[35]

Zappert, by his own account, found the lullaby in the spine of the manuscript. Binding fragments dating from the OHG period are rare, but not unheard-of. The Codex Discissus of Otfrid's *Liber Evangeliorum* is the best known example; fragments survive in Berlin, Bonn and Wolfenbüttel.[36] The soft parchment on which the lullaby survives is scarcely ideal binding material, but medieval binders took what scraps were available, just as modern binders packed newspaper cuttings into the spines of their books. Another circumstance regarded as suspicious was the fact that the other fragments incorporated into the binding were ignored by Zappert and not published until after his death, in Pfeiffer's article in defence of Zappert. These fragments are strips containing thirteenth- and fourteenth-century texts, both Latin and Middle High German. Presumably they were of no interest to Zappert, and the texts remain unidentified. That they are all of later date than the apparent date of the lullaby is odd, but by no means inexplicable. In the later Middle Ages, as paper established itself, parchment became available by the mixed cartload. The later binding fragments lack the beginnings and ends of lines, whereas the lullaby, as fortune would have it, is preserved intact save for half of the last letter of the first line.

When this controversy was resuscitated in 1976, Michael Jacoby, responding to John Howard's defence of the lullaby in the same year, recommended that the parchment, the ink, the script and the traces of glue should be carefully examined.[37] This task had already been undertaken by the Austrian commission which investigated the lullaby on behalf of the Hofbibliothek. Their findings are summarised by Pfeiffer, whose expertise was considerable. The woolly consistency of the parchment is unusual, but not unique in the early Middle Ages; whatever its provenance, the lullaby appears to be written on medieval parchment. Pfeiffer's description is characteristically accurate: "Das Äussere des Blättchens ist kraus und wollig, wie das bei Pergamenten, welche lange Zeit aufgeklebt, dem Staube und der Feuchtigkeit ausgesetzt waren und dann auf nassem Wege abgelöst und gewaltsam vom Leimüberzuge befreit wurden, häufig der Fall zu sein pflegt. Die Dinte zeigt die bei alter Schrift so häufig vorkommende gelbbraune Farbe. . . ."[38]

The colour of the ink, a yellowish ochre hue, suggests that it was made from oak-apple tincture. It is reminiscent of one of the inks employed in the

Wessobrunn Prayer manuscript (Clm. 22053). If the lullaby is a forgery, then the forger in all probability employed medieval parchment, and may well have assembled the ingredients of a medieval ink. The traces of a few letters of the lullaby in reverse on one of the other parchment strips (A.2) prove nothing either way. They may stem from the glueing of the binding in the fifteenth century, or from the work of a nineteenth-century forger. The word *einouga*, now only partially legible and only deciphered with difficulty by Zappert, appears to be written over a speck of dirt. Howard argues that it is illegible because it is written on the hair-side of a leaf. Jaffé's suspicions were aroused by this: "die schrift ist also jünger als der schmutz."[39] Dating dirt is not easy. The impaired surface may be the result of an erasure, but examination under ultra-violet light revealed nothing written below. All in all, the external appearance of the leaf offers no conclusive evidence of a forgery.

(ii) Palæographic and Orthographical Evidence

The character of the German script points to a hand of the first half of the tenth century. The letters are somewhat crudely executed, particularly the *t*, and the *r*, whose long descender, for example in *sarlazes, craftlicho, harta*, is reminiscent of the pre-Carolingian *r* to be found in the *Wessobrunn Prayer* and the *Hildebrandslied*. Another unusual feature is the form of the *z* in *sarlazes* and *zanfana*, thought by Pfeiffer to have been influenced by Hebrew script.[40] Shortly before his death, I had the good fortune to consult Bernhard Bischoff; his opinion was, to say the least, dismissive. In his view, the lullaby is a forgery and was therefore ignored in his authoritative survey of OHG palæography;[41] he held that the script is not traceable to any particular Carolingian school and is essentially a "Mischmasch." If however, as Zappert and Pfeiffer argued, the lullaby derives from some kind of convergence of German and Hebrew learning in the tenth century, then ascribing the hand to a specific school would prove difficult, to say the least.

(iii) Linguistic Criteria

The strange mixture of divergent dialectal features in the lullaby was noted at an early stage. Müller observed the curious juxtaposition of weak and strong inflections in line 10: *plobun rotiu*, and the odd combination of shifted *p* and unshifted *b*.[42] Grimm postulated a Rhenish Franconian dialect, whereas Pfeiffer thought that a Franconian original had been copied in Austria.[43] Arguing for the lullaby's authenticity, Pfeiffer pointed out that the phenomenon of dialect mix in OHG texts only became common knowledge in 1864. If Zappert was a forger, he was, therefore, ahead of his time.

Karl Stackmann, when a version of this paper was given in Göttingen in 1994, pointed to the impossibility of the participle *uuurgianthemo* in the tenth century. Whereas post-consonantal *j* was preserved in OS, in OHG it disappeared entirely in the course of the ninth century.[44] It is, of course, conceivable that the lullaby preserved an archaic form, copied from an older original. On the other hand, a forger might have reconstructed this form of the present participle by working backwards from the umlauted form, *würgend*, in Modern German.

The language of the lullaby cannot provide conclusive evidence as to whether or not it is a forgery. Three factors militate against this: first, the common phenomenon in Old High German of dialect mix; secondly, the equally common chronological gulf between *Urtext* and transmission, and the consequent potential for scribal corruption; and thirdly, the possibility, mooted by Zappert and suggested by the Hebrew "glosses," that the text of the lullaby is the product of a Judaeo-German collaboration.

(iv) Metrical Criteria

Hofmann's essay of 1866[45] illustrates the dilemma which faced the scholars confronted wih the lullaby. A new text that proffered evidence of pagan belief was to be welcomed, but it had to comply with scholarly expectations. Above all, it had to conform with the "rules" thought to obtain, in more absolute fashion than we now entertain, for Germanic alliterative verse. Hofmann found that the lullaby, despite the elucidations suggested by Grimm and Pfeiffer, was open to grave objections on metrical grounds. By dint of numerous emendations, Hofmann succeeded in "improving" the lullaby, with the result that the names of the gods, the most important words in the lines, alliterated correctly. Yet, even in Hofmann's estimation, these are not authentic alliterating staves, but imitations dating from the tenth or eleventh century. Ultimately Hofmann reverted to Jaffé's arguments and accepted that the lullaby is a modern forgery. Undeterred, he proceeded to reconstruct the metrically sound original of the *Lorsch Bee Charm*.

(v) Thematic and Mythological

The lullaby offered a wealth of evidence for the new science of Germanic mythology, which explains Jacob Grimm's enthusiastic welcome of the discovery. In his *Deutsche Mythologie* Grimm defended Bede against the accusation that he had invented the goddess Eástre. The lullaby now confirmed her identity.[46] Equally welcome to Grimm was the first evidence to surface since Tacitus of the Roman goddess Tanfana (by virtue of the Second Sound Shift, *Zanfana* in the lullaby). The temple of Tanfana, the most important religious centre of the Germani, had been razed to the ground by the Romans in A.D. 14 and all trace of her in Germanic sources lost.[47] In the spring of 1859 Grimm went so far as to publish a short essay on the goddess Tanfana. This late work lacks Grimm's customary clarity.[48]

The lullaby invokes two further goddesses, *Triuua* and *Hera*. Zappert's article referred to Grimm's *Deutsche Mythologie* for backing for these.[49] Grimm had derived *Triwa* from the personification of the virtue *Triuwe* (Loyalty) in Middle High German literature. In such personifications Grimm sought to find deities of pagan origin. The evidence for the earth-goddess *Hera* was late, fifteenth-century in origin, so here too the lullaby filled a lacuna. On the other hand, the Merseburg Charms, discovered in 1841 and described by Jacob Grimm in the following year, had also yielded evidence for at least two hitherto unheard-of deities, Phol and Sinthgunt, not to mention the controversial naming of Balder. The authenticity of the Merseburg Charms has, however, rarely been doubted.

Perhaps the oddest of the novelties proferred by the lullaby are the *honacegir*. Zappert again referred to Grimm's *Deutsche Mythologie*, which suggested some kind of sacrificial cake,[50] although he did not exclude the possibility of an allusion to Easter eggs, a suggestion welcomed by Grimm.[51] The *Handwörterbuch des deutschen Aberglaubens* can find no reference to the custom of Easter eggs prior to modern times. It does, however, point to the popularity of a cake made from Easter eggs in Vienna, Bohemia and among Silesian Jews.[52] Here again, the lullaby, if authentic, offers the earliest evidence of a widespread folk custom. Or might the honey-eggs be a forger's anachronism?

Pfeiffer thought Zappert psychologically incapable of forgery: "Zu einem solchen Betruge besass er gar nicht die Ruhe und noch weniger die Befähigung."[53] Whether composure is an essential quality for a successful forger is a moot point. Pfeiffer's defence of the lullaby appeared eight years after Zappert's death, in 1866. Almost a generation later, in 1892, Richard Schuster addressed himself to the controversy. His article has been largely ignored in the few twentieth-century approaches to the lullaby, perhaps because its title indicates that it is concerned only with the purported "ältester Plan von Wien."[54]

Schuster analyses the script of the writing on the map, thought by Zappert to date from the eleventh century. He makes a not altogether convincing attempt to prove that the individual letters are cobbled together from scripts of widely divergent periods. His essay is accompanied by facsimiles of both the map and the lullaby, and in comparing the two Schuster seems closer to the mark. The majority of the letters in the two documents reproduced by Schuster are strikingly similar; a study of the originals in the Österreichische National-bibliothek made the case even more clearly.

Zappert had noted in 1858 that the scribe of the lullaby had a tendency to bend the ascenders of the letters *d*, *h* and *l* to the left. He attributed this to the habits of a Jewish hand, in conformity with his thesis that the text was the work of a Jewish doctor or rabbi. Carolingian minuscule tends to lean slightly from left to right, like Zappert's normal script, to judge from his last will and testament. The ductus of both the lullaby and the "Oldest Map" is somewhat odd: within the same word the letters lean both to the left and to the right. This is particularly evident in *habemus* in the second line of the title of the map, and in *slaslumo* and *uuolfa* in the first two lines of the lullaby. The peculiar *a* that almost falls over itself is also common to both, occurring in *alto* in the middle of the map and in *sarlazes* and *harta* in the lullaby. The *s* and the rather clumsily executed *f* bear a marked similarity. Ligatures are generally avoided in Carolingian minuscule, but there are two letters that frequently form a ligature with the following letter, *f* and *e*. Neither in the map nor in the lullaby is there a single ligature. The degree of coincidence is suspiciously high.

If Zappert did forge the lullaby, what might have served as his model? Even in Vienna, German hands of the tenth century were not two a penny. In 1842 Grimm had published the *Merseburg Charms*, the hand of which dates from the first half of the tenth century. The publication, in the proceedings of the Berlin Academy, was accompanied by a facsimile. Comparing the script of the charms with Zappert's two finds, one is struck by the considerable similarities, particularly with regard to the forms of the *g* and the *n*.

The structure of the lullaby also bears a striking resemblance to that of the Second Merseburg Charm, as Wilhelm Müller pointed out in 1867.[55] In the charm four — or perhaps two — goddesses attempt unsuccessfully to heal Balder's horse; only the intervention of Wodan effects the cure. Similarly, in the lullaby four goddesses (Triuua, Ostara, Hera and Zanfana) act in unison to protect the child and bring him presents, while the final present, the gift of spears, comes from the hand of Wodan. Symmetrically, as in the charm, the four goddesses appear in successive sets of two lines, with Wodan reserved for the last two lines. The degree of structural similarity is striking.

The aids that would have been available to Zappert if he had constructed the lullaby were limited, compared with those available to the modern scholar. Graff's *Althochdeutscher Sprachschatz* (1834–42) and Schmeller's *Bayerisches Wörterbuch* (1827–37) had already been published. He would, of course, have been conversant with such OHG literature as had already appeared in print. The *asca harta* in the last line of the lullaby are strongly reminiscent of the spears of ash, the *asckim* at the end of the *Hildebrandslied* (line 63). But the lexis, like the phonology and morphology of the text, can prove nothing by itself. Where OHG and OS alliterative texts are concerned, *hapax legomenon* is a very common phenomenon.

With regard to the mythology of the lullaby, it would appear that Jacob Grimm underestimated the impact of his own *Deutsche Mythologie*. He generally had a fine eye for forgery in this area, as is clear from the irony with which he demolishes Schönwerth's now forgotten three volumes of *Sitten und Sagen* from the Upper Palatinate: "Wer erstaunt nicht, dasz Schönwerth jetzt aus oberpfälzischen dörfern die geschichte von Woud und Freid ans tageslicht bringt, fast gerade so wie sie in der edda von Odin und Freyja steht; ein bair. ministerialrath und generalsecretär wird sich doch keine fälschung erlauben, er berichtet auch schöne, unerfindliche sagen, denen man die wahrheit schon ansiht, im überflusz."[56]

Zappert, in writing his essay about the lullaby, drew by his own admission upon the second edition of Grimm's *Deutsche Mythologie* (1844), which was provided with a helpful index. There the reader finds the names of all the goddesses in the lullaby, with the exception of *Triuwa*. Looking up *Tanfana*, he finds the reference to Tacitus and the comment that the word must be German in origin: "deutsch sein muss das wort." Grimm regrets the fact that all we are certain of concerning the goddess is her name.[57] Looking up *Ostara*, the reader finds a reference to the custom of Easter eggs, and the baking of "osterfladen" or "ôstertuopha," a cake of pagan appearance. The goddess of Easter is for Grimm a pagan goddess of the morning light, a joyful, benevolent apparition.[58] The word "heidnisch" must again have caught Zappert's eye. On p. 920 there is more to be read concerning *"Ostara, der das volk maiblumen opferte,"* with a further reference to p. 52: "heidnische gewohnheit auf christ-liche feste und abgaben überführt." Hence, perhaps, Hera's flowers in the lullaby. And finally, *einouga*, the one-eyed lord, the barely legible crux which had apparently puzzled Zappert greatly (Pfeiffer, p. 66). In the fifteenth chapter of *Gylfaginning*, it is told how Oðinn had to sacrifice one of his eyes before he could drink from the spring of wisdom. Zappert, however, did not need to look so far afield. The description of the attributes of *Wuotan* in *Deutsche Mythologie* (p. 133) begins: "Von den eigenthümlichkeiten der gestalt und äusseren erscheinung des gottes, wie sie in den nordischen mythen ausgeprägt sind, habe ich bei uns in Deutschland wenige spuren mehr angetroffen. Odin ist einäugig, trägt einen breiten hut und weiten mantel." Zappert looked for holes in Grimm's *Deutsche Mythologie*, and sought to plug them.

Grimm's assessment of the lullaby was undoubtedly coloured by the contin-uity between medieval and contemporary folk motifs which permeates the text, a continuity which forms the theoretical basis for his *Deutsche Mythologie*, as for his better-known activities as a collector. Writing to Pfeiffer, he remarks upon the resemblances between Zappert's lullaby and those still sung in his time: "schlaf, kindchen, schlaf, dein vater hütet die schaf, deine mutter hütet die lämmchen, die schwarzen und die weizsen, die will der wolf beizsen."[59] Grimm laments the fact that the pagan gods have been ousted by the loving parents of more modern times, that lullabies have lost their lustre. For him, Zappert's lullaby demonstrates the strength and longevity of tradition and provides an example of what he calls "der milde sinn des alten heidenthums."

It was Zappert's brilliant achievement to reconstruct the *Ur*-lullaby. In 1984 Emily Gerstner-Hirzel, knowing nothing of Zappert, published her definitive study, *Das volkstümliche deutsche Wiegenlied. Versuch einer Typologie der Texte*.[60] She finds that the sounds preferred in lullabies are *lu* and *slu*.[61] *slaslumo*, whether it means, "sleep, slumber," or "go to sleep quickly," is phonetically ideal. (Uncannily, the comedienne Joyce Grenfell "collected" a lullaby in the 1950s which opened with the words: "Sloop, bubily, sloop.")[62] Gerstner-Hirzel describes the aim of the lullaby as being to create a sense of security. The child's environment is commanded to be silent;

a fictitious disturber of the peace or bringer of danger is addressed directly and turned away, with a more or less explicit echo of pagan defensive magic, assuring the child of the presence of a protector.[63]

The archetypal lullaby combines the threat and the bribe. Red and blue flowers are often part of the bribe offered to the child, as a Silesian example shows:

> Ich ho mei Kindla schlofa gelegt
> ich ho's mit ruta Rusla bedeckt
> mit ruta Rusla und Veigla [. . .][64]

Just as important is the promise or naming of delicacies, such as eggs, cakes or sugar; lambs too can be promised, as in the example quoted by Grimm to Pfeiffer, a widespread lullaby.[65] No wolves are to be found in Gerstner-Hirzel; perhaps here Zappert was influenced by the *Wiener Hundesegen* (Braune XXXI, § 2), whose function is to guard sheepdogs from wolves, or perhaps he was thinking of Fenrir or Fenriswolf, the wolf in Old Norse mythology, who will break free from his fetters at Ragnarok, the end of the world. A modern equivalent of the wolf, the fox, occurs in many lullabies and nursery rhymes. In German lullabies he is frequently to be found lurking behind the house.[66]

This will not be the last word on Zappert's lullaby. Until technology has dated the ink, the arguments are bound to fall short of certainty. Of the six essays which addressed themselves to this subject in the twentieth century, three pleaded for the authenticity of the lullaby (Wolfskehl, Diamant, Howard), three against (Fichtenau, Jacoby, Gerhardt[67].) The story, as it emerges from the letters, essays, and reviews of the mid-nineteenth century, is not a pretty one. Petty, often highly personal arguments and counter-arguments were waged in the first decade after the "discovery." Then, after Pfeiffer's passionate defence, there was a curious gap of almost thirty years until Schuster's denunciation. The lullaby has scarcely merited a footnote in the literary histories; it soon disappeared from the correspondence of the scholars. The open-minded attitude of Jacob Grimm forms an exception to the acrimonious rule. His integrity and his desire to find it in others emerges clearly from his essay on the goddess Tanfana, in which he declares himself "mehr gestimmt, an Wahrheit als an Trug zu glauben."[68] Grimm combined integrity and genius, but there are other kinds of genius. Georg Zappert should not be seen in an altogether negative light. In his lullaby we possess his masterpiece: an unrivalled combination of palaeographic, scholarly, poetic and bookbinding skill — a triumph, above all, of sheer industry.

The fragments of Hebrew quotations from Proverbs on the reverse side of the lullaby read like a commentary on Zappert's work and its reception. They would appear to be authentic, yet have the ring of a forger's signature or confession, rather like the apparently late medieval hand that wrote "scatet erroribus" in the bottom right-hand corner of Zappert's map of Vienna. The biblical texts seem almost to be issuing a challenge to posterity on Zappert's part, a challenge coloured by his dark sense of humour. The quotations read in full: "Happy is the man that findeth wisdom, and the man that getteth understanding" (Proverbs 3:13), and "Go to the ant, thou sluggard; consider her ways and be wise" (Proverbs 6: 6).

There remains at least one question. Why should Zappert opt for a lullaby, of all genres? The post-Freudian scholar might seek an answer in Zappert's isolated, childless existence. As his death neared, his only friend seems to have been his illiterate housekeeper. More probably the answer lies in Zappert's model, the Second Merseburg Charm. The forger needed a genre which was invocatory, which sought to cast a spell.[69] As indeed it did.

Postscripta

I. With regard to the Hebrew script and glosses, in 1996 I consulted Malachi Beit-Arié of the Institute of Microfilmed Hebrew Manuscripts in Jerusalem. His findings are set out below:

1. The Glosses

These are written in a different hand from the lines of Hebrew script. They were probably not written by a trained Jewish hand. The Hebrew of the glosses shows no antiquity; it may be late. They read like a nonsensical attempt to Judaize the lullaby. Thus *Dodi*, "lover," the gloss below *Tocha*, could only refer to a male adult; it could not be a term of endearment addressed to a child.

Jewish interlinear glosses are always placed on top of a word, in contrast to the customary Carolingian technique. The hand of the lullaby glosses is unpractised and not dateable. The lettering of "Zipora" is very clumsy. The Z in *Zanfana* (line 4) is not Hebrew, not zayin. The z in *unza* (line 2) is zayin, not segol.

2. The lines of Hebrew

Both lines are pen-trials, executed by two (probably distinct) trained Jewish hands of the thirteenth, or perhaps the twelfth century.[71] The hair follicles which are clearly to be seen on Fragment A.4 suggest a date prior to 1200, if the fragment is from a Hebrew manuscript written in Germany or Austria. The line on fragment A.4[a] is taken from a lexicon or glossary. No such glossaries survive from the tenth century. The line of Hebrew on the verso side, probably in a different hand, consists of the end and beginning of the two quotations from Proverbs: 1) ". . . wisdom, and . . . understanding," and 2) "Go to. . . ."

The chief difficulty presented by these two lines is the superscript "Tiberian" vocalisation. It is not a known system, and has no obvious parallel. It looks doubtful. Whereas the vocalisation in the lullaby is largely limited to dots, that in the two Hebrew lines employs other signs.

3. The "vocalisation" in the lullaby

This is inconsistent and unsystematic in its representation of vowels, with the dots being placed both above and between the letters.

In conclusion, it appears that Fragment A.4 was cut from a codex with Hebrew pen-trials, probably in the thirteenth century. The OHG lines were in all probability added at some subsequent point, the "glosses" being interpolated and the vocalisation added on the basis of a vague analogy with the Hebrew lines. The vocalisation is not only unsystematic in orthographic terms; it is applied to individual words in an arbitrary manner, for no apparent reason. If it were, as Zappert suggests, a teaching tool, one would expect greater consistency.

That the lullaby was written subsequent to the Hebrew line above it is, furthermore, suggested by the external appearance of the fragment, and by the lack of any overlap between the Hebrew and German script. The "glosses" and the superficial vocalisation of the OHG words would appear to be an attempt to link Germanic and Hebrew culture. That such a link was dear to Zappert's heart is clear from his essay on the lullaby, which adduces evidence for such cultural interrelations in the Middle Ages.[72] The "glosses" might in theory be of any date, but the likeliest explanation is that this dilettante vocalisation is modelled on that in the Hebrew pen-trials. It would be an extraordinary coincidence if two different hands of the tenth and the twelfth/thirteenth century had employed an analogous "system" of vocalisation independently of one another. If the vocalisation in the lullaby is dependant on that in the pen-trials, then it must be of later date. The nineteenth century suggests itself.

II. In 1998, through the kind offices of Hofrätin Dr. Eva Irblich of the Österreichische Nationalbibliothek, a number of tests were carried out in Vienna.

1. Walter Ruhm of the library's Institut für Restaurierung established under a microscope that traces of glue were to be found on the recto side of Fragment A.4 (the lullaby) of Cod. 15.013. These traces were however limited to the unwritten parts of the parchment; no glue was to be found on the script itself. This suggests that the text was written upon an old, originally blank piece of parchment which was then stuck on top of fragment A.3, which is blank save for one line of Hebrew. The pasting was undertaken in such a manner that the writing was not affected.

2. Professor Dr. Franz Mairinger of the Institut für Farbenchemie at the Akademie der bildenden Künste examined Fragment A.4 under the 'Photo-makroskop M400' designed by Messrs Wild. His findings: "The appearance of the ink is untypical. The iron-based gall ink (*Eisengallustinte*) which was employed from classical times through to the modern period, was generally mixed with soot to make the script darker and more legible. When such ink is investi-

gated under a microscope, the soot is revealed in the form of dark points and tiny stains. The following analysis comments upon the presence of soot or otherwise. Soot is present unless otherwise stated:

A.1 recto (dark ink) and verso (glued side)
A.2 verso (glued side) and recto (dark ink)
A.3 verso vertical lines: red cinnabar
           horizontal lines: ink with soot
A.3 recto 1 Hebrew line (mirror image?) shows a soot admixture
A.4 verso 1 Hebrew line: a different kind of ink, with soot admixture
A.4 recto a) 1 Hebrew line: ink dye without soot
           b) the lullaby: dye without soot

Thus neither the Hebrew script nor the German script of Fragment A.4 were executed in the typical medieval "Eisengallentinte" with soot admixture."

The next step would be to apply a fluoroscopic test, applying an X-ray to the original, in an attempt to establish whether the ingredients employed for the dye are of modern date. At the time of writing (February 2001), this test has yet to be carried out.

The evidence adduced above points more than one finger of suspicion, but falls short of certainty. The script of the lullaby steered clear of glue when the fragment was employed for binding purposes, just as it almost entirely avoided being cut by the binder's knife. Recipes for medieval ink were abundant and varied considerably. There is little doubt that the writer of the lullaby employed medieval parchment, but until such time as the ink is dated, whether by X-ray or by carbon dating, the evidence will remain circumstantial.

Notes

[1] This introduction is heavily indebted to Emily Gerstner-Hirzel's study, *Das volkstümliche deutsche Wiegenlied. Versuch einer Typologie der Texte* (Basle: Schweizerische Gesellschaft für Volkskunde, 1984).

[2] Persius, *Satires*, 3, 16–18. On the problem of whether Persius is referring to *cantilenæ*, cf. *Auli Persii Flacci, Satirarum Liber*, ed. Otto Jahn (Leipzig: Breitkopf & Haertel, 1843), 147; *The Satires of A. Persius Flaccus*, trans. and ed. John Conington and H. Nettleship, 3rd rev. ed. (Oxford: Clarendon Press, 1893), 53; Aulius Persius Flaccus, *Satiren*, ed. and trans. Walther Kißel (Heidelberg: Carl Winter, 1990), 390–91; *The Satires of Persius*, ed. and trans. Guy Lee and William Barr (Liverpool: Francis Cairns, 1987), 104.

[3] *Claudii Galeni Opera Omnia*, ed. Carolus Gottlob Kühn (Leipzig: Car. Cnobloch, 1825), VI, 36–37. See Linda M. Paterson, "Sources Féminines et le 'Sentiment de l'Enfance'," 385.

[4] Kuno Meyer, "Bruchstücke der älteren Lyrik Irlands," *Abhandlungen der*

preussischen Akademie der Wissenschaften, 1919, phil.-hist. Kl. Nr. 7. Erster Teil (Berlin, 1919), 69, § 160, includes the poem in the section "Aus Liebesgedichten"; *Irische Texte*, ed. and trans. Wh. Stokes and E. Windisch, III. Serie, H.1 (Leipzig: Hirzel, 1891), 100. For a facsimile see Robert Atkinson, *The Book of Ballymote* (Dublin: Royal Irish Academy, 1887), 291.

[5] Rudolf Thurneysen, "Zu irischen Handschriften und Litteraturdenkmälern," *Abhandlungen der königlichen Gesellschaft der Wissenschaften zu Göttingen. Philosophisch-historische Klasse. N.F.*, vol. 14, no. 2 (Berlin, 1912), 89.

[6] Meinloh von Sevelingen, *Des Minnesangs Frühling*, I,8,1; II,2,5.

[7] *The Penguin Book of English Folk Songs*, ed. R. Vaughan Williams and A. L. Lloyd (Harmondsworth: Penguin, 1959; repr. 1969), 99.

[8] *The Beginnnings of Welsh Poetry. Studies by Sir Ifor Williams*, 2nd ed. by Rachel Bromwich (Cardiff: U of Wales P, 1980), 63; a poetic translation in A. O. H. Jarman and Gwilym Rees Hughes, *A Guide to Welsh Literature*, 2 vols (Swansea: C. Davies, 1976) vol. 1, 101. Brendan Hehir and Jenny Rowland concur that the poem is an "artistic nursery rhyme." See Brendan Hehir, "What is the *Gododdin*?" in *Early Welsh Poetry. Studies in the Book of Aneirin*, ed. Brynley F. Roberts (Aberystwyth: National Library of Wales, 1988), 57–96 (77), and Jenny Rowland, "Genres," *op. cit.*, 179–208 (185). I am grateful to Chris Lewis of the Victoria County History for introducing me to the text.

[9] See Linda Paterson, "L'enfant dans la littérature occitane avant 1230," *Cahiers de civilisation médiévale*, 32 (1989): 233–45 (235). I am indebted to the author for drawing my attention to this article, and to the Galen reference.

[10] Wolfram von Eschenbach, *Des Minnesangs Frühling*, 7,19. Wolfram's few surviving love-lyrics are undatable, but his narrative works date from *c.* 1203–30.

[11] *Die Lieder Neidharts*, ed. Edmund Wießner, 4th ed., rev. Paul Sappler, Altdeutsche Textbibliothek, 44 (Tübingen: Niemeyer, 1984), Sommerlied 18, V, 4–7.

[12] Götfrit von Nifen, song L, *Deutsche Liederdichter des 13. Jahrhunderts* ed. Carl von Kraus, 2nd ed., rev. Gisela Kornrumpf, 2 vols (Tübingen: Niemeyer, 1978), vol. 1, 127.

[13] *Der Sælden Hort. Alemannisches Gedicht vom Leben Jesu, Johannes des Täufers und der Magdalena*, ed. Heinrich Adrian, DTM, XXVI (Berlin: Weidmann, 1927), lines 1603–05.

[14] *Der Mönch von Salzburg. ich bin du und du bist ich. Lieder des Mittelalters*, ed. Franz V. Spechtler (Munich: Heimeran, 1980), 142–43, 189–90.

[15] *English Mystery Plays. A Selection*, ed. Peter Happé (Harmondsworth: Penguin, 1975), 282.

[16] *Medieval English Lyrics. A Critical Anthology*, ed. R. T. Davies (London: Faber and Faber, 1963), 106. The first line acts as the refrain for one of two further "lullabies" of a similar nature contained in the Commonplace Book of John of Grimestone (1372). See *Middle English Lyrics*, selected and ed. Maxwell S. Luria and Richard L. Hoffmann (New York and London: W. W. Norton & Company, 1974), §§ 201 and 202.

[17] *English Verse 1300–1500*, Longman Annotated Anthologies of English Verse, vol. 1, ed. John Burrow (London and New York: Longman, 1977), 28.

[18] E. J. Dobson and F. Ll. Harrison, *Medieval English Songs* (London and Boston: Faber & Faber, 1979), § 20. This song is also in John of Grimestone's Commonplace Book.

[19] *English Mystery Plays*, 283. I am indebted to Andrew Potts for tracking down the source. Both this lullaby and the "adult lullaby" were recorded in 1997 by the "Medieval Babes" ("Salva Nos" CDVE935.7243845157.20).

[20] *English Verse 1300–1500*, 305–06.

[21] Emily Gerstner-Hirzel, "Das Kinderlied," in *Handbuch des Volksliedes*, ed. Rolf Wilhelm Brednich, Lutz Röhrich, Wolfgang Suppan, 2 vols (Munich: Fink, 1973), vol. 1, 923–67 (923–24).

[22] T. G. von Karajan, "Zwei bisher unbekannte Sprachdenkmale aus heidnischer Zeit," *Wiener Sitzungsberichte* 25 (1858): 308–25.

[23] Franz Pfeiffer, "Forschungen und Kritik auf dem Gebiete des deutschen Alterthums II.: IV. Über das Wiener Schlummerlied. Eine Rettung," *Wiener Sitzungsberichte*, 52 (1866): 43–86 (59).

[24] Letter to Pfeiffer, 31 October 1858, published in "Zur Geschichte der deutschen Philologie. I. Briefe von Jacob Grimm. A. J. Grimms Briefe an Franz Pfeiffer," *Germania* 11 (1866): 243.

[25] Georg Zappert, "Über ein althochdeutsches Schlummerlied," *Wiener Sitzungsberichte* 29 (1858): 302–15.

[26] Letter no. 28, *loc. cit.*, 245.

[27] Pfeiffer, "Rettung," 67–68.

[28] Pfeiffer, "Rettung," 47.

[29] Quoted by Pfeiffer, *loc. cit.*

[30] Paul J. Diamant, "Althochdeutsches Schlummerlied. Ein Gelehrtenstreit über deutsch-jüdische Zusammenhänge im Mittelalter," *Jahrbuch des Leo-Baeck-Instituts* 5 (1960): 338–45 (343).

[31] Constantin von Wurzbach, *Biographisches Lexikon des Kaiserthums Oesterreich* (Vienna: Verlag der Universitäts-Buchdruckerei von L. L. Zamarski, 1890), vol. 59, 184–86.

[32] Karl Wolfskehl, "Das althochdeutsche Schlummerlied," in *Aus unbekannten Schriften. Festgabe für Martin Buber zum 50. Geburtstag* (Berlin: L. Schneider, 1928), 58–63; repr. in *Karl Wolfskehl. Gesammelte Werke*, ed. Margot Ruben and Claus Victor Bock (Hamburg: Claassen, 1960), 61–66 (64).

[33] See the bibliography in Diamant, "Althochdeutsches Schlummerlied," 345.

[34] Wilhelm Müller, review of Pfeiffer's "Rettung," *GGA* 27 (1867): 1057–70 (1061).

[35] Pfeiffer, "Rettung," 48–49. Such negligence is not unknown even today. In the 1980s an adopted son of a noble Austrian family was permitted access to the libraries of Kremsmünster and Göttweig, both monasteries cherishing the hope that he might become one of their number, bringing with him considerable wealth. It happened,

however, that the stocks of both libraries diminished at the time in question. The gentleman was loading a sixteenth-century atlas into the boot of his car when he was accosted by a monk, who asked him politely: "Dürfen Sie das eigentlich?" The suspect immediately broke down and confessed. At his trial he offered in his defence: "Ich muß mir doch ein standesgemäßes Leben finanzieren könnnen." I am indebted to Hauke Fill of Kremsmünster for the anecdote.

[36] See *Otfrids Evangelienbuch*, ed. Paul Piper, 2nd rev. ed., 2 vols (Freiburg & Tübingen: J. C. B. Mohr, 1882), 175–77.

[37] John A. Howard, "Über die Echtheit eines althochdeutschen Wiegenliedes," *Studia Neophilologica* 47 (1976): 21–35; Michael Jacoby, "Methodische Gesichtspunkte zur Beurteilung der Frage nach der Echtheit eines 'althochdeutschen Wiegenliedes' (Cod. 15.013, fol. V recto, A)," *Codices manuscripti* 2 (1976), H. 4: 110–13 (111).

[38] Pfeiffer, "Rettung," 53–54.

[39] Ph. Jaffé, "Zum Schlummerlied," *ZfdA* 13 (1867): 496–501 (500).

[40] Pfeiffer, "Rettung," 54.

[41] Bischoff, "Paläographische Fragen." The lullaby is listed under "Forgeries" in Bischoff's *Latin Palaeography. Antiquity and the Middle Ages*, trans. Dáibhí Ó Cróinín and David Ganz (Cambridge: Cambridge UP, 1989), 46.

[42] Wilhelm Müller, review of Zappert, *GGA* 21 (1860): 201–11 (208).

[43] Pfeiffer, "Rettung," 69–70.

[44] Braune, *Althochdeutsche Grammatik*, §§ 118; 303.

[45] Carl Hofmann, "Schlummerlied und Bienensegen," *Sitzungsberichte der königlichen bayerischen Akademie zu München*, 1866, II., H. II: 103–12.

[46] Jacob Grimm, *Deutsche Mythologie*, 2nd ed., 2 vols (Göttingen: Dieterich, 1844), 266.

[47] *Deutsche Mythologie*, 69–70; 236. The Loeb edition of Tacitus quotes the lullaby, noting blithely: "For Tanfana the only other evidence is a ninth- or tenth-century line." Tacitus, *Annals* I, LI, Loeb Classical Library (Tacitus, vol. II), trans. John Jackson (London: Heinemann; Cambridge, MA: Harvard UP, 1931), 328.

[48] Jacob Grimm, "Über die Göttin Tanfana," *Berliner Monatsberichte*, 10 March 1859, 254–58 = *Kleinere Schriften*, ed. Karl Müllenhoff, vol. 5 (Berlin: Dümmler, 1871), 418–21.

[49] Zappert, "Schlummerlied," 313.

[50] Zappert, "Schlummerlied," 313.

[51] Grimm, quoted by Pfeiffer, "Rettung," 76.

[52] *Handwörterbuch des deutschen Aberglaubens*, ed. Hanns Bächtold-Stäubli et al. (Berlin and Leipzig: W. de Gruyter, 1927–42), vol. 6, cols. 1327–33, 1324–25.

[53] Pfeiffer, "Rettung," 47–48.

[54] Richard Schuster, "Zappert's 'ältester Plan von Wien'," *Wiener Sitzungsberichte, phil.-hist. Cl*, CXXVII (Vienna, 1892), 6th section, 1–30.

[55] Müller, review of Pfeiffer, 1068.

[56] Grimm, letter to Pfeiffer, 9 May 1858, *loc.cit.*: 241–42. The honorifics refer to the title page of Fr. Schönwerth, *Aus der Oberpfalz: Sitten und Sagen*, 3 vols (Augsburg:

M. Rieger, 1857–59).

[57] Grimm, *Deutsche Mythologie*, 69–70.

[58] *Deutsche Mythologie*, 267–68.

[59] Pfeiffer, "Rettung," 80–81.

[60] Gerstner-Hirzel, *Das volkstümliche deutsche Wiegenlied* (as note 1).

[61] Gerstner-Hirzel, *Das volkstümliche deutsche Wiegenlied*, 11.

[62] Recollected by David McLintock.

[63] Gerstner-Hirzel, *Das volkstümliche deutsche Wiegenlied*, 12.

[64] Gerstner-Hirzel, *Das volkstümliche deutsche Wiegenlied*, 13.

[65] Gerstner-Hirzel, *Das volkstümliche deutsche Wiegenlied*, 13–14; 27; 332–43.

[66] Gerstner-Hirzel, *Das volkstümliche deutsche Wiegenlied*, 470–71 (§§ 650, 690, 700).

[67] Heinrich Fichtenau, "Die Fälschungen Georg Zapperts," *MIÖG* 78 (1970): 444–67. Fichtenau questions many of Zappert's "finds," without providing conclusive evidence either way. See also Heinrich Fichtenau, *Die Lehrbücher Maximilians I. und die Anfänge der Frakturschrift* (Hamburg: Maximilian Gesellschaft, 1961). The dispute is reconsidered in the context of German-Jewish forgeries by Dietrich Gerhardt, *Süsskind von Trimberg: Berichtigungen zu einer Erinnerung* (Bern: P. Lang, 1997), 283–94.

[68] Jacob Grimm, "Über die Göttin Tanfana," 419.

[69] I am indebted to Paul Kershaw (London) for this suggestion.

[70] For discussion of such little Carolingian Hebrew writing as has survived, see Malachi Beit-Arié, *Hebrew Manuscripts of East and West: towards a Comparative Codicology*, The Panizzi Lectures, 1992 (London: British Library, 1993), 14–15.

[71] Zappert, "Schlummerlied," 308–12.

Bibliography

Dictionaries and other works of reference

Allgemeine deutsche Biographie. Edited by Rochus, Freiherr von Liliencron et al. 56 vols. Leipzig: Duncker & Humblot, 1875–1912.

Atlas zur Kirchengeschichte. Edited by Hubert Jedin et al. Freiburg i. Br.: Herder, 1970.

Biographisches Lexikon des Kaiserthums Oesterreich. Edited by Constantin von Wurzbach. Vienna: Verlag der Universitäts-Buchdruckerei von L. L. Zamarski, 1856–91.

Bosworth, Joseph and T. Northcote Toller, *An Anglo-Saxon Dictionary*. Oxford: Oxford UP, 1964.

Braune, Wilhelm, *Althochdeutsche Grammatik*. 14th ed., rev. by Hans Eggers. Tübingen: Niemeyer, 1987.

Brown, Francis, Samuel R. Driver and Charles A. Briggs. *A Hebrew and English Lexicon of the Old Testament*. Oxford: Clarendon Press, 1977.

Brown, Raymond Edward, Joseph A. Fitzmyer, and Roland Edmund Murphy, eds. *The Jerome Biblical Commentary*. London: Geoffrey Chapman, 1968.

Dalby, David, *Lexicon of the Medieval German Hunt*. Berlin: W. de Gruyter, 1965.

Du Cange, Charles du Fresne. *Glossarium Mediae et Infimae Latinitatis*. Paris: Instituti Regii Franciae Typographi, 1883–87.

Glare, P. G. W. *Oxford Latin Dictionary*. Oxford: Clarendon Press, 1982.

Groseclose, J. S., and B. O. Murdoch. *Die althochdeutschen poetischen Denkmäler*. Sammlung Metzler, 140. Stuttgart: Metzler, 1976.

Handwörterbuch des deutschen Aberglaubens. Edited by Hanns Bächtold-Stäubli et al. Berlin and Leipzig: W. de Gruyter, 1927–42.

Köbler, Gerhard. *Wörterbuch des althochdeutschen Sprachschatzes*. Paderborn: F. Schöningh, 1993.

Maier, Bernhard. *Lexikon der keltischen Religion und Kultur*. Stuttgart: Kröner, 1994.

Masser, Achim, ed. *Die deutsche Literatur des Mittelalters. Verfasserlexikon*. 2nd ed., rev. by Kurt Ruh et al. Munich and New York: De Gruyter, 1977–2000.

Niermeyer, J. F. *Mediae Latinitatis Lexicon Minus*. Leiden: E. J. Brill, 1984.

Noreen, Adolf. *Altisländische und Altnorwegische Grammatik*. Altnordische Grammatik, 1. 3rd rev. ed. Halle: M. Niemeyer, 1903.

Puchner, Karl. *Historisches Ortsnamenbuch von Bayern. Oberbayern, Bd. 1. Landkreis Ebersberg*. Munich: Kommission für Bayerische Landesgeschichte, 1951.

Schützeichel, Rudolf. *Althochdeutsches Wörterbuch*. Tübingen: Niemeyer, 1969.

Souter, Alexander. *A Glossary of Later Latin to 600 A.D.* Oxford: Clarendon Press, 1949.

Splett, Jochen. *Althochdeutsches Wörterbuch: Analyse der Wortfamilienstrukturen des Althochdeutschen, zugleich Grundlegung einer zukünftigen Struktur-geschichte des deutschen Wortschatzes.* Berlin and New York: de Gruyter, 1993.

Versuch eines bremisch-niedersächsischen Wörterbuchs. Edited by the Bremisch Deutsche Gesellschaft. 5 vols. Bremen: Georg Ludewig Forster, 1767.

Wells, John C. *Althochdeutsches Glossenwörterbuch, einschließlich des von Prof. Dr. Taylor Starck† begonnenen Glossenindexes.* Heidelberg: C. Winter, 1990.

Editions, facsimiles and translations

Old High German and Old Saxon

Behaghel, Otto, ed., *Heliand und Genesis.* ATB, 4. 8th ed., rev. by Paul Mitzka. Tübingen: Niemeyer, 1965.

Braune, Wilhelm, ed., *Althochdeutsches Lesebuch.* 17th ed., rev. by Ernst A. Ebbinghaus. Tübingen: Niemeyer, 1994.

Broszinski, Hartmut, ed., *Hiltibraht. Das Hildebrandlied. Faksimile der Kasseler Handschrift.* 2nd ed. Kassel: Stauda, 1985.

Eckardt, Annette von. *Die Handschrift des Wessobrunner Gebets. Geleitwort von Carl von Kraus.* Munich: Kurt Wolff, 1922.

Enneccerus, M., ed., *Die ältesten deutschen Sprach-Denkmäler in Lichtdrucken.* Frankfurt am Main: Enneccerus, 1897.

Fischer, Hanns, *Schrifttafeln zum althochdeutschen Lesebuch.* Tübingen: Niemeyer, 1966.

Grein, Christian Wilhelm Michael, ed., *Das Hildebrandslied nach der Handschrift von Neuem herausgegeben.* Göttingen: Georg H. Wigand, 1858.

Grimm, Jacob and Wilhelm, eds, *Die beiden ältesten deutschen Gedichte aus dem achten Jahrundert. Das Lied von Hildebrand und Hadubrand und das Weißenbrunner Gebet.* Kassel: Thurneissen, 1812.

Hench, George Allison, ed., *The Monsee fragments: New collated text with introduction, notes, grammatical treatise and exhaustive glossary, and a photo-lithographic facsimile.* Strasbourg: K. J. Trübner, 1890.

Müllenhoff, Karl and Wilhelm Scherer, eds, *Denkmäler deutscher Poesie und Prosa aus dem VIII.–XII. Jahrhundert.* 3rd ed., rev. by Elias von Steinmeyer. Berlin: Weidmann, 1892; repr. Berlin & Zurich: Weidmann, 1964.

Otfrids Evangelienbuch. Edited by Oskar Erdmann. 6th ed., rev. by Ludwig Wolff. ATB, 49. Tübingen: Niemeyer, 1973.

Otfrids Evangelienbuch. Edited by Paul Piper. 2nd rev. ed. 2 vols. Tübingen: J. C. B. Mohr, 1882.

Otfrid von Weißenburg. *Evangelienbuch, Auswahl. Althochdeutsch / Neuhochdeutsch*, edited and translated by Gisela Vollmann-Profe. Althochdeutsche Literatur, 3. Stuttgart: Reclam, 1987.

Petzet, Erich and Otto Glauning, *Deutsche Schrifttafeln des IX. bis XVI. Jahrhunderts*. 5 vols. Munich: Carl Kuhn, 1910.

Pez, Bernhard, *Thesaurus anecdotorum novissimus*. 6 vols. Vienna: sumptibus Philippi, Martini & Joannis Veith fratrum, 1721–23.

Steinmeyer, Elias von, ed., *Die kleineren althochdeutschen Sprachdenkmäler*. Berlin: Weidmann, 1916; repr. Berlin: Weidmann, 1963.

Wipf, Karl A., ed., *Althochdeutsche poetische Texte. Althochdeutsch / Neuhochdeutsch*. Althochdeutsche Literatur, 1. Stuttgart: Reclam, 1992.

Works in Other Languages

Adam of Bremen, *Bischofsgeschichte der Hamburgischen Kirche*. Edited by R. Buchner et al. Quellen des 9. und 11. Jhs. zur Geschichte der Hamburgischen Kirche und des Reiches. 5th ed. Darmstadt: Wissenschaftliche Buchgesellschaft, 1978.

Andrieu, Michel, ed., *Les Ordines Romani du haut moyen âge*. 5 vols. Louvain: Spicilegium Sacrum Lovaniense, 1931–61.

Atkinson, Robert, ed., *The Book of Ballymote*. Dublin: Royal Irish Academy, 1887.

Bang, A., ed., *Norske hexeformularer og magiske opskrifter*. Christiania: J. Dybwad, 1901.

Bede's Ecclesiastical History. Edited and translated by Bertram Colgrave and R. A. B. Mynors. Harmondsworth: Penguin, 1969.

Bede, *A History of the English Church and People*. Translated by Leo Sherley-Price. Harmondsworth: Penguin, 1955.

Beyschlag, Siegfried, ed., *Die Lieder Neidharts*. Darmstadt: Wissenschaftliche Buchgesellschaft, 1975.

Böhmer, J. ed., *Die Regesten des Kaiserreichs unter den Karolingern, 751–918*. 1st ed., rev. by E. Mühlbacher. Cologne: Böhlau, 1908.

Böhmer, J., ed., *Regesta archiepiscoporum Maguntiniensum*. Innsbruck, 1877; repr. Aachen: Scientia Verlag, 1966.

Burrow, John, ed., *English Verse 1300–1500*. Longman Annotated Anthologies of English Verse, 1. London & New York: Longman, 1977.

Cagin, Paul, ed., *Le sacramentaire gélasien d'Angoulême*. Angoulême: Société Historique et Archéologique de la Charente, 1919.

Carmina Burana. Edited by A. Hilka, O. Schumann, and B. Bischoff, translated by Carl Fischer and Hugo Kuhn. 3rd ed. Munich: Deutscher Taschenbuch Verlag, 1979.

Carmina Ratisponensia. Edited by Anke Paravicini. Editiones Heidelbergenses, 20. Heidelberg: Carl Winter, 1979.

Caspari, Carl Paul, ed., *Eine Augustin fälschlich beigelegte Homilia de Sacrilegiis. Aus einer Einsiedeler Handschrift des achten Jahrhunderts herausgegeben und mit kritischen und sachlichen Anmerkungen, sowie mit einer Abhandlung begleitet.* Christiania: Jacob Dybwad, 1886.

Cawley, A. C. and J. J. Anderson, eds, *Pearl; Cleanness; Patience; Sir Gawain and the Green Knight.* London & Melbourne: Dent, 1983.

Chambers, R. W., Max Förster and Robin Flower, eds, *The Exeter Book of Old English Poetry.* Exeter: P. Lund, Humphries & Co., 1933.

Charles, R. H., trans., *The Book of Enoch.* London: SPCK, 1912.

Conington, John and H. Nettleship, eds, *The Satires of A. Persius Flaccus.* 3rd ed. Oxford: Clarendon Press, 1893.

Dafydd ap Gwilym: A Selection of Poems. Edited and translated by Rachel Bromwich. Harmondsworth: Penguin, 1985.

Davies, R. T., ed., *Medieval English Lyrics. A Critical Anthology.* London: Faber & Faber, 1963.

Deshusses, Jean, ed., *Le Sacramentaire Grégorien: ses principales formes d'après les plus anciens manuscrits.* Spicilegium Friburgense, vols 16, 24, 28. Fribourg: Éditions Universitaires, 1971–82.

Dobbie, Elliott van Kirk, ed., *The Anglo-Saxon Minor Poems.* The Anglo- Saxon Poetic Records, 6. New York: Columbia UP, 1942.

Dobson, E. J., and F. Ll. Harrison, *Medieval English Songs.* London & Boston: Faber & Faber, 1979.

Edda. Die Lieder des Codex Regius nebst verwandten Denkmälern. Edited by Gustav Neckel. 4th ed., rev. by Hans Kuhn. Heidelberg: Carl Winter, 1962.

Edda: Prologue and Gylfaginning. Edited by Anthony Faulkes. Oxford; New York: Clarendon Press; Oxford UP, 1982.

Einhard, *Vita Karoli.* Edited by O. Holder-Egger. MGH SRG. Hanover and Leipzig: Hahn, 1911.

Einhard and Notker the Stammerer. Two Lives of Charlemagne. Translated by Lewis Thorpe. Harmondsworth: Penguin, 1974.

Geoffrey of Monmouth: Vita Merlini. Edited and translated by Basil Clarke. Cardiff: U of Wales P [for] the Language and Literature Committee of the Board of Celtic Studies, 1973.

Godman, Peter, ed., *Poetry of the Carolingian Renaissance.* London: Duckworth, 1985.

Gordon, R. K., trans., *Anglo-Saxon Poetry.* London; New York: Dent & Dutton, 1926; repr. Dent & Dutton, 1967.

Gradon, P. O., ed., *Cynewulf's 'Elene'.* Rev. ed. Exeter: U of Exeter P, 1977.

Grattan, John Henry Grafton and Charles Singer, eds, *Lacnunga: an Anglo-Saxon magico-medical commonplace book.* Publications of the Wellcome Historical Medical Museum, NS 3. London: Geoffrey Cumberlege, 1952.

Gregorii Magni Dialogi. Edited by Umberto Moricca. Fonti per la storia d'Italia, Scrittori Secolo, 6. Rome: Tipografia del Senato, 1924.

St. Gregory the Great, Dialogues. Translated by Odo John Zimmermann. The Fathers of the Church, 39. New York: Fathers of the Church Inc., 1959.

Hagen, Friedrich Heinrich von der, ed., *Minnesinger. Deutsche Liederdichter des zwölften, dreizehnten und vierzehnten Jahrhunderts.* 4 vols. Leipzig: J. A. Barth, 1838–61.

Happé, Peter, ed., *English Mystery Plays. A Selection.* Harmondsworth: Penguin, 1975.

Hardy, Thomas. *The Return of the Native.* 1878; repr. New York: The New American Library, Inc., 1959.

Heim, Richard, ed., *Incantamenta magica graeca latina. Jahrbücher für Philologie und Pädagogik,* Suppl. NF 19. Leipzig: B. G. Teubner, 1893.

Holtzmann, Robert, ed., *Die Chronik des Bischofs Thietmar von Merseburg.* MGH SRG, IX. 2nd ed. Berlin: Weidmannsche Buchhandlung, 1965.

Jahn, Otto, ed., *Auli Persii Flacci. Satirarum Liber.* Leipzig: Breitkopf & Haertel, 1843.

Jamieson, Robert, ed., *Popular Ballads and Songs.* 2 vols. Edinburgh; London: Archibald Constable & Co.; Cadell & Davies, and John Murray, 1806.

Jerusalem Bible, The. Edited by Alexander Jones. London: Darton, Longman & Todd, 1966.

Johnston, Dafydd, ed. and trans., *Canu Maswedd yr Oesoedd Canol. Medieval Welsh Erotic Poetry.* Cardiff: Gwasg Gomer, Llandysul, 1991.

Jónsson, Finnur, ed., *Den Norsk-Islandske Skjaldedigtning.* 4 vols. Copenhagen and Christiania: Gyldendal, 1908.

Keller, Adalbert von, ed., *Fastnachtspiele aus dem fünfzehnten Jahrhundert.* Bibliothek des litterarischen Vereins in Stuttgart, 28–30. Stuttgart: Litterarischer Verein, 1853.

Kißel, Walther, ed., *Aulius Persius Flaccus. Satiren.* Heidelberg: Carl Winter, 1990.

Klusen, Ernst, ed., *Deutsche Lieder. Texte und Melodien.* Frankfurt: Insel Verlag, 1980.

Kok, J. P. Filedt, ed., *Livelier than Life — the Master of the Amsterdam Cabinet or the Housebook Master, ca. 1470–1500.* Amsterdam: Rijksmuseum, 1985.

Kraus, Carl von, ed., *Deutsche Liederdichter des 13. Jahrhunderts.* 2nd ed., rev. by Gisela Kornrumpf. 2 vols. Tübingen: Niemeyer, 1978.

Kühn, Carolus Gottlob, ed., *Claudii Galeni Opera Omnia.* Leipzig: Car. Cnobloch, 1825.

Larrington, Carolyne, trans., *The Poetic Edda.* Oxford: Oxford UP, 1996.

Lee, Guy and William Barr, eds, *The Satires of Persius.* Liverpool: Francis Cairns, 1987.

Leitzmann, A., ed., *Kleinere geistliche Gedichte des XII. Jahrhunderts.* Bonn: A. Marcus & E. Weber, 1910.

Luria, Maxwell and Richard L. Hoffmann, eds, *Middle English Lyrics*. New York and London: W. W. Norton & Company, 1974.

Mackie, W. S., ed., *The Exeter Book, Part II*. EETS, O.S., 194. London: Oxford UP, 1934.

Meyer, Kuno, ed., 'Bruchstücke der älteren Lyrik Irlands,' *Abhandlungen der preussischen Akademie der Wissenschaften, phil.-hist. Kl.*, Nr. 7. Erster Teil. Berlin, 1919.

Mohlberg, Leo Cunibert, ed., *Liber Sacramentorum Romanae Aeclesiae ordinis anni circuli (Cod. Vat. Reg. Lat. 316 / Paris Bibl. Nat. 7193, 41/56) (SACRAMENTARIUM GELASIANUM)*. Rerum ecclesiasticarum documenta. Series minor. Subsidia studiorum, 5. Rome: Herder, 1960.

Der Mönch von Salzburg. ich bin du und du bist ich. Edited by Franz V. Spechtler. Munich: Heimeran, 1980.

Moser, Hugo and Helmut Tervooren, eds, *Des Minnesangs Frühling*. 38th rev. ed. Stuttgart: S. Hirzel, 1988.

Neff, Karl, ed., *Die Gedichte des Paulus Diaconus*. Quellen und Untersuchungen zur lateinischen Philologie des Mittelalters, III,iv. Munich: C. H. Beck, 1908.

Nordal, Sigurður, ed., *Vǫluspá*. Translated by B. S. Benedikz and John McKinnell. Durham and St. Andrews Medieval Texts, 1. Durham: Durham and St. Andrews Medieval Texts, 1980.

O'Donoghue, Bernard, ed., *The Courtly Love Tradition*. Literature in Context, 5. Manchester: Manchester UP, 1982.

Orderic Vitalis, *The Ecclesiastical History*. Edited and translated by Marjorie Chibnall. 6 vols. Oxford Medieval Texts. Oxford: Clarendon Press, 1969–80.

Paden, William Doremus, ed. and trans., *The Medieval Pastourelle*. Garland library of medieval literature. Series A, vols. 34–35. New York: Garland, 1987.

Pálsson, Hermann and Paul Edwards, trans., *Seven Viking Romances*. Harmondsworth: Penguin, 1985.

Paul the Deacon, *History of the Langobards*. Translated by William Dudley Foulke. Philadephia: Department of History, University of Pennsylvania, PA, 1907.

Pez, Bernhard. 'Monumenta Wessofontana. Diplomatarium Miscellum.' *Monumenta Boica*, 7 (1766), 329–476.

Rees, Rev. William J., ed., *Lives of the Cambro British Saints, of the fifth and immediately succeeding centuries: from ancient Welsh and Latin MSS. in the British Museum and elsewhere*. Llandovery: William Rees, 1853.

Reeves, James, *The Idiom of the People*. 1958. Reprint, London: Mercury Books, 1962.

Richter, Gregor and Albert Schönfelder, eds, *Sacramentarium Fuldense saeculi X: Cod. Theol 321 der K. Universitätsbibliothek zu Göttingen*. Quellen und Abhandlungen zur Geschichte der Abtei und der Diözese Fulda, 9. Fulda, 1912; repr. Farnborough: St. Michael's Abbey Press, 1983.

Rimberti Vita Anskari. Edited and translated by Werner Trillmilch. Quellen des IX. und XI. Jahrhunderts zur Geschichte der Hamburgischen Kirche und des Reiches. 5th ed. Darmstadt: Wissenschaftliche Buchgesellschaft, 1978.

Robinson, P. M. W. "An edition of Svipdagsmál." D. Phil. diss., University of Oxford, 1991.

Der Sælden Hort. Alemannisches Gedicht vom Leben Jesu, Johannes des Täufers und der Magdalena. Edited by Heinrich Adrian. DTM, 226. Berlin: Weidmann, 1927.

Sisam, Celia, ed., *The Vercelli Book.* Early English MSS in Facsimile, 19. Copenhagen: Rosenkilde & Bagger, 1976.

Smith, A. H., ed., *Three Northumbrian Poems: Caedmon's Hymn, Bede's Death Song; and the Leiden riddle.* Rev. ed. Exeter: U of Exeter, 1978.

Snorri Sturluson, *Edda.* Translated by Anthony Faulkes. London & Melbourne: Dent, 1987.

Stokes, W. H. and E. Windisch, eds and trans, *Irische Texte. Dritte Serie H.1.* Leipzig: Hirzel, 1891.

Stuart, Heather. "A Critical Edition of some Anglo-Saxon Charms and Incantations." Ph. D. diss., Flinders University of South Australia, 1973.

Strecker, Karl, ed., *Die Cambridger Lieder.* MGH, SRG 40. Berlin: Weidmann, 1926.

Tacitus, *Annals.* Translated by John Jackson. Cambridge, MA & London: Harvard UP; Heinemann, 1931; repr. 1969.

Vaughan Williams, Ralph, and A. L. Lloyd, eds, *The Penguin Book of English Folk Songs.* Harmondsworth: Penguin, 1959; rpt. 1969.

Vogel, Cyrille and Reinhard Elze, eds, *Le Pontifical Romano-Germanique du dixième siècle.* Studie e Testi, 226. 2 vols. Vatican: Biblioteca Apostolica Vaticana, 1963.

Waldburg Wolfegg, Christoph Graf zu, ed., *The Medieval Housebook.* Translated by Cyril Edwards. Munich: Prestel Verlag, 1997.

Warren, Frederick Edward, ed., *The Leofric Missal: as used in the Cathedral of Exeter during the episcopate of its first bishop. A.D. 1050–10722, together with some account of the Red Book of Derby, the Missal of Robert of Jumièges, and a few other early manuscript books of the English Church.* Oxford: Clarendon Press, 1883.

Walther von der Vogelweide. Leich, Lieder, Sangsprüche. Edited by Karl Lachmann. 14th ed., rev. by Christoph Cormeau with contributions by Thomas Bein and Horst Brunner. Berlin and New York: de Gruyter, 1996.

Widukind von Corvey: Res gestae Saxonicae. Die Sachsengeschichte. Edited and translated by Ekkehart Rotter and Bernd Schneidmüller. Stuttgart: Reclam, 1981.

Wießner, Edmund, ed., *Die Lieder Neidharts.* 4th ed., rev. by Paul Sappler. ATB, 44. Tübingen: Niemeyer, 1984.

Wolfram von Eschenbach, *Werke.* Edited by Karl Lachmann. 6th ed. Berlin and Leipzig: de Gruyter, 1926.

Ziolkowski, Jan M., ed. and trans., *The Cambridge Songs (Carmina Cantabrigiensia)*. Garland Library of Medieval Literature, Series A, 66. New York and London: Garland, 1994.

Secondary Sources

Allard, Jean Paul. "Du Second Charme de Mersebourg au Viatique de Weingarten." *Études Indo-Européennes* 14 (1985): 33–53.

Arntz, Helmut. *Handbuch der Runenkunde*. Halle/Saale: M. Niemeyer, 1944.

Ashcroft, Jeffrey. "Die Anfänge von Walthers politischer Lyrik." In *Minnesang in Österreich*, edited by Helmut Birkhan, 1–14. Vienna: K. M. Halosar, 1983.

Baesecke, Georg. "St. Emmeramer Studien." *PBB* 46 (1922): 430–94.

———. *Der Vocabularius Sti. Galli in der angelsächsischen Mission*. Halle: Niemeyer, 1933.

———. "Contra caducum morbum." *PBB* 62 (1938): 456–60.

———. *Vor- und Frühgeschichte des deutschen Schrifttums*. 2 vols. Halle: Max Niemeyer, 1940; 1953.

———. *Das lateinisch-althochdeutsche Reimgebet 'Carmen ad deum' und das Rätsel vom 'Vogel federlos.'* Berlin: Wissenschaftliche Editionsgesellschaft, 1948.

———. "Die Karlische Renaissance und das deutsche Schrifttum." *DVJS* 23 (1949): 143–216.

———. *Kleinere Schriften zur althochdeutschen Sprache und Literatur*. Bern and Munich: 1966.

Barb, A. A. "The Survival of the Magic Arts." In *The Conflict between Paganism and Christianity in the Fourth Century*, edited by Arnaldo Momigliano, 100–25. Oxford: Clarendon Press, 1963.

Baron, Salo. *A Social and Religious History of the Jews*. 2nd ed. 16 vols. New York: Columbia UP, 1952–69.

Bauerreiss, Romuald. "Das frühmittelalterliche Bistum Neuburg im Staffelsee." *Studien und Mitteilungen zur Geschichte des Benediktiner Ordens* 60 (1946): 375–438.

Beit-Arié, Malachi. *Hebrew Manuscripts of East and West: towards a Comparative Codicology*. The Panizzi Lectures, 1992. London: British Library, 1993.

Bennewitz, Ingrid. "Die obszöne weibliche Stimme. Erotik und Obszönität in den Frauenstrophen der deutschen Literatur des Mittelalters." In *Frauenlieder - Cantigas de amigo. Internationale Kolloquien des Centro de Estudos Humanísticos (Universidade do Minho), der Faculdade de Letras (Universidade do Porto) und des Fachbereichs Germanistik (Freie Universität Berlin) Berlin 6.11.1998; Apúlia 28.–30.3.1999*, edited by Thomas Cramer et al., 69–84. Stuttgart: S. Hirzel, 2000.

Bischoff, Bernhard. "Paläographische Fragen deutscher Denkmäler der Karolinger-zeit." *Frühmittelalterliche Studien* 5 (1971): 101–34.

———. "Paläographie." In *Deutsche Philologie im Aufriß*, 2nd ed., rev. by Wolfgang Stammler, vol. 1, cols 379–451. Berlin: Erich Schmidt, 1957.

———. *Die südostdeutschen Schreibschulen und Bibliotheken in der Karolingerzeit.* 2nd ed. Wiesbaden: O. Harrassowitz, 1960.

———. *Latin Palaeography. Antiquity and the Middle Ages.* Translated by Dáibhí Ó Cróinín and David Ganz. Cambridge: Cambridge UP, 1989.

Blagden, Charles. "Some Observations on ancient Inks, with the Proposal of a new Method of recovering the Legibility of decayed Writings." *Philosophical Trans-actions of the Royal Society of London* 77 (1787): 451–57.

Blumenkranz, Bernhard. *Les auteurs chrétiens latins du moyen âge sur les juifs et le judaïsme.* Paris: Mouton, 1963.

Boase, Roger, *The Origin and Meaning of Courtly Love.* Manchester: Manchester UP, 1977.

Borck, Karl-Heinz. "Zur Bedeutung der Wörter *holz, wald, forst* und *witu* im Althochdeutschen." In *Festschrift Jost Trier zu seinem 60. Geburtstag*, edited by Benno von Wiese and Karl-Heinz Borck, 456–76. Meisenheim/Glan: Westkultur-verlag, 1954.

Bostock, J. Knight. "H." *MLR* 48 (1953): 328.

Bostock, J. Knight. *A Handbook to Old High German Literature.* 2nd ed., rev. by K. C. King and David R. McLintock. Oxford: Clarendon Press, 1976.

Bromwich, Rachel, ed., *The Beginnnings of Welsh Poetry. Studies by Sir Ifor Williams.* 2nd ed. Cardiff: U of Wales P, 1980.

Brown, Giles. "Introduction: The Carolingian Renaissance." In *Carolingian Culture: Emulation and Innovation*, edited by Rosamond McKitterick, 1–51. Cambridge: Cambridge UP, 1994.

Bugge, Sophus. *Studier over de nordiske Gude- og Heltesagns Oprindelse.* Christiania: Gad, 1881–89.

Cabaniss, Alan. "Bodo-Eleazar: a famous Jewish convert." *Jewish Quarterly Review* 43 (1952/1953): 313–28.

Canepari, Petro Maria. *De Atramentis.* Venice: Apud Euangelistam Deuchinum, 1619.

Carstensen, Broder. "Wörter des Jahres 1982." *Deutsche Sprache* 2 (1983): 174–87.

Christiansen, Reidar Th. *Die finnischen und nordischen Varianten des zweiten Merseburgerspruches.* Folklore Fellows Communications, 18. Hamina: Suomalaisen tiedeakatemian kustantama, 1914.

Cook, A. S. "King Oswy and Caedmon's Hymn." *Speculum* 2 (1927): 67–72.

Crossley-Holland, Kevin. *The Anglo-Saxon World. An Anthology.* World's Classics. 1982; repr. Oxford: Oxford UP, 1999.

Dalyell, J. G. *The Darker Superstitions of Scotland.* Edinburgh: Waugh & Innes, 1834.

Danielowski, Emma, *Das Hiltibrantlied. Beitrag zur Überlieferungsgeschichte auf paläographischer Grundlage*. Berlin: Mayer & Müller, 1919.

Davíðsson, Ólafur. "Isländische Zauberzeichen und Zauberbücher." *Zeitschrift des Vereins für Volkskunde* 13 (1903): 150–67; 267–79.

Denecke, O. "Vom Dichter Kazungali." *Zeitschrift für Bücherfreunde* 6:1 (1914): 19–30.

Derolez, René. "Die 'hrabanischen' Runen." *ZfdPh* 78 (1959): 1–19.

Diamant, Paul J. "Althochdeutsches Schlummerlied. ein Gelehrtenstreit über deutsch-jüdische Zusammenhänge im Mittelalter." *Jahrbuch des Leo-Baeck-Instituts* 5 (1960): 338–45.

Dierkens, Alain. "Superstitions, christianisme et paganisme à la fin de l'époque mérovingienne. A propos de l'Induculus superstitionum et paganiorum." In *Magie, sorcellerie, parapsychologie*, edited by Hervé Hasquin, 9–26. Brussels: Université de Bruxelles, 1984.

Docen, Bernhard. *Miscellaneen zur Geschichte der teutschen Literatur*. Munich: Scherer, 1807.

Dronke, Peter. *Medieval Latin and the Rise of European Love-Lyric*. 2 vols. 2nd ed. Oxford: Clarendon Press, 1968.

Ebert, Friedrich Adolph. *Zur Handschriftenkunde*. 2 vols. Leipzig: Steinacker & Hartknoch, 1825–27.

Edwards, Cyril William. "'Die Räuberin' Heinrichs von Morungen im Benediktinerstift Kremsmünster." *PBB* 108 (1986): 206–11.

———. "Die Erotisierung des Handwerks." In *Liebe in der deutschen Literatur des Mittelalters. St. Andrews-Colloquium 1985*, edited by J. Ashcroft, D. Huschenbett, W. H. Jackson, 126–48. Tübingen: Niemeyer, 1987.

———. "The Growth of a Song: Heinrich von Morungen's Robber-Lady (MF 130,9)." *Medium Aevum* 58 (1989): 17–33.

———. "Von Archilochos zu Walther von der Vogelweide. Zu den Anfängen der Pastourelle in Deutschland." In *Lied im deutschen Mittelalter. Überlieferung, Typen, Gebrauch. Chiemsee-Colloquium 1991*, edited by Cyril Edwards, Ernst Hellgardt, and Norbert H. Ott., 1–25. Tübingen: Niemeyer, 1996.

———. "*winileodos*? Zu Nonne, Zensur und den Spuren der althochdeutschen Liebeslyrik." In *Theodisca. Beiträge zur althochdeutschen und altniederdeutschen Sprache und Literatur in der Kultur des frühen Mittelalters*, edited by Wolfgang Haubrichs et al., 189–206. Berlin: de Gruyter, 2000.

Ehrle, Franz. "Über die Erhaltung und Ausbesserung alter Handschriften." *Central-bibliothek für Bibliothekswesen* 15 (1898): 17–33.

Ehrismann, Gustav. *Geschichte der deutschen Literatur bis zum Ausgang des Mittelalters. I. Die althochdeutsche Literatur*. 2nd ed. Munich: C. H. Beck, 1932.

Eis, Gerhard. "Deutung des ersten Merseburger Zauberspruchs." *FuF* 32 (1958): 27–39.

Eis, Gerhard. *Altdeutsche Zaubersprüche*. Berlin: W. de Gruyter, 1964.

Elliott, Ralph W. V., *Runes. An Introduction.* Manchester: Manchester UP, 1959; repr. 1980.

Feist, Sigmund. "Runen und Zauberwesen im germanischen Altertum." *Arkiv för nordisk Filologi* 35 (1919): 243–87.

Fenton, Terry. "CHAOS IN THE BIBLE? Tohu vavohu," in *Jewish Education and Learning, published in honour of Dr. David Patterson on the occasion of his seventieth birthday,* edited by Glenda Abramson and Tudor Parfitt, 203–20. Chur & London: Harwood Academic Publishers, 1993.

Fichtenau, Heinrich. *Die Lehrbücher Maximilians I. und die Anfänge der Frakturschrift.* Hamburg: Maximilian Gesellschaft, 1961.

———. "Die Fälschungen Georg Zapperts." *MIÖG* 78 (1970): 444–67.

Flint, Valerie J. *The Rise of Magic in Early Medieval Europe.* Oxford: Clarendon Press, 1993.

Flood, John L. and David N. Yeandle, eds, *"mit regulu bithuungan." Neue Arbeiten zur althochdeutschen Poesie und Sprache.* GAG, 500. Göppingen: Kümmerle, 1989.

Flowers, Stephen E. *Runes and Magic. Magical Formulaic Elements in the Older Runic Tradition.* American University Series, 1: Germanic Languages and Literatures, vol. 53. New York: Peter Lang, 1986.

Forster, Leonard. "Zum zweiten Merseburger Zauberspruch." *Archiv für das Studium der neueren Sprachen und Literatur* 192 (1955–56): 155–59.

Fowkes, R. A. "Eastern echoes in the *Wessobrunner Gebet?" Germanic Review* 37 (1962): 83–90.

Frazer, James George. *The Golden Bough: a study in magic and religion.* 3rd rev. ed., 12 vols. London: Macmillan, 1907–15.

Fromm, Hans. "Lemminkäinen und Baldr." In *Märchen. Mythos. Dichtung. Festschrift zum 90. Geburtstag Friedrich van der Leyens am 19. August 1963,* edited by Hugo Kuhn, 287–302. Munich: Beck, 1965.

Fuller, Susan. "Pagan Charms in Tenth-Century Saxony? The Function of the Merseburg Charms." *Monatshefte* 72 (1980): 162–70.

Gabrielli, Noemi. "Le miniature delle Omelie di San Grigorio." In *Arte del Primo Millennio. Atti del II⁰ Convegno per lo studio dell' arte dell' alto medio evo tenuto presso l'Università di Pavia nel Settembre 1950,* edited by Eduardo Arslan, 301–11. Turin: Viglongo, 1950.

Ganz, Peter F. "MS Junius 13 und die althochdeutsche Tatianübersetzung." *PBB* 91 (1969): 28–76.

———. "Die Zeilenaufteilung im *Wessobrunner Gebet." PBB* (Tübingen) *Sonderheft* (1973): 39–51.

Gauert, Adolf. "Zum Itinerar Karls des Großen." In *Karl der Große: Lebenswerk und Nachleben,* ed. by Wolfgang Braunfels et al., vol. 1, 307–22. Düsseldorf: L. Schwann, 1966–68.

Genzmer, Felix. "Die Götter des zweiten 'Merseburger Zauberspruches'." *Arkiv för nordisk Filologi* 63 (1948): 55–72.

―――. "Da signed Krist — thû biguol'en Wuodan." *Arv* 5 (1949): 37–68.

Gerstner-Hirzel, Emily. "Das Kinderlied." In *Handbuch des Volksliedes*, edited by Rolf Wilhelm Brednich, Lutz Röhrich, Wolfgang Suppan, 2 vols, vol. 1, 923–967. Munich: Fink, 1973.

―――. *Das volkstümliche deutsche Wiegenlied. Versuch einer Typologie der Texte.* Basle: Schweizerische Gesellschaft für Volkskunde, 1984.

Gräter, F. D. "Das älteste teutsche Gedicht." *Bragur* V:i (1796): 118–55.

Green, Dennis E. *The Carolingian Lord: Semantic studies on four Old High German words: balder, frô, truhtin, hêrro.* Cambridge: Cambridge UP, 1965.

Greenacre, Phyllis. "Fetishism." In *Sexual Deviation*, edited by Ismond Rosen, 2nd ed., 79–108. Oxford & New York: Oxford UP, 1979.

Grein, C. W. M. "Das Wessobrunner Gebet." *Germania* 10 (1865): 310.

Grienberger, Theodor von. "Althochdeutsche Texterklärungen." *PBB* 45 (1921): 212–38.

Grimm, Jacob and Wilhelm. *Die ältesten deutschen Gedichte aus dem achten Jahrhundert: Das Lied von Hildebrand und Hadubrand und das Wessobrunner Gebet.* Kassel: Thurneissen, 1812.

Grimm, Jacob. "Über zwei entdeckte Gedichte aus der Zeit des deutschen Heidenthums." *Abhandlungen der Berliner Akademie der Wissenschaften, philologische und historische Abtheilung*, 1842: 1–26.

―――. *Deutsche Mythologie.* 2nd ed., 2 vols. Göttingen: Dieterich, 1844.

―――. "Über die Göttin Tanfana." *Berliner Monatsberichte*, 10 March 1859: 254–58.

―――. "Zur Geschichte der deutschen Philologie. I. Briefe von Jacob Grimm. A. J. Grimms Briefe an Franz Pfeiffer." *Germania* 11 (1866): 111–28; 239–56.

―――. *Kleinere Schriften*, 5 vols, edited by Karl Müllenhoff. Berlin: Dümmler, 1864–71.

Grimm, Wilhelm. [Untitled] announcement of his facsimile edition of the *Hildebrandslied. GGA* I:48 (1830): 466–67.

Gutenbrunner, Siegfried. *Die germanischen Götter in antiken Inschriften.* Halle/Saale: Niemeyer, 1936.

―――. "Der zweite Merseburger Zauberspruch im Lichte nordischer Überlieferungen." *ZfdA* 80 (1943): 1–5.

―――. "Ritennamen — Kultnamen — Mythennamen der Götter." In *Namenforschung. Festschrift für Adolf Bach zum 75. Geburtstag*, edited by Rudolf Schützeichel and Mattthias Zender, 17–31. Heidelberg: C. Winter, 1965.

Gunkel, Hermann. *Schöpfung und Chaos in Urzeit und Endzeit: eine religionsgeschichtliche Untersuchung über Gen 1 und Ap John 12.* Göttingen: Vandenhoeck & Ruprecht, 1895.

Gunkel, Hermann. *Genesis.* 7th ed. Göttingen: Vandenhoeck & Ruprecht, 1966.

Haubrichs, Wolfgang. *Geschichte der deutschen Literatur von den Anfängen bis zum Beginn der Neuzeit. Band I: Von den Anfängen zum hohen Mittelalter. Teil I: Die Anfänge: Versuche volkssprachiger Schriftlichkeit im frühen Mittelalter (ca 700–1050/60).* Frankfurt am Main; Tübingen: Athenäum, 1988.

———. ed., *Theodisca. Beiträge zur althochdeutschen und altniederdeutschen Sprache und Literatur in der Kultur des frühen Mittelalters: eine internationale Fachtagung in Schönmühl bei Penzberg vom 13. bis zum 17. März 1997.* Ergänzungsbände zum Reallexikon der Germanischen Altertumskunde, 22. Berlin: W. de Gruyter, 2000.

Hauck, Karl. *Goldbrakteaten aus Sievern. Spätantike Amulett-Bilder der 'Dania Saxonica' und die Sachsen-'Origo' bei Widukind.* Münstersche Mittelalter-Schriften, 1. Munich: W. Fink, 1970.

———. "Völkerwanderungszeitliche Bilddarstellungen des zweiten Merseburger Spruchs als Zugang zu Heiligtum und Opfer." In *Vorgeschichtliche Heiligtümer und Opferplätze in Mittel- und Nordeuropa.* Abhandlungen der Akademie der Wissenschaften, Historisch-philologische Klasse III.74. Göttingen, 1970: 297–319.

Haug, Walter. *Literaturtheorie im deutschen Mittelalter. Von den Anfängen bis zum Ende des 13. Jahrhunderts: eine Einführung.* Darmstadt: Wissenschaftliche Buchgesellschaft, 1985.

Hellen, Eduard von der. "Zur Kritik des Wessobrunner Gebetes." *Germania* 31 (1886): 272–80.

Hehir, Brendan. "What is the *Gododdin*?" In *Early Welsh Poetry. Studies in the Book of Aneirin*, edited by Brynley F. Roberts, 57–96. Aberystwyth: National Library of Wales, 1988.

Henkel, Nikolaus. "Carmina Ratisponensia." In *Ratisbona sacra: das Bistum Regensburg im Mittelalter*, exhibition catalogue (Munich/Zurich, 1989), 161–62.

Hofmann, Carl. "Schlummerlied und Bienensegen." *Sitzungsberichte der königlichen bayerischen Akademie der Wissenschaften* (Munich, 1866), vol. 2: 103–12.

———. "Ueber Docens Abschrift des Muspilli." *Sitzungsberichte der königlichen bayerischen Akademie der Wissenschaften. Philosophisch-philologische Classe* (Munich, 1866), II: 225–35.

Howard, John A. "Über die Echtheit eines althochdeutschen Wiegenliedes." *Studia Neophilologica* 47 (1976): 21–35.

Jacoby, Michael. "Methodische Gesichtspunkte zur Beurteilung der Frage nach der Echtheit eines 'althochdeutschen Wiegenliedes' (Cod. 15.013, fol. V recto, A 4)." *Codices manuscripti* 2 (1976): H. 4, 110–13.

Jaeger, C. Stephen. *Ennobling Love. In Search of a Lost Sensibility.* Philadelphia: U. of Pennsylvania P, 1999.

Jaffé, Ph. "Zum Schlummerlied." *ZfdA* 13 (1867): 496–501.

Karajan, Theodor von. "Zwei bisher unbekannte Sprachdenkmale aus heidnischer Zeit." *Wiener Sitzungsberichte* 25 (1858): 308–25.

Jarman, A. O. H. and Gwilym Rees Hughes, *A Guide to Welsh Literature*. 2 vols. Swansea: C. Davies, 1976.

Katz, Solomon, *The Jews in the Visigothic and Frankish Kingdoms of Spain and Gaul*. Cambridge, MA: The Medieval Academy of America, 1937.

Klaeber, Friedrich. "Zum *Wessobrunner Gebet.*" *Archiv für das Studium der neueren Sprachen*, 174 (1938): 204.

Kluge, Friedrich. "Geschichte des Reimes im Altgermanischen." *PBB* 9 (1883): 422–50.

Ködderitsch, Rolf. "Der 2. Merseburger Zauberspruch und seine Parallelen." *Zeitschrift für Celtische Philologie* 33 (1974): 45–57.

Koegel, Rudolf and Wilhelm Bruckner. *Geschichte der althoch- und niederdeutschen Literatur*. Grundriss der germanischen Philologie, edited by Hermann Paul et al., II, VI, 2. 2nd rev. ed. Strasbourg: K. J. Trübner, 1901.

Kraus, Carl von. Review of *Geschichte der deutschen Litteratur bis zum Ausgange des Mittelalters. Bd. I, Theil I. Die stabreimende Dichtung und die gothische Prosadichtung*, by Rudolf Koegel. *Zeitschrift für die österreichischen Gymnasien* 47 (1896): 306–49.

Krause, Wolfgang and Herbert Jankuhn, *Die Runeninschriften im älteren Futhark*, Abhandlungen der Akademie der Wissenschaften in Göttingen, philologisch-historische Klasse, dritte Folge, nr. 65. Göttingen: 1966.

Krogmann, Willy. "Die Mundart des Wessobrunner Gebets." *Zeitschrift für Mundartforschung* 13 (1937): 129–49.

———. "Phol im Merseburger Pferdesegen." *ZfdPh* 71 (1951/52): 152–62.

Krohn, Kaarle. "Wo und wann entstanden die finnischen zauberlieder?" *Finnisch-ugrische Forschungen* 1 (1901): 147–81.

Kühnel, Jürgen. *Dû bist mîn, ih bin dîn. Die lateinischen Liebes- (und Freundschafts-) Briefe des clm. 19411. Abbildungen, Text und Übersetzung*. GAG, 52. Göppingen: Kümmerle, 1977.

Kuhn, A. "Indische und germanische segenssprüche." *Zeitschrift für vergleichende Sprachforschung* 13 (1864): 49–74 and 113–57.

Kuhn, Hugo. "Es gibt kein balder 'Herr'." In *Erbe der Vergangenheit: germanistische Beiträge. Fs. für Karl Helm zum 80. Geburtstag*, 37–45. Tübingen: M. Niemeyer, 1951.

Laistner, M. L. W. "Some early medieval commentaries on the Old Testament." *Harvard Theological Review* 46 (1953): 27–46.

———. *Thought and Letters in Western Europe AD 500 to 900*. 2nd ed. London: Methuen, 1957.

Leclercq, Jean, *L'amour des lettres et le désir de Dieu, initiation aux auteurs monastiques du moyen âge*. Paris: Éditions du Cerf, 1957.

Leitzmann, Albert. "Zu den kleineren althochdeutschen Denkmälern." *PBB* 39 (1914): 548–58.

Lewis, C. S. *The Allegory of Love. A Study in Medieval Tradition*. London: Oxford UP, 1936.

Lowe, E. A. *Codices latini antiquiores; a palaeographical guide to Latin manuscripts prior to the ninth century*. Oxford: Clarendon Press, 1950.

Lubac, Henri de. *Exégèse médiévale. Les quatre sens de l'écriture*. Théologie, 41, 42 and 59. Paris: Aubier, 1959–64.

Lühr, Rosemarie. *Studien zur Sprache des Hildebrandliedes*. Europäische Hochschulschriften. 2 vols. Frankfurt am Main: Peter Lang, 1982.

Manganella, Gemma. "Il 'caos' del *Wessobrunner Gebet*." *Istituto Orientale di Napoli, Annali, Sezione Germanica* 8 (1965): 285–91.

McKitterick, Rosamond, ed., *Carolingian Culture: Emulation and Innovation*. Cambridge: Cambridge UP, 1994.

McLintock, David R. "The negatives of the 'Wessobrunn Prayer'." *MLR* 52 (1957): 397–98.

———. "The language of the *Hildebrandslied*." *OGS* 1 (1966): 1–9.

MacPhail, Malcolm. "Folklore from the Hebrides. IV." *Folk-Lore* 11 (1900): 439–50.

Mayer, C. A. "Die Heimat des Wessobrunner Gebets." *Alemannia* 31 (1903): 161–70.

Mazal, Otto. *Lehrbuch der Handschriftenkunde*. Elemente des Buch- und Bibliothekswesens, 10. Wiesbaden: Reichert, 1986.

Meid, Wolfgang. "Gallisch oder Lateinisch? Soziolinguistische und andere Bemerkungen zu populären gallo-lateinischen Inschriften." In *Principat, 29, II. Sprache und Literatur*, edited by Wolfgang Haase, 1019–44. Berlin and New York: Walter de Gruyter, 1983.

Müllenhoff, Karl. *De Carmine Wessofontano et de versu ac stropharum usu apud Germanos*. Berlin: typis academicis, 1861.

Müller, Wilhelm ["W.M."]. Review of "Ein althochdeutsches Schlummerlied," by Georg Zappert. *GGA* 21 (1860): 201–11.

———. Review of "Forschungen und Kritik auf dem Gebiete des deutschen Alterthums II.: IV. Über das Wiener Schlummerlied. Eine Rettung," by Franz Pfeiffer. *GGA* 27 (1867): 1057–70.

Murdoch, Brian O. *Old High German Literature*. Twayne's World Authors Series, 688. Boston, MA: Twayne Publishers, 1983.

———. "Peri Hieres Nousou: Approaches to the Old High German Medical Charms." In *'mit regulu bithuungan'. Neue Arbeiten zur althochdeutschen Poesie und Sprache*, edited by John L. Flood and David N. Yeandle, 142–59. GAG, 500. Göppingen: Kümmerle, 1989.

Musset, Lucien. *Introduction à la runologie*. Bibliothèque de la philologie germanique, 20. Paris: Aubier: Montaigne, 1965.

Neckel, Gustav. *Die Überlieferungen vom Gotte Balder*. Dortmund: F. W. Ruhfus, 1920.

Neuser, Peter-Erich. "Das karolingische 'Hildebrandslied'. Kodikologische und rezeptionsgeschichtliche Aspekte des 2⁰ Ms. theol 54 aus Fulda." In *Architectura Poetica. Festschrift für Johannes Rathofer zum 65. Geburtstag*, edited by Ulrich Ernst and Bernhard Sowinski, 1–16. Cologne: Böhlau, 1990.

Northcott, Kenneth. "An Interpretation of the Second Merseburg Charm." *MLR* 54 (1959): 45–50.

Ochs, Ernst. "Das 'Wessobrunner Gebet'." *Archiv für das Studium der neueren Sprachen und Literatur* 194 (1958): 43.

Page, Raymond I. "Anglo-Saxon Runes and Magic." *Journal of the British Archaeological Association*, 3rd Series, 27 (1964–65): 14–31.

Paterson, Linda. "L'enfant dans la littérature occitane avant 1230." *Cahiers de civilisation médiévale* 32 (1989): 233–45.

———. "Sources Féminines et le 'Sentiment de l'Enfance' dans certains textes médicaux et didactiques du XIIe au XIVe siècle." In *Histoire et Littérature au Moyen Âge. Actes du Colloque du Centre d'Études Médiévales de l'Université de Picardie (Amiens 20–24 mars 1985)*, edited by Danielle Buschinger, 381–88. GAG, 546. Göppingen: Kümmerle, 1991.

Paul, Hermann, ed., *Grundriß der germanischen Philologie*. 2nd. rev. ed. 4 vols. Strasbourg: K. J. Trübner, 1901–09.

Perrett, W. "On the *Wessobrunner Gebet* — I and II," *London Medieval Studies* 1 (1937): 134–38; 2 (1939): 139–49.

Pfeiffer, Franz. "Forschungen und Kritik auf dem Gebiete des deutschen Alterthums II.: IV. Über das Wiener Schlummerlied. Eine Rettung." *Wiener Sitzungsberichte* 52 (1866), 43–86.

Pfister, Friedrich. *Deutsches Volkstum im Glauben und Aberglauben*. Berlin and Leipzig: de Gruyter, 1936.

Plummer, John F., ed., *Vox feminae: studies in medieval woman's songs*. Studies in Medieval Culture, 15. Kalamazoo, MI: Medieval Institute Publications, Western Michigan University, 1981.

Pongs, Hermann. *Das Hildebrandslied. Ueberlieferung und Lautstand im Rahmen der althochdeutschen Literatur*. Marburg: W. Hütter, 1913.

Porta, Giovanni Battista della. *Magiae naturalis*. Cologne: Hannes Birckmann & Werner Richvuin, 1562.

Porta, Giovanni Battista della. *Natural Magick in XX Bookes*. Translated anonymously. London: Thomas Young & Samuel Speed, 1658.

Preusler, Walther. "Zum zweiten Merseburger Spruch." In *Beiträge zur Deutschkunde. Festschrift Theodor Siebs zum 60. Geburtstag*, edited by Helmut de Boor, 39–45. Emden: Davids, 1922.

Puchner, Karl. *Historisches Ortsnamenbuch von Bayern. Oberbayern, Bd. I. Landkreis Ebersberg*. Munich: Kommission für Bayerische Landesgeschichte, 1925.

Rad, Gerhard von. *Genesis: A Commentary*. Translated by John H. Marks. 3rd rev. ed. London: SCM Press, 1963.

Reynolds, L. D. and N. G. Wilson. *Scribes and Scholars. A Guide to the Transmission of Greek and Latin Literature*. 3rd ed. Oxford: Clarendon Press, 1991.

Richter, Michael. *The Formation of the Medieval West. Studies in the Oral Culture of the Barbarians*. Dublin: Four Courts Press, 1994.

Rieger, Max. Review of *Der Heliand und die angelsächsische Genesis* by Eduard Sievers. *ZfdPh* 7 (1876): 114–16.

Rieger, Stadtrabbiner Dr. "Wer war der Hebräer, dessen Werke Hrabanus Maurus benutzt hat?" *Monatsschrift für Geschichte und Wissenschaft des Judentums* 68 (1924): 66–68.

Riesel, Elise. "Der erste Merseburger Zauberspruch." *Deutsches Jahrbuch für Volkskunde* 4 (1958): 53–81.

Rietzler, Sigmund. "Die Ortsnamen der Münchener Gegend." *Oberbayrisches Archiv für vaterländische Geschichte* 44 (1887): 33–110.

Rösel, Ludwig. *Die Gliederung der germanischen Sprachen nach dem Zeugnis ihrer Flexionsformen*. Erlanger Beiträge zur Sprach- und Kunstwissenschaft, 11. Nuremberg: H. Carl, 1962.

Rosenfeld, Hellmut. "*Phol ende Wuodan vuorun zi holza*. Baldermythe oder Fohlenzauber?" *PBB* (Tübingen) 95 (1973): 1–12.

Rowland, Jenny, "Genres." In *Early Welsh Poetry. Studies in the Book of Aneirin*, edited by Brynley F. Roberts, 179–208. Aberystwyth: National Library of Wales, 1988.

Sandmann, Mechthild. "Hrabanus Maurus als Mönch, Abt und Erzbischof." In *Hrabanus Maurus und seine Schule. Festschrift der Rabanus-Maurus Schule 1980*, edited by Winfried Böhne, 13–47. Fulda: Hrabanus-Maurus-Schule, 1980.

Sawyer, Birgit, Peter Sawyer and Ian Wood, eds, *The Christianization of Scandinavia. Report of a Symposium held at Kungälv, Sweden, 4–9 August 1985*. Alingsås: Viktoria Bokförlag, 1987.

Schieffer, Theodor. "Erzbischof Richulf (787–813)." *Jahrbuch für das Bistum Mainz* 5 (1950): 329–42.

Schier, K., "Balder." In *Reallexikon der germanischen Altertumskunde*, edited by Johannes Hoops, 2nd ed., rev. by Heinrich Beck et al., 2–7. Berlin: de Gruyter, 1977.

Schirokauer, Arno. "Der Zweite Merseburger Zauberspruch." In *Corona. Studies in Celebration of the Eightieth Birthday of Samuel Singer*, edited by Arno Schirokauer and Wolfgang Paulsen, 116–41. Durham, NC: Duke UP, 1941.

Schirokauer, Arno. "Der mareo seo." *PMLA* 65 (1950): 313–18.

Schlesinger, Walter. *Kirchengeschichte Sachsens im Mittelalter*. 2 vols. Cologne and Graz: Böhlau, 1962.

Schlosser, Horst Dieter. "Die Aufzeichnung des *Hildebrandslieds* im historischen Kontext." *GRM* 28 (1978): 217–24.

————, *dtv-Atlas zur deutschen Literatur. Tafeln und Texte.* 2nd ed. Munich: Deutscher Taschenbuch Verlag: 1985.

Schmid, Karl, ed. *Die Klostergemeinschaft von Fulda im früheren Mittelalter.* Münstersche Mittelalter-Schriften, 8. Munich: W. Fink, 1978.

Schmidt, Joseph. "Die germanischen präpositionen und das auslautssystem." *Zeitschrift für vergleichende Sprachforschung* 26 (1883): 20–45.

Schmitt, Ludwig, ed. *Kurzer Grundriß der germanischen Philologie bis 1500.* 2 vols. Berlin: de Gruyter, 1971.

Schneider, Hermann, ed. *Germanische Altertumskunde.* 2nd ed. Munich: C. H. Beck, 1951.

Schneider, Karin. *Paläographie und Handschriftenkunde für Germanisten. Eine Einführung.* Sammlung kurzer Grammatiken germanischer Dialekte, B. Ergänzungsreihe Nr. 8. Tübingen: Niemeyer, 1999.

Schnell, Rüdiger. *Causa Amoris. Liebeskonzeption und Liebesdarstellung in der mittelalterlichen Literatur.* Bern: Francke, 1985.

Schönwerth, Fr. von. *Aus der Oberpfalz: Sitten und Sagen.* 3 vols. Augsburg: M. Rieger, 1857–59.

Schröder, Werner. "Otfried von Weißenburg." In *Verfasserlexikon,* vol. 7, cols. 179–80.

Schuster, Richard. "Zappert's 'ältester Plan von Wien'." *Wiener Sitzungsberichte, phil.-hist. Cl,* CXXVII. Vienna, 1892. 6th section, 1–30.

Schwab, Ute. *Die Sternrune im 'Wessobrunner Gebet': Beobachtungen zur Lokalisierung des clm. 22053, zur Hs. BM Arundel 393 und zu Rune Poem V. 86–89.* Amsterdamer Publikationen zur Sprache und Literatur, 1. Amsterdam: Rodopi, 1973.

————. "Das althochdeutsche Lied 'Hirsch und Hinde' in seiner lateinischen Umgebung." In *Latein und Volkssprache im deutschen Mittelalter 1000–1500,* edited by Nikolaus Henkel and Nigel Palmer, 74–122. Tübingen: Niemeyer, 1992.

————. "Sizilianisiche Schnitzel. Marcellus in Fulda und einiges zur Anwendung volkssprachiger magischer Rezepte." In *Deutsche Literatur und Sprache von 1050–1200. Festschrift für Ursula Hennig zum 65. Geburtstag,* edited by Annegret Fiebig and Hans-Jochen Schiewer, 261–96. Berlin: Akademie Verlag, 1995.

Schwarz, Hans. "Ahd. Liod und sein sprachliches Feld." *PBB* (Halle) 75 (1952): 321–68.

Seiffert, Leslie. "The metrical form and composition of the *Wessobrunner Gebet.*" *Medium Aevum* 31 (1962): 1–13.

Siebs, Theodor. "Beiträge zur deutschen mythologie. I. Der todesgott ahd. Henno Wôtan = Mercurius." *ZfdPh* 24 (1892): 146–57.

Sievers, Eduard, ed. *Das Hildebrandlied, die Merseburger Zaubersprüche und das fränkische Taufgelöbnis, mit photographischem Faksimile.* Halle: Verlag der Buchhandlung des Waisenhauses, 1872.

de Smet, Gilbert. "Die *winileot* in Karls Edikt von 789." In *Studien zur deutschen Literatur und Sprache des Mittelalters. Festschrift für Hugo Moser zum 65. Geburtstag*, edited by Werner Besch et al., 1–7. Berlin: E. Schmidt, 1974.

Smalley, Beryl. *The Study of the Bible in the Middle Ages.* 2nd ed. Oxford: Basil Blackwell, 1952.

Snaith, Norman H. *Notes on the Hebrew Text of Genesis I–VIII.* London: The Epworth Press, 1947.

Soeteman, Cornelis. "Venus apud Germanos." *Neophilologus* 45 (1961): 45–54.

Sonderegger, Stefan. *Althochdeutsch in St. Gallen. Ergebnisse und Probleme der althochdeutschen Sprachüberlieferung in St. Gallen vom 8. bis ins 12. Jahrhundert.* St. Gall; Sigmaringen: Verlag Osterschweiz; Tan-thorberke-Verlag, 1970.

———. "St. Galler Spottverse." In *Verfasserlexikon*, vol. 2, cols. 1051–53.

Spamer, Adolf. "P(h)ol ende Uuodan." *Deutsches Jahrbuch für Volkskunde* 3 (1957): 347–65.

Stanley, Eric G. "Alliterative Ornament and Alliterative Rhythmical Discourse in Old High German and Old Frisian Compared with Similar Manifestations in Old English." *PBB* 106 (1984): 184–217.

Steele, Valerie. *Fetish. Fashion, Sex and Power.* Oxford: Oxford UP, 1996.

Steinhoff, Hans-Hugo. "Contra caducum morbum." In *Verfasserlexikon*, vol. 2 (1980), cols. 8–9.

———. "Merseburger Zaubersprüche." In *Verfasserlexikon*, vol. 6 (1987), cols. 410–18.

Steller, Walther. "'Phol ende Wodan'." In *Volkskundliche Studien. Festschrift Friedrich Schmidt-Ott zum siebzigsten Geburtstage dargebracht*, 61–71. Berlin: de Gruyter, 1930.

Störmer, Wilhelm. *Adelsgruppen im früh- und hochmittelalterlichen Bayern.* Studien zur Bayerischen Verfassungsgeschichte und Sozialgeschichte, 4. Munich: Kommission für Bayerische Landesgeschichte, 1972.

———. *Früher Adel. Studien zur politischen Führungsschicht im fränkisch-deutschen Reich vom 8. bis 11. Jahrhundert.* Monographien zur Geschichte des Mittelalters, 6. Stuttgart: A. Hiersemann, 1973.

Storms, Godfrid. *Anglo-Saxon magic.* The Hague: Nijhoff, 1948.

Stuart, Heather. "A Critical Edition of some Anglo-Saxon Charms and Incantations." Diss., Flinders University of South Australia, 1973.

Stuart, Heather and F. Walla. "Die Überlieferung der mittelalterlichen Segen." *ZfdA* 116 (1987): 53–79.

Süßmann, Gustav. *Das Hildebrandlied — gefälscht?* Staufenberg: Gustav Süßmann Eigenverlag, 1988.

Taeger, Burkhard. "Heliand." In *Verfasserlexikon*, vol. 3, cols. 960–961.

Teyssèdre, Bernard. *Le Sacramentaire de Gellone et la figure humaine dans les manuscrits francs du VIIIe siècle.*Toulouse: E. Privat, 1959.

Thurneysen, Rudolf. "Zu irischen Handschriften und Litteraturdenkmälern." *Abhandlungen der königlichen Gesellschaft der Wissenschaften zu Göttingen. Philosophisch-historische Klasse. N.F.*, vol. 14, no. 2. Berlin, 1912.

Timparano, Sebastiano jr. "Angelo Mai." *Atene e Roma*, N.S. 1 (1956): 3–34.

Van der Kolk, Heinrich. *Das Hildebrandlied. Eine forschungsgeschichtliche Darstellung*. Amsterdam: Scheltma & Holkema, 1967.

Vogel, Cyrille. "Pratiques superstitieuses au début du XIe siècle d'après le *Corrector sive medicus* de Burchard, évêque de Worms (965–1025)." In *Études de civilisation médiévale (IXe–XIIe siècles). Mélanges offerts à Edmont-René Labande*, 751–761. Poitiers: Centre d'Études Supérieures de Civilisation Médiévale, 1974.

Vogel, Walther. *Die Normannen und das fränkische Reich bis zur Gründung der Normandie, 779–911*. Heidelberger Abhandlungen zur mittleren und neueren Geschichte, H. 14. Heidelberg: C. Winter, 1906.

Vogt, Friedrich and Max Koch. *Geschichte der deutschen Litteratur von den ältesten Zeiten bis zur Gegenwart*. 2nd rev. ed. Leipzig and Vienna: Bibliographisches Institut, 1904.

Vollmann, Benedikt K. "'O admirabile Veneris idolum' (Carmina Cantabrigiensia 48) — ein Mädchenlied?" In *Festschrift für Paul Klopsch*, edited by Udo Kindermann, Wolfgang Maaz and Fritz Wagner, 532–43. GAG, 492. Göppingen: Kümmerle, 1988.

Wackernagel, Wilhelm. *Das Wessobrunner Gebet und die Wessobrunner Glossen* (Berlin: Schmidt, 1827).

———. "Der Heliand und das Wessobrunner Gebet." *ZfdPh* 1 (1869): 291–309.

Wadstein, Elis. "Zum zweiten Merseburger Zauberspruch." *Studia Neophilologica* 12 (1939/40): 205–09.

Waldman, Glenys A. "The Wessobrunn Prayer Manuscript, Clm. 22053: a transliteration, translation and study of parallels." Diss., Pennsylvania State University, 1975. Ann Arbor, Mich.: University Microfilms, 1975.

———. "The Scriptorium of the Wessobrunn Prayer Manuscript." *Scriptorium* 32 (1978): 249–50.

———."The German and geographical Glosses of the Wessobrunn Prayer Manuscript." *Beiträge zur Namenforschung*, N. F. 13 (1978): 261–305.

Wallner, Anton. "Eiris sazun idisi." *ZfdA* 50 (1908): 214–18.

Warnatsch, Otto. "Phol und der 2. Merseburger Zauberspruch." *ZfdPh* 64 (1939): 148–55.

Wattenbach, Wilhelm. *Das Schriftwesen im Mittelalter*. 3rd ed. Leipzig, 1896; repr. Graz: Akademische Druck- und Verlagsanstalt, 1958.

Weidmüller, Wilhelm. "Das *Wessobrunner Gebet* und seine 'Runen'." *Volk und Schrift* 10 (1939): 2–11.

Weissthanner, Alois, ed., *Die Klostergemeinschaft von Fulda im frühen Mittelalter.* Quellen und Forschungen zur bayerischen Geschichte, N. F., 10. Munich: Beck, 1953.

Wessels, P. B. "Zur Wesensbestimmung des Winelieds." *Neophilologus* 41 (1957): 19–25.

Whitbread, L. "Line 8*a* of the *Wessobrunner Gebet." MLR* 34 (1939): 426–27.

Wickham, Chris. *Early Medieval Italy. Central Power and Local Society 400–1000.* New Studies in Medieval History. London: MacMillan, 1981.

Wiegel, Karl Adolf. "Die Darstellungen der Kreuzauffindung bis zu Piera della Francesca." Diss., Cologne, 1973.

Willson, H. B. "'bluotrenki'." *MLR* 52 (1957): 233–35.

Wilson, Joseph B. "A Conjecture on the Opening of the Second Merseburg Charm." In *Studies in German in memory of Andrew Louis,* edited by James E. Copeland and Robert Ludwig Kahn, 241–50. Rice University Studies, vol. 55, no. 33. Houston, TX: William March Rice University, 1969.

Wolfskehl, Karl. "Das althochdeutsche Schlummerlied." In *Aus unbekannten Schriften. Festgabe für Martin Buber zum 50. Geburtstag,* 58–63. Berlin: L. Schneider, 1928. Reprinted in *Karl Wolfskehl. Gesammelte Werke,* edited by Margot Ruben and Claus Victor Bock, 61–66. Hamburg: Claassen, 1960.

Wormald, Patrick. "Bede, 'Beowulf' and the conversion of the Anglo-Saxon aristocracy." In *Bede and Anglo-Saxon England,* edited by Robert T. Farrell, 32–95. British Archaeological Reports, 46. Oxford: British Archaeological Reports, 1978.

Wrede, Ferdinand. "Zu den Merseburger Zaubersprüchen." *Sitzungsberichte der Preussischen Akademie der Wissenschaften.* Berlin, 1923: 85–90.

Wutz, Franz. *Onomastica Sacra; Untersuchungen zum Liber interpretationis nominum Hebraicorum des hl. Hieronymus.*Texte und Untersuchungen zur Geschichte der altchristlichen Literatur, 41. 3. Reihe, 11. Leipzig: J. C. Hinrichs, 1914–15.

Zappert, Georg. "Über ein althochdeutsches Schlummerlied." *Wiener Sitzungsberichte,* 29 (1858): 302–15.

Zoepfl, Friedrich. *Das Bistum Augsburg und seine Bischöfe im Mittelalter.* Augsburg: Schnell & Steiner, 1955.

Index

(References to scholars and librarians are limited to those of the nineteenth century or earlier; these relate in particular to chapters 3 and 7).